Real Estate Finance

Edited by:

Stephen L. Barter   MA (Cantab.), ARICS

Partner, Richard Ellis
Director, Richard Ellis Financial Services

Butterworths
London, Boston, Dublin, Edinburgh, Kuala Lumpur,
Singapore, Sydney, Toronto, Wellington
1988

United Kingdom	Butterworth & Co (Publishers) Ltd, 88 Kingsway, LONDON WC2B 6AB and 4 Hill St, EDINBURGH EH2 3JZ
Australia	Butterworths Pty Ltd, SYDNEY, MELBOURNE, BRISBANE, ADELAIDE, PERTH, CANBERRA and HOBART
Canada	Butterworths Canada Ltd, TORONTO and VANCOUVER
Ireland	Butterworth (Ireland) Ltd, DUBLIN
Malaysia	Malayan Law Journal Sdn Bhd, KUALA LUMPUR
New Zealand	Butterworths of New Zealand Ltd, WELLINGTON and AUCKLAND
Singapore	Butterworth & Co (Asia) Pte Ltd, SINGAPORE
USA	Butterworths Legal Publishers, ST PAUL, Minnesota, SEATTLE, Washington, BOSTON, Massachusetts, AUSTIN, Texas and D & S Publishers, CLEARWATER, Florida

A CIP Catalogue record for this book is available from the British Library.

ISBN 0406115 001

Typeset by Cotswold Typesetting Ltd, Gloucester
Printed and bound by MacKays of Chatham

To Alyson

1 3 6
1

'When I first heard his name, I said, just as you are going to say, "But I thought he was a boy?"
"So did I," said Christopher Robin.
"Then you can't call him Winnie?"
"I don't."
"But you said—"
"He's Winnie-ther-Pooh. Don't you know what '*ther*' means?"
"Ah, yes, now I do," I said quickly; and I hope you do too, because it is all the explanation you are going to get.'

A. A. Milne
Winnie-the-Pooh

Foreword by Sir Christopher Benson, FRICS

It used to be said that investment in property was a long-term affair. However, a look at the features of property and its financing over the past 25 years reveals a picture of constant change and innovation.

Building forms and techniques, to say nothing of the architecture of shopping malls, office blocks and business/industrial parks, have improved greatly in quality, speed and innovation. In the past, the essence of property development was 'finding the deal'. Nowadays, achieving the right financing is just as important as finding the right site. Furthermore, many of the larger UK property companies are now international corporations and, consequently, they need to understand the complexities of international money markets as much as local property markets.

As a result, the finance director of today's modern property company has to marshal a plethora of new financing ideas. Not only must he have a thorough understanding of individual property finance and the mysteries of modern taxation, but he also has to be a corporate financier, innovative and diligent in seeking new financial vehicles and markets. He needs banking knowledge and sound relationships with merchant bankers and financial services organisations. The finance director is now a key asset to the modern property company.

For the rest of us, the managers of the companies and those who advise them, we grapple daily with the products of finance directors, fertile minds, and we try to look knowledgeable when MOFs, PINCs and SAPCOs, trip off their tongues. We listen with fascination to talk of caps, swaptions, commercial paper programmes and deep discount bonds.

Amidst this sophistication we remind ourselves that, fundamentally, property is a commodity to be built, occupied, bought, sold and managed as an asset, and that property investment companies are judged on a combination of asset growth and increasing earnings and dividend payments. Thus, the success of the property company now depends as much upon the entrepreneurial flair of the manager as upon the skill of his financial officer.

To date, there has been no authoritative work in the United Kingdom which reviews the range of financing opportunities which have emerged over the years and which are now available to the modern operators in the real estate business.

Real Estate Finance is not intended to be a textbook, but Stephen Barter has brought together an outstanding group of experts whose knowledge and experience will be invaluable to student and practitioner alike. I can vouch that the book is very readable and, even to someone who lives every day in the forest, it has helped me to see some of the trees more clearly.

My only question is: when will it need to be re-written to accommodate changes which even now are taking place and rendering some of today's innovations redundant?

September 1988

Sir Christopher Benson, FRICS
Chairman, MEPC plc

Preface

At a time when investment markets have become more critical of traditional attitudes, more liberalised in structure and more demanding in the desire for performance, the property market has remained something of an enigma. For many, property provides a unique fascination and in recent years its appeal has been matched by impressive investment performance.

Yet behind the facade of this traditionally private market, significant innovation and change has been taking place in recent years, particularly concerning the ways in which property investment and development are financed. The importance of pension funds and insurance companies as direct investors and equity financiers of property has been eclipsed by a trend towards debt funding from banks and the increasing use of capital market instruments. The funding requirements of property companies have radically altered, not only because the characteristics of such companies have become more diverse, but also because efficient funding has become such an integral part of their business success.

The physical characteristics of the commodity itself have also changed. No longer is the distinction simply between office blocks, shops and industrial buildings; new forms of development have evolved to meet the needs of an occupier-led market. The last decade has seen the emergence of, for example, the retail warehouse, the out-of-town shopping centre (often with a significant leisure content), the business park and the so called 'high-tech' office. The funding solutions for such developments often involve a complex blend of different types of finance from different sources; the standards of appraisal now demanded are rigorous and dependent upon a tightly managed computerised cashflow analysis.

At the same time, strong competition has emerged among advisers offering expertise in these new areas. Investment banks and other professional firms are now competing with chartered surveyors to provide property funding advice. A new, multi-disciplined business sector in property financial services has been created, combining property with corporate finance expertise and, in some cases, considerable capital resources. In addition, the impact of the Financial Services

Act has imposed new regulations, capital requirements and disclosure obligations on those firms which seek to offer such services.

The potential for property securitisation (shares in single properties which can be traded on The Stock Exchange) brings property investment and finance even closer to the securities markets. It transforms property from a private into a public market and may encourage international investment and trading through the screen-based global securities network. It also raises a number of new key issues for professionals concerning disclosure and conflicts of interest.

Yet despite such radical changes, little has been written to describe and explain them in any depth. Indeed, comparatively few books have been written specifically about the UK real estate market at all, and fewer still for the practitioner.

My objective in preparing this book was to provide a comprehensive guide to the ways in which UK property is currently being financed and how property investment is being undertaken. To achieve this, it seemed appropriate to invite leading practitioners to write about the specific area of property finance in which they have particular expertise and experience. In so doing, the book offers a unique insight into the attitudes of the major players. It is, therefore, a book by practitioners essentially for practitioners, although it will undoubtedly appeal to a wider audience.

The book reviews the trends in equity finance, debt finance and the use of the capital markets; it examines the technical aspects of off-balance sheet funding and the structure of joint ventures; it outlines the objectives and practical issues facing a leading property company and it provides a comprehensive study of the prospects for property securitisation in the UK and its application to development funding.

In all respects, the intention has been to avoid academic debate and to concentrate on describing how property is financed in practice in a UK context. At the same time, some discussion of key professional issues, such as valuation methodology and the future role of the chartered surveyor, have been included.

Inevitably, the personal views and corporate attitudes of the authors and their individual organisations or professions emerge from the chapters. This was a deliberate objective; property finance is a multi-disciplined business and it is the collection of views which forms market opinion. Equally, although efforts have been made to avoid overlap of subject matter, there has been no attempt to ensure a uniform view between contributors on a particular issue. Consequently, the book does contain a number of contrasting explanations and opinions, seen from different perspectives, which I hope will enhance the reader's interest and understanding.

However, because the property finance market is continuously changing, certain technical details (for example, concerning off balance sheet financing) are accurate at the time of writing, but may be subject to further change in the months to come. Equally, by early 1989 the prospects for a successful securitisation market will also have become considerably clearer. The financial statistics used in the text are, as far as possible, the latest available as at August 1988; the conclusions drawn reflect these results. It is not unlikely that future trends may differ, but an appreciation of the underlying characteristics is the key objective.

Finally, some acknowledgements. Firstly, I must thank Butterworths, who originally suggested that this book should be written and convinced me that I should take it on. Their encouragement and enthusiasm for the project was infectious from the start.

Fundamentally, the task depended upon the co-operation and commitment of my fellow contributors, all of whom met demanding deadlines in a suitably business-like fashion, worthy of their personal and corporate standing in the property world. Most had previously presented some of their views and ideas on conference platforms which we have shared in recent times, but I know that in all cases, much new work was needed to prepare the material for their chapters. They deserve to be pleased with the results and I thank them for their efforts.

As for my own contributions, it would not have been possible for Neil Sinclair and myself to have written such a detailed chapter on securitisation, had the concept not been as far advanced in this country as it currently is. For that, the credit must be shared with our fellow members of The PINCs Association Executive Committee. They have individually contributed the intellectual ability and enormous capacity for speculative hard work which has produced a badly needed financial instrument and a regulated market-place within a comparatively short time-period. I am particularly grateful to Alison Cawley and Paul Walker for their comments on the text. It is now for investors to decide whether or not the concept will be a success.

In preparing the introduction, I should acknowledge the contributions made to my views, wittingly and unwittingly, by my Partners at Richard Ellis, as well as by numerous friends and colleagues over the years. I am particularly grateful to Colin Barber and his team in Richard Ellis Research for the preparation of the excellent graphs and diagrams.

I am especially grateful to Sir Christopher Benson for contributing the foreward to this book. MEPC is one of the giants which has been at the hub of the UK property market for many decades. As a company, it is sufficiently large and internationally diversified to be able to take full advantage of the innovative property financing techniques currently prevailing. Under Sir Christopher's stewardship, this has been a keen philosophy.

I would like to thank The International Stock Exchange of the United Kingdom and the Republic of Ireland Ltd for their kind permission to reproduce the listing provisions for single property schemes as an appendix to the chapter on Securitisation.

The physical production of this book would not have been possible without the superhuman efforts of my secretary, Lynn Sharp. If there was an Egon Ronay Gold Star award for secretaries, she would win five. Not only does she remain tirelessly cheerful (when all around is anything but cheerful), she is also consistently successful in deciphering amendments drafted in my appalling handwriting!

Above all, the greatest acknowledgement must be made to my wife, Alyson, who suffered the real opportunity cost of my wish to publish this book as quickly as possible. However, in producing our first child, Olivia, within days of the book's completion, she herself provided the perfect deadline.

I hope that this book will be read in the spirit in which it has been written, by those who seek explanation, but who recognise that the explanations they receive may well differ and that they themselves must make the ultimate decisions.

September 1988   Stephen L. Barter
                                                                London

The Contributors

Editor and Author

Stephen Barter is a Partner of Richard Ellis, and a Director of Richard Ellis Financial Services Limited. After graduating from Gonville & Caius College, Cambridge, he joined Richard Ellis in 1979 and specialised in portfolio asset management and investment policy advice for five years, before becoming involved in the creation of Richard Ellis Financial Services in 1984. A chartered surveyor, he became an Associate Partner of Richard Ellis in 1984 and a Partner in 1987.

He has been involved in the development of a number of important property financing innovations, including The Property Equity Fund and PINCs. He has international experience, having worked in both the United States and Western Europe and has delivered seminars in Tokyo, Hong Kong, Singapore and Amsterdam, in addition to receiving regular invitations to speak at conferences in London. He is the author of several articles on property finance and securitisation. He was a member of The Royal Institution of Chartered Surveyors' Financial Services Committee which prepared the first guidance note on conflicts of interest in the securitised property market.

He is married and lives in South West London. His wider interests include music, (particularly opera), and keeping fit.

Authors

Michael Mallinson FRICS was educated at Marlborough College, and during National Service was commissioned in the Royal Artillery. On 'retirement' from the army, he enjoyed a brief, and financially rewarding, period making asbestos cement before joining The Prudential Assurance Company Limited as a trainee surveyor. He qualified as an Associate of the RICS in 1960, and became a Fellow in 1974.

He has served his entire career with the Prudential, becoming Chief Surveyor and Property Director of Prudential Portfolio Managers Ltd, the investment subsidiary of Prudential Corporation plc, in 1986.

He is a member of the Council of the British Property Federation, being Vice-President for 1988/89. He became a member of The Commission for the New Towns in 1986 and has been a member of the Property Advisory Group to the Department of the Environment since 1985. He is a Director of the Barkshire Committee Ltd, one of the two groups who have actively been pursuing the securitisation of property. In another sphere altogether he is also a Governor of the South Bank Polytechnic.

Richard Wolfe has been involved in merchant banking, mainly in the City of London, for some 24 years.

On leaving Arkworth School in Yorkshire he joined N. M. Rothschild as a management trainee and subsequently worked with British Continental Building Co. and Hill Samuel as an investment fund manager.

In 1980, Richard Wolfe moved to Security Pacific National Bank as a corporate finance executive. In 1981 he was given the task of forming a permanent real estate financing capability in London. The Security Pacific Real Estate Financing Unit is now one of the most important real estate lenders in the UK. A further unit has since been established in Frankfurt to service property financing needs in West Germany and to explore other European initiatives.

Richard Wolfe is an Associate of the Institute of Bankers.

Michael Peat was born in 1949 and studied Law at Oxford University from 1969 to 1972. He joined Peat Marwick Mitchell in 1972 and qualified as a Chartered Accountant in 1975, obtaining an MBA at INSEAD in 1976/77. In 1985 he became a Partner. He is Chairman of the Peat Marwick McLintock UK Property and Construction Industry Group.

David Bramson was born in 1942 and obtained an LLB degree from University College London in 1963. He was admitted as a solicitor in 1966. After a short spell in industry, he joined Nabarro Nathanson in 1968 and is now senior property partner.

He specialises in all aspects of property development and financing, acting for developers, institutions and public sector clients. He has a particular interest in the structuring of partnership arrangements in which commercial developers enter into joint ventures with local authority and public utility landowners to provide for the more efficient use of the landowner's property assets.

David Bramson is a frequent lecturer on legal aspects of commercial real property to lawyers, surveyors and other professionals involved in the industry.

Jim A. Beveridge graduated from Edinburgh University in 1970, taking up Articles the same year with Tansley Witt & Company, a then medium-sized firm of Chartered Accountants in London. He qualified as a Chartered Accountant in 1973. For the next two years he worked with the British Tourist Authority on special project work, including computerisation of the accounting system.

Jim Beveridge joined MEPC in 1975 and has held several positions with the Company. He began as MEPC's European Accountant and then became Group Chief Accountant the following year. He was appointed Finace Director in 1984, a position he still holds.

Stewart Millman was educated at New College, Oxford where he read Chemistry, and joined Lazards in 1971 straight from University. He specialised in fund management, especially offshore funds and fixed-interest investments, becoming a director of Lazard Securities.

In 1981 he joined de Zoete Bevan, now part of BZW, becoming a partner in the Corporate Finance Department in 1984. He is now a director of BZW Securities and of the corporate stockbroking subsidiary. Clients and recent major transactions include: Arlington Securities; Coats Viyella; European Home Products; the British Telecom privatisation; the formation of BZW, and various international transactions involving the USA or Australia.

He has been a member of Council of The Society of Investment Analysts for some years and has published articles on a range of financial subjects.

Neil Sinclair graduated from Gonville & Caius College Cambridge with a double first in law, and qualified as a solicitor in 1962. He has been a senior partner of Berwin Leighton since 1970 and is a specialist in corporate finance and company taxation. Author of 'Warranties and Indemnities on Share Sales', he is also a general editor and contributor to 'Practical Commercial Precedent'. He is the creator of the PINCs property securitisation vehicle.

Contents

Chapter 1

Introduction

Stephen Barter

When you ask people to identify the key characteristics of UK commercial property as an investment, what do they say? Many will use phrases such as 'special', 'secure bricks and mortar', 'long-term', 'slow moving', or 'stable inflation hedge'; some might add 'illiquid' and some might even treat you to a lecture on the fundamental importance of possessing land.

Yet there have been sufficient examples during the past ten years to question all of these statements, although illiquidity remains a key issue, particularly for the larger developments. At the same time, a better understanding of property as a medium for investment has brought with it radical changes to the ways in which property is financed.

The purpose of this introduction is to review the background to these changes in order to set the scene for the more detailed considerations by the individual contributors in their own chapters. In so doing, I shall consider the impact of these changes on traditional attitudes to property investment and the reactions of the property industry to the new business opportunities which they present.

I THE IMPACT OF PERFORMANCE MEASUREMENT

The late 1970s was something of a watershed for property investment. A quick glance at the limited performance statistics available at the time shows that property was comfortably out-performing inflation. Yet by the early 1980s it was not; average rental growth significantly under-performed inflation and capital values in certain sectors were actually falling. According to the Richard Ellis Monthly Index, only since 1986 has property begun to show significant real returns again.

A more careful observation of the late 1970s figures by independent commentators of the time shattered many illusions by correctly identifying that the favourable performance was due more to falling yield levels (supposedly based upon higher rental growth expectations) than to underlying rental growth itself.

The timing of this particular observation betrays much about the comparatively recent application of reliable performance measurement systems to property. One of the first formal external valuations of a major institutional portfolio was undertaken as recently as 1969 for an insurance company. It was not until the late 1970s, in the wake of the rapid growth in property investment by pension funds, that a few of the leading firms of surveyors began to develop basic performance measurement systems for their in-house clients. The apparently late start was due not in small measure to reluctance by certain of the larger institutions for a diversity of reasons.

Wider performance measurement, matched by increasingly sophisticated market research and analysis as property returns fell in the early 1980s, produced a much keener understanding of the components of property investment – of yield and rent, of valuation benchmarks, of valuation methods. This understanding, magnified by the large number of institutions who by then held direct property portfolios, encouraged radical changes in the traditional attitudes to property investment. By the mid-1980s, property was being measured relatively as much as absolutely and, at a time when equities were producing substantially better returns, this merely exaggerated the shortcomings of property as an investment medium and increased the need for innovation.

II NEW REALISM

The past few years have seen significant changes in real estate finance which have begun to address many of these concerns. While property is now an accepted part of a balanced institutional portfolio, it is appreciated that its performance can and should be analysed, tested and explained so that it can be more accurately compared with other investment media. It is therefore no longer 'special'. It is a financial investment backed by a physical asset with certain unique characteristics which will require specialised management. But essentially there is an income element and a capital element which can be valued and appraised as an investment opportunity like any stock or bond.

For some – I think now comparatively few – all attempts to unveil the mystique of property have been greeted with acute suspicion, to be regarded as a threat to professional skill. The property profession has never been short of emotion, but it is fundamentally based upon enterprise and shrewd commercialism – pro-active rather than re-active – and contains some of the sharpest business brains around. For the few, the pure 'seat of the pants/gut feel' remains the style and provides the key to an exciting day. For the many, however, the wider availability of well researched information, if not the greater disclosure of transactions, is seen as a crucial aid to (but no substitute for) the professional judgment which the client fundamentally seeks from his adviser. The brilliance of the decisions is never the issue, rather the consistency of the results and the professionalism with which they are executed.

Take away the sentiment of land and buildings and consider a property investment as an asset backed flow of income which can be distributed in many different ways to offer investors differing degrees of risk and hence differing yields and capital values, and there lies the basis of property securitisation and the innovative forms of real estate finance which are now being developed. These new financing techniques not only create, as a mirror image, new and diverse investment opportunities, they also help to overcome the traditional concerns about property's inherent illiquidity and inflexibility.

III KEY CONCERNS

Key concerns about property as an investment medium remain:

i. *Illiquidity*

A property usually takes at least three months to buy or sell and (in English law) there is no certainty of the price or terms until contracts have been exchanged. This greatly inhibits investment timing. The problem is particularly acute for properties with capital values of around £20m and above because of the relatively small supply of potential single purchasers in the market. This causes significant problems in appraising and financing the more substantial developments.

ii. *Inflexibility*

Direct property investment has a relatively high unit cost and offers little flexibility at the individual property level; one usually buys, as it were, either the whole thing as an equity investment with all its contingent risks, or not at all. This causes particular problems in portfolio diversification and management. Property shares and property unit trusts offer some consolation here, but property companies are taxed in the same way as other companies and unauthorised property unit trusts, are only available to pension funds and certain types of charities and cannot be listed. It is proposed that property unit trusts will soon be able to operate as authorised unit trusts; this will extend their investor base to include the general public, but they may remain unlisted and will suffer corporation tax on income.

iii. *The Growth of Debt Finance*

Some commentators view the substantial increase in bank lending to the property sector in recent years, relative to new equity investment by institutions, as a major threat to the stability of the property market.

iv. *Valuation Methodology and Precision*

Conventional valuation methods increasingly appear inflexible and unable to meet the rigorous demands of modern property investment appraisal. The 'all risks yield' approach is particularly difficult to apply to the larger, relatively more illiquid properties, such as major shopping centres and substantial office buildings.

v. *The Future Role of The Property Professional*

The liberalisation of financial markets and the increasing importance of debt in property funding has brought new competition to chartered surveying firms from investment banks and other professions in the provision of property advice. The impact of the Financial Services Act has introduced a new tier of regulation and new requirements for disclosure. For some firms these changes have been accelerated by the need for external capital; for most, the changes have prompted the need to redefine business objectives and the role which should be fulfilled.

This list is by no means exhaustive, but it summarises those issues on which, to a greater or lesser degree, most of my fellow contributors comment in their individual chapters from their own perspectives.

IV   RECENT TRENDS IN PROPERTY PERFORMANCE

So, with hindsight, what can be learned from the lessons of the past decade?

Graphs 1 and 2 (right) illustrate the relative movements of rental and capital growth for the office, retail and industrial sectors over the past eight years and compare the results with inflation. Notice how they differ in strength of performance and how it is only since 1987 that all three sectors show both rental and capital growth which significantly out-performed inflation. The graph also neatly confirms that the cycles of activity are by no means consistent across the sectors.

Graph 3 shows the relationship between capital and rental growth for the three sectors combined over the same period. Whereas the strong performance of property in the late 1970s was due principally to capital growth (falling yields), this graph confirms that the current bull phase has been fuelled principally by strong real rental growth. There is also evidence of a distinct time lag between rental movements and yield changes, which in part reflects the inherent illiquidity of the market and in part the caution of institutional investors towards property over the past few years, faced with persistently strong equity performance. Graph 4 combines the capital and rental results to show the overall trend between total return and inflation over the same period.

Putting these results in a relative context, Graph 5 compares the annual total returns from equities and gilts with property over the past ten years. This

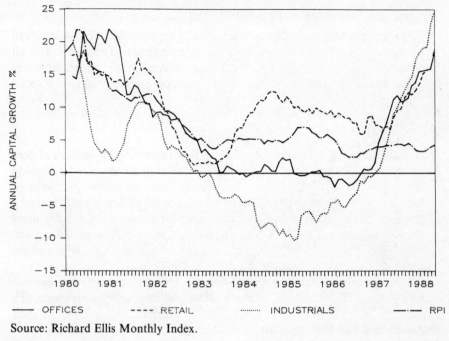

OFFICES ——— RETAIL - - - - INDUSTRIALS ·········· RPI —·—·—

Source: Richard Ellis Monthly Index.

Graph 1. Capital Change 1980–1988.

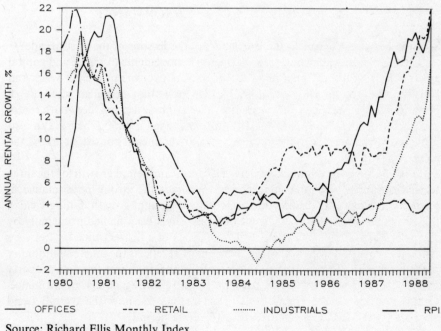

OFFICES ——— RETAIL - - - - INDUSTRIALS ·········· RPI —·—·—

Source: Richard Ellis Monthly Index.

Graph 2. Rental Change 1980–1988.

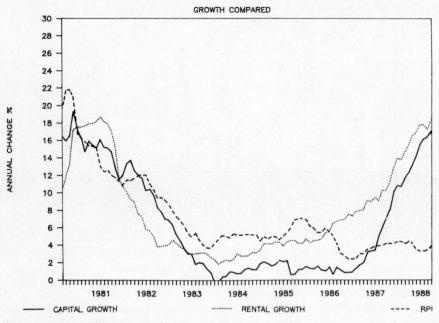

Source: Richard Ellis Monthly Index.

Graph 3. Capital, Rental, Inflation.

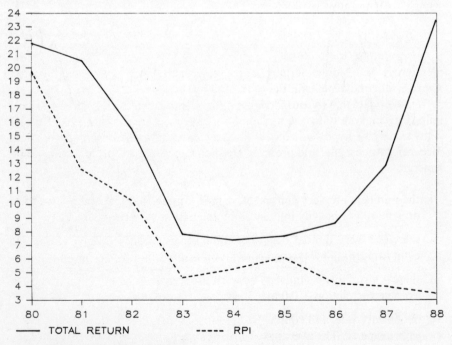

Source: Richard Ellis Monthly Index.

Graph 4. Year on Year Growth Total Return and RPI.

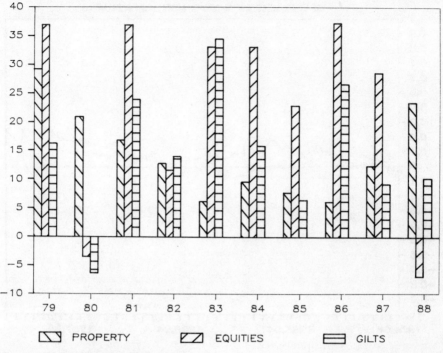

PROPERTY   EQUITIES   GILTS

Source: Richard Ellis Monthly Index.

Graph 5. Comparative Total Return.

demonstrates the longer term nature of the property cycle as compared with the more erratic movements in the other two markets.

It is often said that the property market moves countercyclically to equities and gilts, thus making it a good medium for diversification. Early in 1988, Richard Ellis tested this hypothesis over a five year period and the relative correlations between equities, gilts and property are shown in Graph 6. The following points emerge:

i. the numbers are very consistent, demonstrating that the conclusions to be drawn are not heavily influenced by the time period considered;

ii. there is a very limited degree of similarity between property returns and equity returns. The average correlation is 0.10;

iii. there is virtually no similarity between property returns and gilt returns. The average correlation is 0.03;

iv. in contrast, gilts and equities move much more in line with each other than with property. The average correlation between gilts and equities is 0.44.

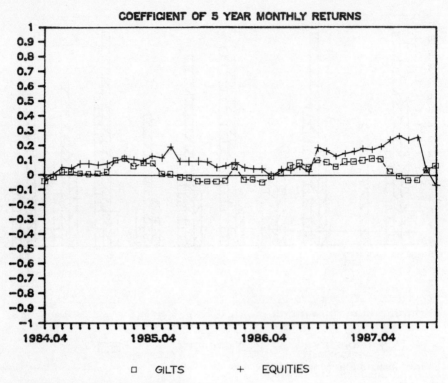

COEFFICIENT OF 5 YEAR MONTHLY RETURNS

□   GILTS   +   EQUITIES

Source: Richard Ellis Monthly Index.

Graph 6. Correlation of Property Returns.

While these results seem to confirm the hypothesis, a detailed discussion of the reasons is beyond the scope of this book, although an analysis over a longer time period would be worthwhile.

However, in the context of my earlier comments, the apparent countercyclical trend, matched by the time lag between rental growth and yield movements, emphasises property's relative illiquidity and the difficulties facing fund managers who are unable to time their property investments as precisely as equities.

The significance of this time lag and the inefficiency of the property pricing mechanism is well illustrated in Graph 7. This compares the trend in average rental growth since 1980 (ie, property's underlying performance) with the movement in average equivalent yields (ie, its price). It is an extraordinary result. In particular, the graph reveals that despite the upturn in rental growth from mid-1983 onwards, property yields actually rose (putting downward pressure on capital values) for two further years. At the time of writing (August 1988) yields are showing some signs of having begun to fall slightly, but this does not alter the overall impression of an inefficient pricing mechanism and an illiquid property market.

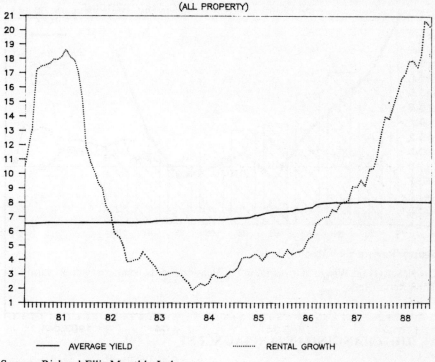

(ALL PROPERTY)

———— AVERAGE YIELD   ··········· RENTAL GROWTH

Source: Richard Ellis Monthly Index.

Graph 7. Rental Growth Average Yields.

Some argue that the time lag and pricing inefficiency is principally because fund managers are characteristically slow to react and that, as a result, they consistently make poorly timed policy judgments in relation to their property allocations. In the early 1980s, so the argument goes, many fund managers (particularly the pension fund managers) bought too much, too late, became overweight in the sector, could not sell properties without suffering book losses when the market turned down and paid the penalty of aggregate under-performance when equities roared ahead. Graph 8 sheds some questioning light on this argument.

The commercial reality is that, right or wrong, fund managers are now being judged increasingly by short-term performance targets. Therefore, unless property investments can be timed more precisely or unless property's countercyclical performance can be made available at sufficiently attractive yields in a sufficiently liquid form, institutions who already hold significant direct property portfolios will remain selective in their commitments and the pricing conundrum will persist.

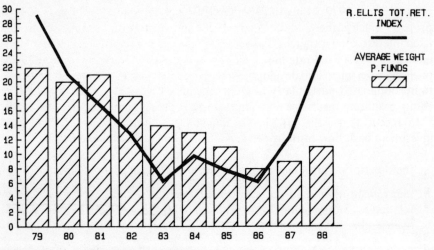

Source: Richard Ellis Monthly Index.

Graph 8. Average Weight of Property in UK Pension Funds, compared with Richard Ellis Total Return Index.

V   THE CHANGING FINANCIAL SCENE

Overview

Historically, the UK commercial property market has been a market financed mainly by equity, dominated by the insurance companies and pension funds. However, during the past five years, debt has become increasingly important and, in my view, is likely to become a permanent feature. At the same time, the capital markets have been increasingly used to finance property, both at the company level and at the individual property level. Financial instruments which were originally designed for corporate funding are now being applied to single properties. There is now, therefore, a significantly wider choice of funding sources, types and vehicles than there was ten years ago. In all areas there has been considerable innovation to create flexible financing arrangements which, by being designed to fit the specific characteristics of the individual property asset, have the capacity to reduce risk and to provide many new opportunities for investment.

1   Equity finance

1   DIRECT PROPERTY INVESTMENT BY UK INSTITUTIONS

Commercial property investment is a relatively new market. It has only become significant to institutions during the past 30 years and most of its growth has occurred since 1970. Many of the older insurance companies had begun to hold property much earlier and during the 1950s and 1960s provided finance through fixed interest rate mortgages. However, as inflation accelerated during the 1960s and early 1970s, fixed rate mortgages became less economic. By the mid-1970s, property investment and development had become a significant market in its own right, dominated particularly after the secondary banking crisis of 1973/4 by equity cash from insurance companies and a growing number of pension funds.

In recent years, the UK institutions have committed less of their total investment cash flow into property. This may be partly explained by:

i. the superior performance of equities since 1981 (at least until October 1987);

ii. many institutions had enough property in their investment portfolios in relation to a notional long-term target weighting, and some were significantly overweight;

iii. a greater understanding of the performance characteristics of property investment (ie, risk and reward), matched by an increasing appreciation of its relative illiquidity and limited short-term volatility, resulting in greater caution and selectivity. A low yielding property does not necessarily imply a low risk/high reward investment. Higher yielding industrial property, for example, has been one of the best performing sectors in recent years.

There are numerous other explanations, but a common factor between them seems to be a maturing of understanding about property as an investment, matched by more rigorous performance requirements as the institutions themselves and their own customer base have become more financially sophisticated. Some commentators have labelled this attitude 'progressive short-termism' and no doubt that particular debate will continue in the years to come.

A related concern of many institutions about property ownership has been the need for management, not just through collecting the rent and supervising maintenance, but also through asset improvement to enhance performance produced solely by market forces. Management, under both headings, represents an obligatory cost for a crucial service. For many smaller funds, the obligation prohibits direct investment; for the larger funds, the issue is who does it and how should it be paid for? Michael Mallinson examines the concern in some depth in his chapter.

Graph 9 summarises the trend in direct property investment by pension funds and insurance companies. The question for many at the time of writing is how far the substantially improved performance of property, relatively and absolutely, will reverse the trend, particularly for the pension funds. There are many who believe that history will not simply repeat itself. The equity crash of October 1987 did not produce a flood of institutional investment back into property; the arithmetical shift in value weighting did the job automatically. Moreover, it is not possible significantly to increase a fund's holding of property in the short term. Consequently, substantial new investment, other than at the margin, will require

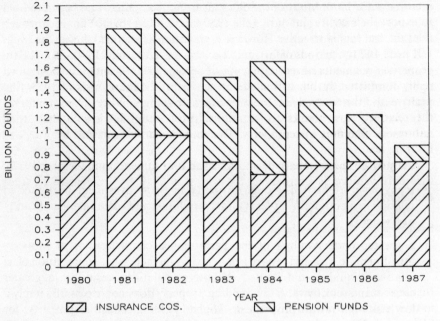

Source: Central Statistical Office.

Graph 9. Institutions Net Investment in Property.

a change in longer term target weighting, which may be more a reflection of the institutions' disenchantment with equities than their appetite for property.

2   OVERSEAS EQUITY INVESTORS

Apart from the domestic insurance companies and pensions funds, in recent years other sources of equity finance have emerged. Overseas investors, drawn by a strong UK economy and the increasing financial importance of the City of London, have begun to invest more noticeably. Of particular significance has been the Japanese. For some years, the Japanese have been major investors in US real estate and now their attention has begun to spread towards Australia and latterly the UK. To date, virtually all Japanese UK investment has been committed by contractors and developers, and to some extent by corporations for owner occupation or trading. However, the longer term investors, such as the life companies, are actively seeking opportunities, and may soon make significant commitments, but it will be a gradual process.

Equity finance has also come from Europe, particularly from the larger pensions funds of Holland – starved of opportunities at home for their substantial cash flows – and from the property companies (soon also the insurance companies) of Sweden, as a result of exchange control relaxation. The inertia of EEC harmonisation in 1992 may encourage other European countries to export their capital into UK property. Funds from the Middle East remain relevant, but highly selective. US equity, such an obvious opportunity given the UK need and the periods of favourable exchange rates from US to UK in recent years, has not materialised to any significant degree. Perhaps the US market really is sufficiently big to remove the need for external diversification; but perhaps also the relatively higher property yields in the US are misleading, given the relatively lower risks to be derived from the UK's sophisticated and nationwide planning system and the benefit in yield terms of full repairing and insuring leases.

Many of the new overseas investors are joint venture players and the revival of the joint venture is considered later in this chapter. Unfortunately, in a confidential property market, there are insufficient figures available accurately to quantify the impact of the overseas players, but the perception in London and the South East is that it has been significant.

3   INVESTMENT IN PROPERTY SHARES

Institutional caution towards direct property in recent years has not been echoed in their attitude towards property shares. UK institutions contributed between £1.5bn and £2bn to the equity issues made by property companies during 1987 before the October crash. This compares with total net, institutional direct investment to property for the whole of that year of only £975m. Since early 1987 (and despite the crash), at least to the time of writing, property shares have outperformed the market. In his chapter, Stewart Millman reflects on the relationship between direct property and property shares; Jim Beveridge, in his chapter, considers how property companies are taking advantage of the innovations in property finance to improve their performance.

2   Debt finance

1   RECENT TRENDS AND PARTICIPANTS

As I noted at the outset, the UK property market has been funded traditionally by equity. However, one of the most striking features of the past five years has been the increasing availability and use of debt. Graph 10 compares the growth of bank lending to property companies with new net investment by pension funds and insurance companies since 1980. As at August 1988, the total of loans outstanding to the property sector was some £19bn, a figure which has trebled in four years. Although loans to residential developers are included in this figure, the bulk of it relates to the commercial sector.

The reasons for this rapid growth are varied, but include:

i. the shortage of institutional equity for development funding at a time of strengthening letting markets and increasingly profitable development

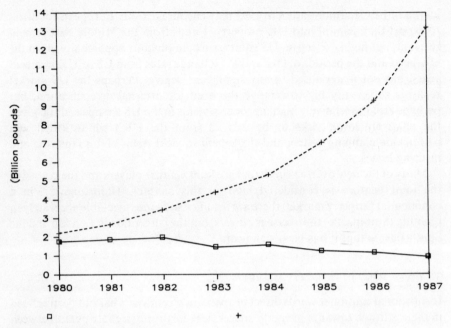

Source: Financial Statistics.

Graph 10. Comparison: institutional investment and bank lending.

opportunities. At the same time, there has been a distinction between those schemes which institutions would forward purchase and finance and those which they would only buy as completed investments;

ii. an appreciation that the margins on property lending were significantly greater than for mainstream corporate lending;

iii. the availability in London of a growing number of overseas banks eager to participate in or lead syndicates; while the Americans were the key players in the early 1970s, most of the recent growth has come from the Europeans and Japanese, as well as the Australian banks;

iv. the specific need for finance to develop a number of substantial office buildings in the City of London to house the new investment banking conglomerates which have arisen from 'Big Bang'. For example, the new office developments at Liverpool Street (Broadgate), Cannon Street and Charing Cross Stations and the former Spitalfields Market alone have to date committed some £1.7bn of bank lending.

Perhaps the most important new arrival in the property lending market during the next few years will be the building societies. As a result of the Building

Societies Act 1986, societies can lend up to 10% of their loan portfolio into non-residential opportunities. The Abbey National was the first major lender from this sector, providing a £40m facility for a substantial mixed-use development at Paddington in London; others are beginning to follow. The building societies' financial resources are such as to make them potentially substantial players – the biggest societies are as big as some of the largest UK clearing banks – providing strong competition in the market. Some are planning to be floated as public companies. However, it seems unlikely that their involvement will be significant until the early 1990s.

2 LIMITED RECOURSE LENDING

Particular attention has concentrated on the so-called limited recourse loan. This is designed to limit the recourse of the bank to the project itself, within certain limits, and thereby to restrict the potential liability and risk to the borrower. In essence, in the case of a development, the bank bears the risk of a shortfall in the repayment of the principal from the sale proceeds of the property, usually provided the developer guarantees practical completion of the building. The treatment of interest and cost overruns is negotiated in each case, but, usually, the bank will absorb some of the equity risk of the development in return for a slightly higher interest margin than if the developer had received a corporate loan.

For income producing investments, a limited recourse loan would be secured only against the property and the debt interest would be serviced by the rental income. Any interest shortfall may well have to be underwritten by the borrower but in certain cases can be rolled up. In effect the loan is principally secured against the tenants' covenants and their obligations under the occupational leases, but the bank takes the risk on the future capital value of the property.

The prospect of linking the security of a loan to the property rather than to the borrower has a particular appeal to the private developer who lacks a substantial balance sheet. However, in practice, the attraction of the limited recourse label can be over-stated; few developers would wish to walk away from any banking commitments, their entire reputation is at stake. The fact that the value of a development scheme can be substantially in excess of the net worth of the developer emphasises the responsibility on both sides and the significant care which the bank must take in verifying both the borrower and the project.

Having said that, the limited recourse principle has allowed the introduction of many ingenious innovations, designed to maximise the percentage of value which can be borrowed, secured only against the property itself. These methods rely on separating the loan risk between the 'hard core' amount, which can be well secured and serviced by current rental income, and the 'top-slice' of value, which relies on growth in rental and capital values within prudent levels. As a result, a distinction is made between the pure debt risk and the equity or quasi-equity (mezzanine) risk. It is the treatment of the top-slice element which has attracted much of the innovative interest in recent years.

3   AN OVER-GEARED MARKET?

The growth in bank lending has caused some concern to those who have memories of 1973/4. Fears have been growing of an over-geared property market and it is known that The Bank of England has indicated its concern to the property lending banks. While this concern is likely to continue, particularly if the economy enters a period of relatively high interest rates, circumstances are materially different from those prevailing in the early 1970s. In my view:

i. the quality of credit risk analysis by the banks and their understanding of property is significantly higher than it was 15 years ago;

ii. the underlying economy has been strong and there is little doubt that the current development boom is fuelled more by tenant demand than by the supply of finance;

iii. most of the larger loans are syndicated and hence the credit exposure to any individual bank is contained;

iv. banks are now particularly sensitive to the distinction between the equity risk and the debt risk which they are being asked to take in making their lending decisions. 100% finance is available (see below) but only on terms which adequately reflect the risks involved;

v. the development of a sophisticated interest rate swap market and the introduction of other hedging techniques has significantly reduced the vulnerability of both borrower and lender to unforeseen changes in interest rates.

Clearly, the more which can be done to encourage greater equity investment into the market whether by direct institutional investment or by indirect means, such as securitisation, the sooner this apparent gearing pressure and concern about the repayment of construction loans outstanding on major developments will be alleviated. In this respect, cashflow is critical to the appraisal of modern property developments and to property development companies. Identifying the key pressure points of the funding, particularly when the scheme is phased, is an important first step towards assessing risks and the capacity for gearing. Most leading developers, banks and advisers are familiar with computerised spread sheet techniques and these are now essential tools in credit risk analysis.

Aside from securitising the property itself, there may also emerge the opportunity for the banks to securitise their own loan portfolios. Common in USA, this has already occurred in the UK residential mortgage lending market. The bonds created, backed by secure real estate assets, have proved very popular with investors. For the banks, the approach would successfully refinance their commercial property lending by taking the loans off balance sheet.

In his chapter Richard Wolfe considers limited recourse lending and the role of the banks in property finance in further detail.

3 Off balance sheet financing

Many of the more innovative debt arrangements in recent years have been designed to be 'off balance sheet'. For developers, raising debt off balance sheet is often essential to the extent that, as noted above, many development companies have only a small capital base relative to the value of the projects which they undertake. The technique is also helpful to owner occupiers, particularly retailers and breweries, because it avoids confusion between the company's trading operations and its property activities. Burtons, Wickes and Safeway have all financed property portfolios through off balance sheet techniques in recent years.

However, the recent sharp growth in property lending has caused increasing concern about gearing disclosure in property company accounts. The widespread use of controlled non-subsidiary companies through so-called 'diamond structures' to achieve off balance sheet, tax efficient financing arrangements looks set to become outlawed. In March 1988, the Institute of Chartered Accountants published a draft SSAP on Accounting for Special Purpose Transactions (Exposure Draft 42). Moreover, the EEC has also been considering the matter and its Seventh Directive on company law which deals with group accounts will shortly be implemented in the UK by an amendment to the Companies Act.

Off balance sheet financing is a complex area and one which Michael Peat considers in more detail in his chapter. The key objective must be to ensure that where the financing arrangement demands recourse to the company, the potential extent of that liability is properly reflected in the company's accounts.

4 The joint venture revival

The combination of a rising property market, the wide availability of limited recourse development finance and a selective institutional funding market, has revived the use of joint venture arrangements in recent years. The attraction to a developer is that by being able to delay disposal until development completion, the full benefit of any rental or capital growth which might occur during the development period can be retained. The developer thus avoids the need to forward sell to an institution at a discounted yield and at a pegged base rent.

The attraction to the joint venture partner depends upon the nature of the partner and the purpose of the joint venture. A key issue is whether or not the partner brings to the party more than just money. For example, the partner may be a landowner, a contractor, or an overseas investor seeking a longer term business relationship.

In a typical deal, the joint venture partner will provide most of the equity finance required for the development, in return for a share of the profits. The joint venture vehicle will raise the required debt, with a view to selling the completed investment, thus providing the equity partner with an attractive leveraged return. Minimum target internal rates of return on equity of 20% are not untypical, although certain investment trusts and institutions who are more familiar with management buy-out deals may be much more demanding. It all depends on the perceived risk.

Fundamentally, it is essential that the partners understand and think through at the outset how they will work together in practice, what each really wants out of the relationship and how decisions will be made. The potential problems which are identified at this stage can be provided for in the documents; those left undeclared or implied merely fester to irritate later.

David Bramson examines the legal mechanics of negotiating joint ventures in more detail in his chapter.

5   New products – The Property Equity Fund

The shortage of equity finance for property development in the mid-1980s encouraged a number of new initiatives. In my own experience was the creation of The Property Equity Fund (PEF). This was devised by Richard Ellis Financial Services, in conjunction with Barclays de Zoete Wedd and was launched in 1987. It was the first special purpose facility to provide 100% finance for developments from a single source and thereby to avoid the need for a developer to seek, independently, equity from a joint venture partner and a construction loan from a bank. PEF shares the trading developer's philosophy in that once the scheme has been completed, it will be sold. PEF was therefore, deliberately, a short-term financing facility and not a long-term investment fund.

PEF initially provided a total facility of £100m, comprising £25m of committed equity from four investors and up to £75m of limited recourse debt from a syndicate of eight banks. As a result, there was a gearing ratio of approximately 3:1, which provided an attractive leveraged profit share to the equity participants. PEF is aimed at developments having completed values of between £5m and £20m. A minimum target internal rate of return on equity committed of 20% is required unless the project is particularly low risk. In practice, PEF usually requires only a minority share of the development profit to generate an acceptable level of return.

Other, similar, facilities have been introduced and although the structures and working arrangements may differ between them, the objectives are largely identical. PEF was the pioneer and neatly demonstrated the pooling of expertise between firms of chartered surveyors and the investment banks in real estate finance.

6   The capital markets

One of the most fundamental developments in recent years has been the increasing ability to use the capital markets to finance both public property companies and individual buildings. This is partly a reaction to the growing appreciation that property is as much a financial commodity as a physical asset and can be appraised on the basis of its cashflow characteristics. It is also partly a function of the liberalisation of the UK capital markets, post Big Bang, and the increasing competition and push for innovation which these changes have encouraged.

1   PROPERTY COMPANIES

There are now so many different types of property company that a universal definition is impossible. My fellow contributors attempt some distinctions and I shall not add to the confusion here, other than to reflect on a significant change in attitude.

The past few years have seen a gradual transition from the preconception of a property company as a company which purchased and held properties as investment assets to generate a stream of income from rents, to the acceptance of a company which traded property investments and developments to generate a stream of income from trading and development profits. Some of our leading property companies are now, in practice, a combination of the two.

The transition was therefore from valuing property companies purely in terms of net asset value – a rather static analysis, to be able to analyse them in terms of an earnings multiple – a rather more dynamic analysis. At the time of writing, examples of the former include Hammerson and MEPC, while examples of the latter include Arlington Securities and London & Metropolitan.

Each type of property company has different financing requirements, not just because of differing business objectives, but also because of the financial pressures on its profit and loss account and share price. For one, the objective is to finance to retain, for the other, it is to finance to sell.

A third variant is the company for which property is one of many diversified activities. This includes those companies, such as the multi-national conglomerate, which acquires property as a by-product of its corporate acquisitions and others, such as the retailer, for which property is intrinsically fundamental to the success of its business. Retailers in particular have come to realise that they are just as much in the property business as in retailing; some have set up separate property subsidiaries which have been financed independently, in order to distinguish between property profits and retailing profits. Sleepy retailers with potentially valuable property portfolios often provide tempting takeover targets.

In general terms, the fickle pendulum of fashion tends to swing over time between the analysts' preference for assets and their preference for trading profits – between a net asset value basis and an earnings multiple basis. At the time of writing, with rising interest rates and increasing concern about the duration of the current property boom, assets are again in the ascendancy. Attention therefore concentrates on the relationship between the share price and the company's net asset value and whether or not a discount or a premium can be

LONDON & EDINBURGH TRUST PLC

OFFER FOR SALE BY TENDER
BY
BARCLAYS MERCHANT BANK
LIMITED

[Photo. London and Edinburgh Trust prospectus – the first of the quoted merchant developers, now a diversified property and investment group.]

justified. This creates enormous problems for the so-called hybrid companies (of which there are many), whose activities embrace both trading and investment. The issue is no longer black and white, and, with approaching 130 property companies now listed on The Stock Exchange, it merits a more intelligent approach. Stewart Millman considers the arguments in detail in his chapter.

For all property companies, however defined, this book will seek to illustrate how recent innovations in corporate funding techniques, helped by new competition within the international capital markets, have considerably increased the flexibility of financing property. Most of the larger public companies, such as British Land, MEPC and Hammerson, have taken advantage of these new arrangements, which are detailed elsewhere in this book, and include multiple option facilities, tender panel loans, Eurobond issues and commercial paper programmes. It is not unusual now to find some of the larger property companies enjoying debt facilities at virtually LIBOR interest rates.

The development of these techniques has offered important alternatives for those property companies who might otherwise rush towards a stock market flotation. The key issue is, what is the purpose of flotation? The reporting requirements and profitability demanded from public companies are such as can put a great burden on management. Property companies, for their size, employ relatively few people; if the main objective is to increase the capital base and public profile of the business, other significantly less onerous and costly methods are now readily available.

2 INDIVIDUAL PROPERTIES

There have been many examples in recent years of financial instruments which were originally designed for corporate funding being applied to single properties. Deep discount bonds have been used to finance both standing investments in a non-recourse form (for example Samuel Montagu's headquarters at Billingsgate by S & W Berisford), and developments in an unsecured form (for example, the Charing Cross Station redevelopment by Greycoat Plc). The financing of Rosehaugh/Greycoat's joint venture development at 1 Finsbury Avenue in the City of London – the pioneering scheme for the massive Broadgate complex – provides a good example of innovation in the adaptation of familiar financial investments to meet particular circumstances and was a milestone in UK real estate finance.

To finance the construction of this development in 1982, the developers assembled a syndicate of institutions and major corporates who, together, put up the required equity of approximately £34m. The developers issued to the syndicate shares in the special purpose development company and nil paid debentures. The shares were for a small amount and were fully subscribed whereas the debentures were issued without any cash being paid but subject to a call to pay the face value at a future date. Because of the strength of the covenants

[Photograph 1, Finsbury Avenue, London EC2 – the pioneer for Broadgate.]

making the commitment, Rosehaugh/Greycoat were able to raise an interim loan for the entire cost of the development at very competitive interest rates from a bank assured of repayment from the debenture.

Through their shares the debenture holders were entitled to receive a proportion of the development profits. In the event, the debenture monies were never called because, by the time of the exercise date, in November 1987, the development had been completed and let and was sufficiently profitable for the interim loan to be re-financed. The debenture holders had therefore received an attractive share of a substantial development profit in return for providing only a guarantee, rather than cash. A remarkable achievement.

The interim loan was re-financed by a listed mortgage debenture, also noteworthy because it was secured only on the property (although the property itself did not have to be listed), totally without recourse to Rosehaugh/Greycoat. The £40m issue was priced at only 65 basis points above a comparable Treasury gilt.

The key feature about both debenture issues was that the investors were prepared to take a view on the property alone, without corporate support. The listed debenture on the completed property helped to establish an important principle and was, in effect, the first example of securitisation in the UK.

7 Securitisation

Securitisation takes the application of the capital markets to single properties to its logical extent. At the current time, it is probably the most important development of all for the future of real estate finance.

Securitisation, quite simply, means the conversion of assets into tradeable paper securities. The concept has been common in other financial markets for many years. Its application to property – such an obvious solution to the fundamental problem of illiquidity – has only begun to evolve seriously during the past four years. I suspect that this is partly due to the many technical problems which needed to be overcome, coupled with a fundamental change in attitude, trading style and competition within the securities markets as a result of Big Bang.

This change in attitude was exemplified by The Stock Exchange's decision in August 1986 to permit the flotation of single properties on the main market. It is now possible for both professional and private investors to buy an equity share in a single property investment which can be traded on The Stock Exchange, without the obligation of management and having only limited liability, which produces a direct proportion of the property's rental income and capital growth, at a yield which is (on average) double the dividend yield from a property company share, and which is taxed only once – in the hands of the investor – at his own rate of tax, if any.

For £1 a share, the investor obtains the same benefits as direct ownership of a property worth many millions more, but with the advantage of immediate liquidity and without the obligation of management. The trading price of the share will offer an immediate indication of value and performance and property investments made in this way can be timed as precisely as investments in other securities through the global screen-trading markets.

The technique allows property owners to release substantial amounts of capital previously locked into valuable property assets without having to sacrifice management control. Moreover, because single property companies can be geared, it is possible to create layered structures, offering investors the choice of both equity and debt securities, backed by the same property, and offering the original owner or developer the ultimate flexibility in financing its asset.

1   STEPPING STONES TO A NEW MARKET

With hindsight, it is quite remarkable that three independent groups of professionals, Richard Ellis/County NatWest, The Barkshire Committee and the Royal Institution of Chartered Surveyors (RICS), should have begun to investigate a suitable approach to property securitisation in the UK at almost exactly the same time.

Richard Ellis began its work with County in 1985, on the initiative of Andrew Huntley, then head of Richard Ellis's Investment Department. Both firms had been investigating the subject independently already for some months. A working party was established which met frequently and had a clear sense of urgency. The fundamental objectives were to find a vehicle which was both tax transparent and viable within the current law and to establish a satisfactory market system for trading.

The initial group included myself and Paul Rivlin[1], together with Neil Sinclair and Robert John, then a director of County Bank. It was immediately obvious that a completely new vehicle would have to be developed to meet these objectives. We each offered ideas and philosophies of approach, but it was ultimately Neil's brilliant invention which gave us our breakthrough.

The key was the thought that the financial benefit of a property investment could be separated from ownership and hence the sharing between investors could be of a financial participation rather than of an interest in land or a physical part of the property. As a result, management control and ownership could be expressed in corporate terms rather than property terms. Securitisation essentially involves a division among many different investors of the right to receive an income stream generated by a property investment. Neil took this thought and with it created what became known as the PINC.

Having refined the vehicle, we then needed to build the framework within which it could operate. Paul Rivlin and I spent many long hours during the subsequent year developing the system with our colleagues. Using the existing

---

1   Paul D Rivlin became a director of County NatWest Ltd, and in March 1988 he accepted an appointment to become a director of Rosehaugh Plc.

regulations and market practice of companies, we applied these principles to single properties. Much of it demanded a totally new approach. Yet, when we attended the initial presentation of The Barkshire Committee's[2] proposals for the single property unit trust in April 1986, it was gratifying to discover that their approach to the concept (though not the vehicle nor, at that time, the market system) was very similar to our own ideas.

Soon afterwards, our working group was expanded to include the accountants, Peat Marwick McLintock and, later, ANZ Merchant Bank and the solicitors, Lawrence Graham.

Our proposals for PINCs were launched in May 1986, having been reassured by the Inland Revenue of the vehicle's tax transparency as to both income and capital gains. At that time, we were suggesting a matched bargain dealing system for PINCs through Reuters' screens. However, in August 1986, The Stock Exchange confirmed that PINCs and other single asset property vehicles could be listed on the main market, and, in May 1987, following discussion with The PINCs Association, The Barkshire Committee and the RICS, detailed listing provisions were published in The Stock Exchange's Yellow Book. We had therefore established within two years a satisfactory securitisation vehicle and the opportunity to trade the securities within a proven market place.

There was a major psychological barrier to be overcome in persuading investors, chiefly the institutions, that the vehicle could work and that the market could be successful. We had tested our ideas at an early stage with leading insurance companies, pension funds and property companies and had gathered around us a nucleus of support. In March and October 1986, we had also commissioned two comprehensive, independent surveys of some 200 institutions, property companies and advisers. Gradually, it became apparent that our ideas had a very widespread appeal and that securitisation had the potential to become a major force in property finance. The formation of The PINCs Association[3], like

2 The Barkshire Committee was established during 1985 under the Chairmanship of John Barkshire to develop and promote the property securitisation market and, in particular, to develop the Single Property Ownership Trust (SPOT). Many of its members are also members of The PINCs Association.
3 The PINCs Association was formally established in October 1986 as the association for single property vehicles. It acts as an interest group for the property securitisation market and encourages education and awareness of the securitisation concept, including PINCs. Its membership (approaching so as at August 1988) represents a broad cross-section of institutions, property companies, advisers and financial organisations. Many of its members are also members of The Barkshire Committee.
   The Executive Committee of The PINCs Association currently comprises: Andrew Huntley (Chairman – Richard Ellis Financial Services), the Author, Simon Purser (County NatWest), Sarah Grünewald (County NatWest), Bryan Cavill (ANZ Merchant Bank), Alison Cawley (ANZ Merchant Bank), Neil Sinclair (Berwin Leighton), John Fenner (Berwin Leighton), Chris Beresford (Peat Marwick McLintock), David Forge (Peat Marwick McLintock), Paul Walker (Lawrence Graham), Dan Sheridan (The Stock Exchange), Michelle White (Legal & General Group), Chris Daniels (Legal & General Group), Paul Rivlin (Rosehaugh Plc), Paul Orchard-Lisle (Healey & Baker), Neil Taylor (Secretary – Richard Ellis Financial Services).

the formation of The Barkshire Committee, enabled a wider audience to be reached. Having developed the vehicle, the principal concern of the Association's multi-disciplined committee was to ensure that there would be an active, liquid market. Much has been written and spoken on this subject and, even after the first issues of PINCs, the education process will need to continue.

The development of this market has not been without its setbacks; PINCs were to have been issued on three properties in October 1987, but the flotations had to be postponed after an unexpected ruling by The Department of Trade and Industry that the PINC should fall within the collective investment scheme regulations under the Financial Services Act (1986). At the time of writing (August 1988) these regulations are about to be finally published and hence the first issues of PINCs can again be contemplated. The Barkshire Committee announced in June 1988 that the Treasury had not permitted full tax transparency to its single property trust vehicle (SPOT). As a result, at the time of writing, the PINC is the only fully tax transparent securitisation vehicle available which can be geared. Chapter 8 considers these alternative approaches and the development of the market in further detail.

During the concept's formative stages, there was much comment in the press about the commercial rivalry between The PINCs Association and The Barkshire Committee. I have no doubt that the foundations of this market would not be as well advanced as they are today, in such a relatively short period of time, were it not for the determined pressure from two, highly motivated groups of professionals, speculating their hard work and time to seek a common objective by slightly different routes. It is therefore not surprising to see that similar working parties have now been formed in Australia, Hong Kong and Singapore. This further implies the exciting prospect in the future of an international dimension to property securitisation through the global securities markets.

2   THE WAY FORWARD

Securitisation is an important innovation for property finance. Its impact on development funding, on public participation in the property market and on attitudes to property generally will be far reaching. To be able to trade both debt and equity investments backed by the same property asset offers a new dimension to property ownership and a powerful tool for real estate finance.

The challenge now is to ensure that the securitisation market achieves its full potential. There may well be further single property vehicles created in the future, but, at a time of a fundamental adjustment to new regulatory regimes within financial markets, it is vital that the property securitisation market has the confidence of its users. The operation of the market in practice may well reveal certain problems which may require further regulation. A key consideration here is that it will be a public market, with full disclosure of information, operating alongside the traditional property market, which will remain private and unaccountable. This will require understanding and monitoring by investors, advisers and regulators in the years to come.

The anticipated liquidity will take some time to evolve, not least because of the number of properties which will need to have been successfully floated. Let us hope that the determination and commitment which saw the LIFFE market through its initial teething problems will prevail here; there should be enough opportunities for most potential market users to recognise that the ends will justify the means.

VI KEY ISSUES

At the beginning of this introduction, I outlined five key concerns which currently face the UK property finance market. The list was not intended to be exhaustive; I have already commented on three of the issues and my co-authors add their own perspectives in later chapters. In conclusion, I now offer thoughts on the remaining two issues which are currently being widely debated, valuation methodology and the impact of new competition on the professional firms.

1 Valuation methodology

1 TRADITIONAL WEAKNESSES

Conventional valuation methods, while relatively simple and convenient to use, are often criticised for their lack of flexibility and their impractical application to modern commercial property. Yet consumers of property, be they occupiers, developers, or investors rely heavily on the answers which valuers produce.

The conventional 'all risks yield' approach, most commonly used, has a number of significant weakness, widely recognised by valuers. These include:

i. rent is assumed to be received annually in arrears, whereas it is usually received quarterly in advance;

ii. irregular, non-recoverable management costs are difficult to provide for;

iii. likely future capital expenditure and/or depreciation of the existing building fabric cannot be readily incorporated;

iv. leasehold properties (particularly where the lease has less than 70 years unexpired or there is a complicated ground rent gearing formula) are notoriously difficult to interpret by reference to a single yield. Moreover, the notional sinking fund which market practice usually applies, is either irrelevant to the investor or inadequate for the actuary.

In essence, the all risks yield approach can often make unreasonable demands on the valuer's judgment in order to distill into a single yield figure the diversity of characteristics which an individual property might possess. A typical modern shopping centre may have in excess of 100 occupiers, holding a mixture of standard leases, turnover rents and licences. Major capital expenditure on refurbishment or re-modelling is likely to be needed within a ten year period and the investment is likely to be owned on a joint venture basis, often through a leasehold structure in conjunction with a local authority. Similar characteristics often apply to central city office buildings, in that they may be multi-let, held in joint ownerships and require active management.

2   THE DISCOUNTED CASHFLOW APPROACH (DCF)

These weaknesses have led some valuers to use a discounted cashflow method, as a cross check against a more conventional approach, in considering the more substantial or complex properties. This approach has the advantages of flexibility. A 10 or 15 year cashflow for the interest in the property to be valued is projected, against explicit assumptions of rental income, expenditure and other variables such as inflation and interest rates. The cashflow is then discounted back to a present value against the required internal rate of return. Modern spread sheet computer programmes make the iterative calculations involved automatic. Whereas the all risks yield approach implies an internal rate of return and a level of future performance from a capital value, the DCF method works back from an assumed cashflow and a minimum target level of return, to produce a present capital value. As a result, the valuer is judged as much on the quality of his assumptions as on the accuracy of his capital value answer. It therefore does not diminish the need for a valuer's judgment and, while no less an art than a science in that respect, the basis of computation is perhaps made easier to comprehend by the client.

The DCF approach is not without its weaknesses, some mathematical, some practical. For example, the nature of the calculations invariably produces two answers (one of them is usually clearly inappropriate) and negative cashflows can cause problems, although these can usually be overcome. At a practical level, certain assumptions – particularly future refurbishment costs – defy accurate assessment years in advance as to both timing and amount, yet some form of refurbishment at some stage may be inevitable. It is now recognised that the depreciation of buildings, both physically and economically (ie, relative to the letting market), is significant to valuation and performance. As a result, much more attention is now being paid towards providing valuers with more reliable statistics and information in this respect[4].

Inevitably, there are those who would rather not put their faith in internal rates of return (IRR) in making their investment judgments. Property, after all, they argue, is a physical asset and demands a fundamental analysis as much as a technical analysis. But although feel and experienced judgment remain critical to

4   Richard Ellis and Hill Samuel Property Services Ltd published in 1988 'Property Investment Depreciation and Obsolescence', based on a report commissioned from The Centre for Studies in Property Valuation and Management at The City University, London.

the property risk appraisal process, investors – particularly the institutions – measure performance by IRR and their individual competitive edge in the financial services market depends on it. It is therefore not unreasonable for them to wish to value their property investments rather more explicitly in this way, particularly as all of the property performance measurement services now available use the IRR approach. Part of the difficulty is that to assess target rates of return demands an express consideration by the investor of the minimum time period for holding the investment. For such an illiquid commodity as property, that is never easy.

3   THE IMPACT OF SECURITISATION

Will the introduction of a securitised property market have any effect on the valuation debate and will it provide any solutions? Securitisation, by providing continuous pricing for individual properties from trading in the market, not only produces a wider supply of comparable evidence for the larger property, it encourages the valuer to apply a discounted cashflow basis of appraisal. The Stock Exchange has specifically eschewed the need for regular revaluations of each property by the managers (except where new capital is to be raised), in order that the value should be indicated by the trading price of the securities in the market.

Consequently, a property may be judged explicitly in terms of its income and capital growth potential, as expressed by a total return from a projected cashflow, which can then be compared directly with the anticipated returns from other investment media. Analysts will be expected to make suitable assumptions for future capital expenditure, management costs and the effect of new lettings. With the benefit of full disclosure from each management company, combined with three yearly building surveys, sensible projections may be made easier. Moreover, the time period of investment can be considered directly because of the immediate liquidity of the securities. In practice, a diversified portfolio of securities, both in terms of property type and anticipated investment time period can be readily acquired. How often has property been described as 'slow moving' and 'long-term' simply because in the past it has been difficult to take short-term positions in specific properties and to appraise them with reasonable accuracy?

It will be interesting to see in the years to come how far the appraisal of securitised property begins to influence valuations in the conventional market. Some argue that it must, if only because fund managers will need a common basis to choose between purchasing direct and buying securities in the target property sectors.

4   CONCLUSIONS

The complexity of modern commercial properties and the likely impact of a securitised property market both demand a careful review of property valuation methodology as it is currently applied. A move from the present static approach to a more dynamic approach merely accepts the reality of continuously changing market circumstances, both in the letting markets and in the financial markets. This review will not and should not diminish the critical importance of the valuer's judgment in the appraisal process, but it may help to foster a new realism in meeting the increasing demands of investors and thereby to allow valuers to interpret these requirements with even greater clarity.

A property valuation essentially involves calculating the present value of the stream of income which a property is capable of generating in the future. It is therefore concerned with assessing a multiple of earnings produced by an asset which happens to be a property rather than a company. This may be an over simplified comparison, but the intention is to emphasise that the valuation of a property is no more a static exercise than the valuation of a company; the property valuer simply takes a snapshot of the asset as it is at a particular point in time. The letting markets which underpin that income stream are continuously changing. The capital value may *appear* to be slow moving, but that may be partly due to the relative infrequency of valuations, for understandable practical reasons. Graph 7 on page 9 clearly showed the significant time delay in practice between the growth in rents and the change in equivalent yields.

2   Impact on the professional firms

1   NEW COMPETITION

The new forms of finance have brought increased competition for the property professionals, the chartered surveyors. As debt finance and the capital markets have become more important, so the investment banks have attempted to compete more directly and openly with surveyors in providing specialist property financing services. Competition has also come from the accountants, particularly in the areas of project management and corporate advice. Major surveying practices have reacted with equal conviction and many have followed Richard Ellis' lead in establishing in 1984 a multi-disciplined property financial services team.

2   PRINCIPAL OR ADVISER

The key issue is how far surveyors should seek to act as a principal rather than solely as an adviser. Clearly, in certain corporate finance transactions, not least the flotation of a securitised property, the ability to take a principal position is fundamental to executing the deal for the client. However, many professional partnerships have historically established their reputations by providing independent objective advice. What does the client want? The answer is probably a bit of both, hence the dilemma currently facing the larger and more diversified practices.

3 THE NEED FOR CAPITAL

The key consideration is capital; the property world has watched the securities market's transformation from single capacity to dual capacity since 1983 and has seen the substantial capital investment which has proved to be essential for the leading players to retain their market share and competitive edge. Mergers have already taken place between investment banks and surveying practices; more recently, a number of surveying firms have been floated and, in the residential sector, many provincial estate agencies have been adsorbed by financial institutions. The need for new capital for chartered surveying partnerships arises partly to finance the business and partly – perhaps more so in the future – to be able to take principal positions.

Capital is needed for the business, not just to recruit key staff or to acquire other firms or services, but also, from time to time, to buy out retiring partners! The issue of flotation is a thorny one. For some, the potential to be made an equity partner of a firm remains an important and motivating ambition. Flotation usually removes that opportunity; everyone becomes an employee rather than an employer and even for the most senior director, remuneration tends to comprise salary, bonus and share options rather than the voting profit share which equity demands. The additional administrative and psychological burden of disclosure and public accountability is a further, not insignificant, consideration.

There are, of course, many different methods of balancing the equity, share option, profit share/bonus and salary variables to offer an attractive package; this is a demanding problem for those firms seeking to retain or introduce key staff at the time of flotation. However, this problem may be counterbalanced by the dilemma which might face the firm if it cannot secure the capital to retain its competitive position in the market by expansion or by restructuring its activities.

The solution need not necessarily involve flotation, at least not of the whole practice. Some significant investment banks in the US, for example, were originally established as private partnerships and have subsequently remained privately controlled, although part of their business may now be either publicly quoted or involve substantial external shareholders.

Of particular interest to the more financial services orientated firms at present is the need for capital to be able to take principal positions. This could mean the ability to underwrite a debt financing facility or an equity placing for a single development or a property company; in the context of the securitised property market, it could mean underwriting the flotation of a property or making markets in the securities.

To date, all the firms of chartered surveyors, private and public, who have so far created financial services divisions, operate as advisers only. Yet, in providing advice on property finance, they are increasingly competing directly with investment banks and brokers who are able to combine their advice with an ability to commit money to make a deal happen. A structuring and arranging ability alone are often not enough to secure the more worthwhile mandates;

many clients frequently wish to see the arranger taking the lead with its own funds, accepting that the majority of the funding facility may be prudently syndicated elsewhere.

Distinctions can be made between differing client needs – between those who already have detailed knowledge and appropriate contacts (usually the larger companies), and those who may need additional help in (for them) a new or complex funding arena (often the smaller and medium sized companies). It remains to be seen how firms of surveyors progress in this climate and whether there will remain a significant niche for the pure independent adviser in an increasingly competitive market.

4   TYPE OF FIRM

The new competition for firms of chartered surveyors does not stop at property financing. Certain overseas investment banks and some institutions have the clear intention of offering diversified property services to their UK clients, including investment agency, project management and valuation. The issue is therefore the style of practice which firms wish to adopt in the future. Part of the reason for the present challenge is that, as the debt and capital markets have become as important to property financing as the institutions' equity, so the expertise and market knowledge which property advisers need to possess has broadened accordingly. In the past, most of the leading surveying firms have enjoyed considerable placing power among the property fund managers of the larger institutions; but now, in order to offer their clients the same quality of advice in the future, these firms are having to demonstrate (by external recruitment) the same degree of placing power in the debt and securities markets.

The RICS is making determined efforts to broaden the training and awareness base of its members. The Investment Surveyors Forum has been founded to spearhead an education campaign during the coming years among those at the 'sharp end' of the profession. However, it is really for the individual firms to make corporate decisions and to take business initiatives to meet the new challenges.

As in the securities markets, it has been the medium sized firm, without the benefit of a specialist niche or a strong client base, which has been the most vulnerable. The larger, more diversified practices, have great strength in their integrated, international agency networks and comprehensive research departments – facilities which even the biggest investment banks might envy.

As a result, there may emerge a distinction between the larger, multi-disciplined and international firms, who offer their property financing skills in a competitive manner, the very small niche agencies – the traditional market catalysts (some of whom may be owned externally), and the totally independent, professional practices which concentrate on a specific range of purely advisory services, such as valuation, research, and project management, none of which demands principal positions. Examples are rapidly emerging of all three types although, in practice, there may be many other variations.

5 THE IMPACT OF THE FINANCIAL SERVICES ACT

The Financial Services Act and its requirement for authorisation have brought new administrative complexities and disclosure obligations to those firms involved in financing property. Because of the breadth of the Act's net, the requirement for authorisation has also extended to include certain investment agency work, elements of property management and other services. Different firms have reacted in different ways. Some have incorporated and authorised their financial services division, channelling all relevant business through that company. Others have authorised several different parts of the firm under different headings, while a few have authorised their entire business.

The Act has brought with it a new tier of regulation, as well as some thorny issues to resolve in the areas of compliance and conflicts of interest. Aside from the impact of the securitisation market itself, it is clear that property transactions can have a major impact on a company's performance, even if it is not strictly a property company. Flotations, takeovers and asset revaluations can all involve surveyors in some capacity and all involve confidential, price sensitive information and hence the risk of insider dealing. Whilst there will have to be formal compliance requirements within the authorised part of a surveyor's business, the inevitable consequence for the more diversified firms may be – as some have already established – a need for a compliance policy and a compliance officer for the whole firm. The compliance officer would have knowledge of all transactions being undertaken within the firm as a whole (including the authorised investment businesses), and would have the power to enforce disclosure of conflicts, to establish chinese walls and to discipline staff.

At the time of writing, the RICS has just published its first guidance note on conflicts of interest, having established a multi-disciplined working party to consider the problem. But the key areas of compliance and insider dealing will require even more careful consideration in the years to come. These areas bring the surveyors directly under the same scrutiny and codes of conduct as those now being introduced into the securities industry. Recently, well-publicised cases provide salutary warnings to all those involved in financing property, however well qualified or experienced; the rules have changed.

6 CONCLUSIONS

Surveyors are not alone in facing these issues. Lawyers and accountants are, to a degree, having to contend with similar challenges; however, they are equally aware of the opportunities which the new approaches to property finance and professional competition can bring. The next few years will be testing times for everyone.

Chapter 2

Equity Finance

Michael Mallinson

This chapter will briefly define 'equity', and consider the attributes of property in relation to that definition. It will consider who are the providers of equity and, drawing the conclusion that the principal providers are long-term savings institutions, it will look at their needs and review how well property meets those needs.

The chapter will then describe how such institutions reach their property investment decisions utilising research and information, the appraisals they carry out, their attitude to risk and gearing, and their need for management.

Finally, the chapter will review certain special opportunities available to investors: development, property shares, overseas property and the prospects for securitisation. The concluding paragraphs look at some of the changes facing long-term savings institutions and the impact of those changes on their attitude to the equity of property.

I THE MEANING OF EQUITY

It is true that all investment involves risk, but it is also true that all investment involves choice. The most fundamental choice an investor must make is between 'debt' investments and 'equity' investments. Each class has wholly different characteristics but, as a working analysis of the approach to their differences:

> a rational investor will seek to maximise his returns but in doing so he will demand a higher return for taking a higher risk. His choice between the monetary security and certainty of debt and the relative uncertainty and insecurity of equity will therefore depend upon his individual assessment of risk and the differential between the returns available.

To understand the analysis, debt and equity must first be defined:

A debt investment is based upon borrowing. The borrower offers the investor a guaranteed money return, expressed in fixed terms, usually over a finite period. The investment return is not directly related to the financial success of any particular enterprise and it is usually secured in some way. Apart from the risk of default by the borrower, the investment return is therefore quite precisely predictable in money terms and is comparatively secure.

A conventional government stock would clearly fall into this definition, as would a mortgage, but all debt investments are not necessarily secure, for example 'junk bonds' which have been issued as a defence against takeover.

An equity investment is a financial interest in an economic venture where the return to the investor is residual in character and entirely dependent upon the financial profitability of the venture and will therefore generally be variable, volatile and insecure.

Most readers of this book will have lived all their working lives when the choice under the analysis would appear to point strongly towards equity. Those who have kept their savings in building societies or gilt-edged or other debt type investments would appear to have lost out heavily to those who have chosen equity-type investments. But that experience can be contrasted with the nineteenth century when, to have a good sum of money 'in the funds' made a bachelor highly eligible! It can also be contrasted with the fact that investors actually purchased large amounts of debt, particularly government debt, during recent decades.

The reason for this contrast lies, of course, in 'the assessment of risk'. A wide range of factors affect that assessment, but they can usefully be categorised as follows:

1. Vulnerability to changes in the value of money, ie, inflation.

2. The need for competitive investment returns.

3. The business need to earn returns above debt returns in order to service debt.

4. The attitude to pure risk – the desire or otherwise to attain high returns despite the risk and the uncertainty.

These four categories will carry varying weight within and between the four principle sources of equity finance today, the long-term savings institutions, property companies, the private investor and 'other sources', which are described below.

Debt is discussed in detail in chapter 3. This chapter deals with equity.

One characteristic of equity is worthy of emphasis at this stage. The definition given expresses the variability of the return to the investor. This variability springs both from the financial way in which equity interests are structured and from the way returns to the investor are produced. Those returns are usually produced by changes in the capital value of his asset, and from a flow of income derived from the asset. Capital value changes are usually identified from some perception of 'market value' which value may be quite well defined, as for a small line of ordinary shares quoted on The Stock Exchange, or it may be ill-defined as for a large line of such shares, or shares in an unquoted company. Property tends towards the ill-defined end of the spectrum because of the problems and intrinsic uncertainties which surround valuations. The clarity with which market value can be identified, and the ability to realise it, strongly conditions attitudes to different forms of equity. For example many investors will deliberately exclude unquoted shares from their portfolio.

Capital values are not, of course, freestanding; they are the product of perceptions of the present value of future income flows. Those income flows will derive more or less directly from the earning capacity of the underlying real assets adjusted for any prior calls upon that income, eg, from debt participants. In the case of ordinary shares the income flows (or dividends) may be intrinsically highly variable from year to year as the fortunes of the company vary. For large companies it is normal for the directors to retain some of the income stream for reinvestment in the business. This will be held in the form of 'shareholders reserves' but they may, on occasion, be used to smooth out to some degree any dividend variations which would otherwise be necessary. Even so dividends are viewed by investors as a less certain flow of income than debt payments.

In this context direct property is significantly different in that the income flows may well be secured by quite long-term contracts (ie , leases) and contracts which, certainly at the top end of the market, seek to pass to the occupier all or most of the costs of running and maintaining the building; it is a deliberate policy of these contracts to minimise variability in the investor's income and a 'landlord's market' for many years has brought success to this policy in the British property market, in marked contrast to many overseas markets which have more of a 'tenant's market'. It is relevant to observe that the nature of these contracts is bringing increasing criticism from occupiers and can be a strong determinant in their decision to buy or to rent; this is discussed further later. Quite apart from this stability it is also observable in some property markets that rent levels are not particularly variable in money terms. This is best demonstrated at a market level by reference to one of the published indices. For example, the table on p 37 sets out an index of the actual income flow from the portfolio which comprises the JLW Index.

This stability is not an intrinsic quality of property, but derives from a common general condition of the property market of a relative shortage of accommodation. Although that shortage can disappear, generally in many markets it does not and rents are therefore perceived to be a more secure flow of income than dividends. However, despite this *comparative* stability the definition of 'equity' is clearly met to a large degree in any flow of rent which is dependent upon a renewal of leases to occupiers. It is also strong where leases are long but subject to reviews of the rent at frequent intervals. The timing and frequency of the reviews

Growth in Net Rental Income

June 1967	62	June 1978	117
June 1968	62	June 1979	129
June 1969	62	June 1980	140
June 1970	62	June 1981	157
June 1971	59	June 1982	178
June 1972	78	June 1983	186
June 1973	79	June 1984	209
June 1974	80	June 1985	222
June 1975	83	June 1986	234
June 1976	90	June 1987	256
June 1977	100		

Source: JLW Property Index

will, however, be important; five or seven yearly reviews, whilst giving a considerable degree of certainty when compared with dividends, must retain a strong equity character, 21 yearly reviews start to look more like debt in that, at the commencement of the term, the bulk of the value will be derived from the present value of the current income, and little value will be derived from income after the review (probably at most one or two years purchase). As the review approaches an ever higher proportion of the value will derive from an estimate of the income obtainable at the review, but it is likely to be observed that this flow of income is particularly uncertain or at hazard because its quantum depends upon the particular market and legal circumstances at the day of the review; it is then fixed at that level for a further 21 years with no opportunity to recover an adverse rent review result.

For practical purposes, all rents deriving from short leases or long leases with reviews will be classed as equity. The marginal characteristics will be invisible in freehold situations, because valuation and analysis practice do not normally divide rental flows into secure and less secure slices; 'hardcore' methods of valuation do have that effect, but not in a disciplined manner because they only differentiate between the rent which is being paid and rental value; whilst this is a valid differentiation the resultant arithmetic is rarely rigorous. However, marginality will start to emerge in leaseholds with a significant ground rent. If the ground rent is 'side by side', ie, with the parties participating in income and capital flows in due proportion and with equal status, marginality will again disappear, but most ground rents leave the leaseholder with a top slice or marginal income and a high degree of capital and income liability through the repairing covenants of the lease. Further it is not uncommon for ground rents to contain reviews in themselves, often out of phase with an occupation lease. Thus the intermediate income can acquire not only marginality, but also a degree of gearing making it even more similar to income flows from the stockmarket.

From this it is clear that property can produce rent flows which fulfil the definition of equity, but which are also quite divergent in character.

II THE PROVIDERS OF EQUITY

1 Long-term savings institutions

This generic title is intended to differentiate pension funds and insurance companies and similar 'institutions' from banks, etc. They primarily invest in equity to support products which have a long duration and have open liabilities, that is to say products for which the pay-out is not fixed in money terms. They are thus particularly averse to inflation. That is demonstrably true of pension funds who must struggle to match earnings growth, which for some years has exceeded inflation but it is also true of many insurance company products which offer bonuses to policyholders. Whilst many of the bonuses are not contractual in nature, they are offered to the public on the basis of providing an investment return, with the implicit understanding that this return is likely to be a 'real' one.

Earnings Growth and Inflation 1980–87

Year	Earnings growth	Inflation
1980	100.00	100.00
1981	112.93	111.87
1982	123.52	121.50
1983	133.93	127.08
1984	142.10	133.41
1985	154.13	141.52
1986	166.34	146.34
1987	179.35	152.41

Source: Department of Employment

The liabilities of both pension funds and insurance companies may extend over long periods (40 years or more) and the very extensiveness of the period enhances the risks and uncertainties surrounding inflation. An equity investment may appear to offer some protection.

Because they are selling a product in a competitive market, insurance companies are also exposed to the need to provide enhanced returns; bonuses ultimately reflect investment returns. Pension funds prima facie do not need to be competitive; provided that they meet the calls made upon them by their participants they will have achieved their aim. However competition enters at the management level – many pension funds are managed by external managers for a fee. These managers attempt to differentiate themselves by the competitive performance they provide and their position in the 'league tables'.

Long-term savings institutions are the main source of equity finance. This has arisen because government policy since 1945 has tended to favour them, both by direct action (tax breaks), and indirect. For example the tendency to spread wealth has brought custom to them. The 'man in the street' recognises the risks of equity investment and is tempted by products (eg, unit trusts) which relieve him of the burdens of judgment and of management but offer him most of the benefits. Thus the proportion of national wealth managed by institutions has tended to grow when expressed as a percentage of GDP:

1958–62	1963–67	1968–72	1973–77	1978	1979	1980	1981	1982
3.1	3.3	3.6	4.3	4.5	4.9	4.8	4.6	4.3

Source: Financial Statistics, 1988
Reproduced with the permission of the Controller of HMSO.

It will be seen that the figures tail off in recent years, partly as government has sought to reduce the advantages. Many institutions are seeking to redress this situation by increasing their range of products, and by adapting to government policies (for example, the introduction in 1987 of Personal Equity Plans, which has been met by products from long-term savings institutions although the purpose was supposed to encourage the private investor).

2 Property companies

Property companies are discussed in more detail later in this chapter and in chapters 6 and 7. Their activities are financed partly by equity via their share capital and reserves, which will be drawn from investors, both financial institutions and private individuals (this money, by definition, is equity money seeking equity employment; few equity investors in property companies would be content if their money were only laid out for debt returns) and partly by the debt market, borrowing over short- and long-terms as the market permits and their needs dictate. In certain circumstances this market will offer money in copious amounts as investors are attracted to debt by high real interest rates which they wish to lock into, or by the relative attractions of property as a security. This is well illustrated in recent years where a decline in institutional interest in direct property has been more than compensated by increased involvement by debt

Net annual investment in property by institutions, compared with change in bank lending to property companies

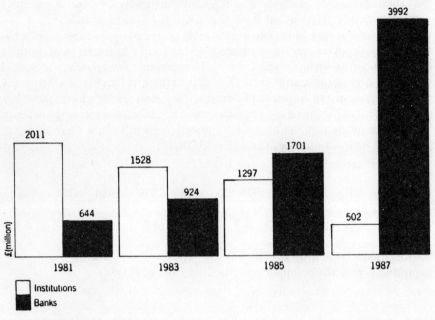

Source: CSO/Bank of England

lenders. This debt, in the hands of the property companies, becomes available for equity investment.

Property companies, by their nature, must invest in equity because they receive their money either in the form of debt, as already described, upon which they must make a turn if they are to survive, or in equity money invested in their ordinary shares. As a source of equity money to the property market they tend to be cyclical for two reasons. The money they can draw from the stock market via rights issues, etc will be cyclical depending upon the mood of the general market as well as attitudes to property in relationship to that mood. Their ability to attract debt will depend upon the willingness of long-term investors to provide it, or the willingness of short-term investors (the Banks) to provide it, coupled with the confidence of both parties in their ability to refinance with debt or equity later on; a confidence which appears high at the time of writing.

Absence of debt does not, of course, make the property companies inactive, but they will tend to become traders – building to sell immediately, whether to occupiers or investors – and occasionally little more than project managers for a fee or a small slice of the profit. It is salutary to remember that this was considered to be the future for property companies in the late 1970s when direct institutional activity was rampant.

3 Private investors

Private investors are excluded from direct participation in many areas of the property market because of the sums of money involved. Whilst it is not uncommon for closed-end funds to be created for a limited group of investors to participate together in particular situations (eg, capital growth from reversions), this remains a small area of the market. Whilst recent events have perhaps demonstrated a greater willingness by the man in the street to invest equity in shares, he is denied the opportunity to invest in property beyond his own house, property company shares and a limited range of insurance-related property products. This situation may be about to change as during 1988 the government intends to allow authorised property unit trusts, and arrangements are in train for the 'unitisation' of property (see below).

At the lower end of the property market, high yielding secondary and tertiary commercial property, individuals do start to play a part. The size of this sector should not be understated, by number of properties or even by total sums of money involved. It is an area where the world of the property company meets that of the private individual. Investment prices often produce running yields which might appear more appropriate to a debt investment, but it is undoubtedly equity, usually with a particularly high void and management risk, and it is to some degree a raft of activity upon which the rest of the market floats.

The role of the private investor in the property market within the UK is smaller than in a number of other countries, particularly those where disparities of wealth are greater such as the US. It is therefore relevant to note the considerable reduction which has occurred in marginal tax rates for the individual in the UK over the last nine years, with the Finance Act 1988 reducing it to 40%, amongst the lowest in the world. Provided that this is maintained, and given continued economic health, it must lead to a considerable number of very wealthy people who would at least have the financial capacity to participate more widely in the property market.

However, it is hard to quantify the likely effect. The Treasury estimate the increase in the pay packets to be £2,070m (1989/90). This amount is therefore added to the disposable income of richer people. Any estimate of the proportion of this they will allocate to personal investment can be no more than a guess, and the share for commercial property must be even more uncertain. Such amounts as they do allocate are likely to be geared up by a degree of bank borrowing, but it is clear that the sums involved are unlikely to be significant at the prime end of the market. However, at the secondary end, greater interest does appear likely.

4 Other sources

There is a considerable variety of other sources of equity, but at most times they only have a small influence upon the investment market, although the value of their activities may well be quite high. The largest group is commercial bodies who choose to own properties they occupy for their business. Their presence in the market will be variable depending to a large degree upon perceived returns from property compared with returns available within their business. The relationship between interest rates for borrowing and property yields will also be relevant. If it appears to be as cheap in cashflow terms to borrow money and buy a property as to rent it, there are obvious advantages in buying. There may be problems for a company's balance sheet in such borrowing (although the more sophisticated can circumvent this by off balance sheet borrowing), but they acquire the accounting benefit of a wider asset base which may, if values rise, provide an opportunity for further borrowing in the future.

During the 1960s and 1970s owner-occupiers were major suppliers of stock to the investment market in the form of sales and leasebacks. However in recent years there has been some reversal of this trend which could well be related to the development of specialist needs which the normal commercial market has been unable or unwilling to provide either physically, or perhaps on the right terms; there has been much criticism of the standard 'institutional' 25 year lease. From an occupier's viewpoint such leases have a number of disadvantages:

- The length of term itself places a considerable liability upon the tenant extending beyond any normal business horizon he may have. Because of the common law doctrine of 'privity of contract' the liability lasts for the full term whether or not he assigns his interest.

- Because of the regular rent reviews he is unlikely to have the opportunity of creating any valuable asset in his hands which might offset these risks.

- The lease also places comprehensive repairing and other obligations on the tenant even as the building obsolesces.

Such issues provide a big incentive to a business to own its properties if it is able to do so.

Construction companies may also be modest providers of equity, though this will normally be short-term money to facilitate their construction activities with the opportunity to earn an enhanced profit. A few construction companies have chosen to participate over a longer period and to hold a continuing investment stake, but it is usual now for such assets to be held in a 'property company' subsidiary, thus acquiring property company attributes.

Overseas purchasers are increasingly seen as a potential source of equity. Such purchasers are likely to fall into one of the categories already described and will carry those attributes. However they are likely to participate in only a small area of the market, one which they will be able to recognise from their home experience and thus feel that they are able to control the inevitably greater risks of entering an alien market; at present this largely limits their activity to central London. Despite occasional rumours of imminent invasion by the Americans or the Japanese, they have so far proved to be small players, and generally quite cautious, in some cases seeking partnerships with established British organisations.

In the current market, as already explained, the long-term savings institutions dominate the provision of equity to the property market. The remainder of the chapter will therefore focus more closely on their needs, their attitudes and their techniques, all of which will tend to mirror to some degree those of the other participants.

III   THE NEEDS OF LONG-TERM SAVINGS INSTITUTIONS

Although commonly lumped together, such institutions are not particularly homogeneous in character; the difference between insurance companies and pension funds has already been referred to. However some common threads in the form of needs will be identified first, with later reference to their degree of importance to each type of participant. The threads can be summarised as certainty, marketability, income preference, manageability, spreadability, and risk and opportunity.

1   Certainty

Certainty is an intrinsically desirable characteristic of investment. However, as the definition implies, returns from equity are inevitably uncertain to some degree. Although willing to accept the disbenefit of uncertainty for the hoped for added benefit of higher return, institutions will be critical of the return potentially available. Although for some proportion of their assets they may be willing to accept a high degree of uncertainty in the hope of high reward (eg, venture capital), generally they will find attractions in keeping uncertainty to a minimum. They therefore seek equity in the most secure forms available. This approach leads to some criticism of their lack of adventure, but this criticism overlooks a real need; the assets of financial institutions are mostly held to match and meet liabilities, often within a statutory or semi-statutory framework, for instance the Insurance Companies Act 1982. Too much adventure will, if it fails to come off, cause problems quite rapidly; an extreme example occurred with UK Provident Life Assurance who were over-exposed to a very adventurous investment sector, oil exploration shares, and had to be rescued by Friends Provident. The reason for any element of statutory control is, of course, that the institutions are repositories of relatively risk-averse money belonging to risk-averse clients; few of us would care to think that *our* retirement pension was at risk to any degree beyond the absolute minimum. That attitude is not irrational because, if we belong to a company pension scheme, we cannot participate in the fruits of successful adventurousness; our pension is unaffected whether or not the investment managers make a killing, but it might disappear if they make a hash of it. Although many products of life assurance companies do offer a sharing in the 'profit' from investment, it is probably true that most policyholders are more concerned that forecast bonuses should be achieved than that risks should be taken to exceed them.

For these reasons institutions look for certainty, and indeed attempts to measure the 'volatility' in the performance of an asset or asset class are made, and this volatility is classed as one type of risk to be controlled.

2 Marketability

Although most long-term savings institutions are seen as 'long-term' investors, and indeed they are so by some measures, they increasingly demand that their individual assets should be marketable. This apparent paradox derives from two causes. The most powerful is the growing importance attached to 'managing' even the largest portfolios. Such managing can often only be at the margin, as discussed below, but the ability to do it gives the opportunity to enhance returns at the margin, but a margin which may be competitively crucial. Management is also aimed towards changing the structure of portfolios. Investment needs and attitudes to markets or classes of asset are constantly changing, and a fund manager who cannot adapt to the new demands will be lost.

Marketability also implies that there will be a clearer picture of 'market value'. Obscurity of value makes performance measurement difficult, obstructs portfolio analysis and confuses the match with liabilities; it therefore makes competitive portfolio management difficult.

3 Income preference

Present income is always to be preferred in nature to deferred income or capital growth. Discounting, usually at a gilt rate plus an allowance for risk, is designed to compensate for this, and indeed a zero coupon or deep-discounted bond may be intrinsically attractive but the preference remains and reflects the natural preference for 'a bird in the hand' (the desire for certainty). Perhaps more important it also reflects the opportunities early income gives not only to pay out calls on the fund without selling assets at what may be an inconvenient time, but also the chance to invest that income in new opportunities. The influence of tax confuses the issue, but many funds, particularly as they 'mature', may have quite a small inflow of funds compared with the existing pool of assets. Whilst assets can always be sold for re-investment this can be difficult to achieve in certain market conditions, may well be expensive in terms of dealing costs and tax, and can give rise to other market stresses.

4 Manageability

Compared with the quantum of assets under their control, most long-term savings institutions will have limited management resources. This will be true of funds of all sizes. They therefore seek assets which make low management demands. It is true that management can always be subcontracted; in the case of ordinary shares to a board of directors, in the case of property to managing agents. But that management must still be supervised, and the supervision must increase as the riskiness increases or as the holding increases in relation to the size of the fund. There are therefore intrinsic attractions in a spread portfolio of trouble-free assets. Whilst large funds who do carry, perhaps quite extensive, management capacity are able to absorb management intensive assets, they will only do so to earn additional return, and even they must seek to control the total management demand.

5 Spreadability

It is beyond the scope of this book to describe the concept of 'spread' or diversification as a method of risk control in portfolio management. However it is a widely accepted concept (even if debated at the margin) and implies that a fund manager should seek to disperse his assets quite widely. From this it must follow that he will seek classes of asset which, by their nature, will assist him in this aim. As part of the same objective, he will also not want too large a holding of a particular asset in relation to the size of his fund. He will also seek assets where he is able to vary the size of his holding depending upon his attitude to it; for example, few fund managers would choose not to hold ICI ordinary shares because they form a significant element of the market, and therefore not to hold them at all would be a large risk. But each will wish to vary his holding in response to his perception of whether they are likely to out perform or under perform the market.

6 Risk and opportunity

Even for the risk-averse fund, risk is inevitable and must at the least be controlled. That may well involve the taking of particular, deliberate risks which match or counter each other. For funds seeking competitive performance there will be a desire to exploit the opportunities of risk and to seek certain types of risk which can give an opportunity for enhanced return. Attitudes to risk are referred to later, but suffice it to say here, that institutions will, for competitive funds, seek investment types, particularly equity investment, which offer them an exposure to as wide a range as possible of opportunities to take and benefit from risk, but they will require the risk to be in a form which gives adequate control, and in which it can be identified and even measured.

Having established the broad classes of 'need', each type of institution will give them different priorities.

1 LIFE ASSURANCE FUNDS

In the broadest terms their business can be classified as either immediate annuity and without profit products where the liabilities are clearly expressed in money terms, or deferred annuity and with profit products where they are not. The former will normally be matched by fixed income investments only, as it is an interest rate matching business. With profits business is open to competition on bonuses offered, and being of long duration also it will be vulnerable to inflation and to competitive needs. For these products companies will therefore be driven to equity investments.

They will be seeking all six of the needs described above, but because of the sheer size of many of the funds involved, they may feel free to take a number of 'exceptional' positions, often with what, in absolute terms, seem quite large sums of money, and they will seek competitive advantage from so doing. Nevertheless this will remain within a cautious framework, and no 'exceptional position' will be held to a degree which in any way imperils the stability of the fund.

The resulting investment performance is veiled by actuarial intervention. With profit bonuses do not emerge as a direct result of investment returns, but are set by the company actuary in the light of achieved performance, but influenced also by likely future performance, by risk control, by evaluation of the liabilities and by many other factors. This veiling or dilution of course ensures the stability of the fund, but it may also affect investment policy and allow the taking of greater *controlled* risk, albeit at the margin only.

2 PENSION FUNDS

Pension Funds are more closely analogous to with profit insurance products. They too will be seeking long duration assets which meet the six needs. They may however be more exposed. Whilst their actual investment performance may be concealed from the ultimate beneficiaries (although this is now being broken down), those beneficiaries are represented by the trustees. Trustees must tend to be risk averse by virtue of their legal status, thus craving greater certainty, and they will wish to take regular soundings as to where they stand (utilising the performance league tables for this process in part). They will find it even harder than an insurance company actuary to accept a short-term loss of performance for a long-term gain and achieved return will be a strong need for them.

However their liabilities are even more real than for a with profit insurance fund which can at least cut some of its bonuses if it must. They are therefore particularly averse to inflation and will, in the end, place control of this risk above the need for competitive performance, and will cherish equity in an unfavourable or uncertain inflation climate.

3 GENERAL INSURANCE FUNDS

Much of general business is a cashflow business. Whilst the company will attempt to ensure that its underwriting is intrinsically profitable, profit emerges from managing the cashflow between the time you pay your premium and your neighbour crashes his car. That is an over simplified view, and whilst general insurance business contains many short-term accounts, others, such as employers or product liability insurance, are quite long-term. Irrespective of the term of the policy, companies build reserves on a large scale to enable them to meet their liabilities. These will be invested in both gilts and equities and the size and nature of these reserves are subject to very close scrutiny by governmental agencies. Marketability is an important consideration for shorter term policies where claims can arise at short notice and are required to be paid quickly.

4   UNIT-LINKED FUNDS

These are a very particular subsection of the financial institutional market with two special features, the obligation upon the manager to redeem units at short notice, and the opportunity for the unitholder to switch between different funds. Many unitholders choose to leave this decision to the managers, investing in a 'managed' fund which is spread across many investment sectors.

Prudential Holborn Managed Funds

Asset Distribution 31.12.87

	%
UK equities	59.00
Overseas equities	17.53
Fixed interest	13.90
Property	8.49
Cash	1.08

Unitised funds also have one other characteristic; they are often no more than a means of shifting control of assets within the long-term savings institutions; for example the many authorised unit trusts are run by such institutions for pension funds only.

However, whatever their antecedents, such funds live by the sword. They are selling in a highly competitive market place with their prices, and thus their investment performance, quoted daily, or at most monthly, in the press, and with their investors able to leave on short notice. Their 'product' is delivered unit performance and they can have no view of the purposes for which those units are held. Thus they will have no intrinsic aversion to inflation, but live solely by their own achievements and a view of what their competitors are doing. Their greatest need is marketability, and they are little concerned whether their performance derives from capital or income, and only fret about certainty if they are choosing a particular and differentiated position.

The sector is so wide, around 4,000 (excluding overseas and offshore) that these are inevitably generalisations.

IV   THE INVESTMENT UTILITY OF PROPERTY

As will be seen, the needs of each type of investor do revolve around the same fundamental needs. How is property seen in the light of those needs?

1   CERTAINTY

Most forms of property, particularly those which lie at the 'prime' end of the market, appear to meet this need to a high standard for an equity type investment. Rent income proves to be reasonably predictable even over quite extended periods, and it appears to be secure when compared with ordinary share dividends. In part this derives from the existence of extended contracts (ie, leases) with the occupants. Such properties generally have a low void rate because they form a part of the occupation market with a high and fairly consistent demand; if one tenant fails another is usually available. The direction and rate of change in rents is less predictable, but is nevertheless reasonably stable. It is a common perception that rents are more stable than share dividends because the latter are 'reviewed' annually by the directors, and are a demonstrable residue of the company's profitability. At the individual company level the perception may have some validity, but at the market level it appears to be untrue and dividends are not measurably more volatile or uncertain than rents.

For the concomitant capital movement, there does appear to be considerably less volatility in property prices than share prices, although whether property prices are really as stable as some suggest is discussed later in this chapter.

This general perception of predictability appears to be true of many areas of the property investment market, but it is certainly believed to be particularly true of prime property which delivers an initially low but very secure income flow, with quite stable prospects of growth in income and capital value. This accounts, in part, for institutional preference for prime property. They are willing to accept the lower returns for the benefit of the higher certainty (they thus define to some degree their willingness to take risk), but it must be observed that the low initial yield of a prime property carries with it an intrinsic enhanced risk that future rental growth will not match expectations. It is therefore a compromise between greater confidence because of the quality of the property and allowance for inherent uncertainty of the future. It is also important to realise that institutions, in preferring prime property, are not only accepting a lower initial return, but the probability of a lower total return over time as well. Although this threatens one of the myths of the property world, it is unlikely that any reasonably efficient market pricing system would permit an asset which offered greater security to trade at a price which also offered a better return than a less secure asset. Indeed the hypothesis at the beginning of this chapter postulates that investors will, as a whole, attempt to ensure that that is not the case.

For higher yielding secondary properties, the income appears to be less secure because the covenants are weaker and there is greater risk of voids, although some argue that this risk can be diversified away to quite low levels. Capital enhancement may be fundamentally more uncertain, but because of the higher yield it is a less important element of the total return. Indeed the pattern of change in values at the lower end of the secondary market usually bears more relationship to general interest rates than to any changes in the prospects for the properties themselves. The buyers of such assets relate the current income flow to the cost of borrowing the money to buy the asset, looking for a margin of perhaps 2 or 3%, and viewing any prospect of rental growth as offsetting void and management risks in a general and unenumerated way.

2 MARKETABILITY

Here property appears to suffer badly. Property takes months or even years to deal in, trading is expensive, and prices can be very uncertain. There is no central marketplace in which prices can be seen and in which deals can be done; everything is subjected to negotiation and the risks of 'gazumping' or withdrawal. Investors attempt to reduce this problem by investment in prime property which is believed to be more marketable than other categories, but even that marketability is highly imperfect compared with other investment sectors.

3 INCOME PREFERENCE

The property market appears to offer a range of options here as properties can be bought which are more or less 'reversionary' within a surveyor's meaning of the word. They can also be acquired at different initial yields excluding a surveyor's reversion. Thus a prime shop can be bought to show an initial income yield of say 4% let at a full modern rent, or a multi-storey factory can be bought to show 15% on a modern rent. The choice of a reversionary or non-reversionary investment does give an investor some real choice as to when and how he receives his total return, but the yield differences quoted do not express simple alternatives; both figures say as much about the riskiness of the income, through voids and the duration of any income through obsolescence, as they do about a genuine choice between options on timing and income versus capital. That said, there is an intrinsic choice, and even after making adjustments for a risk premium, the high yielding property is likely to be offering the investor early returns with an uncertain future, whereas the low yielding property can only offer a deferred return. This simple differentiation can be further heightened by the use of leasehold interests where the duration of the income is set by the length of term. An interesting yield curve is observable in the leasehold market. For long unexpired terms, say over 100 years, the yield differential from freehold is small, say around 1%, but as the term shortens to 20 years or less the yield offered approaches, and indeed may exceed, fixed income returns. Between these extremes, the curve is by no means smooth. Again, these yields reflect in part particular property characteristics, but they also offer a timing choice. Leasehold interests can also offer geared future returns built on the relationship between the rack rent and the ground rent.

In summary therefore property can offer a wide range of options to the investor, but the choice of income flow may restrict the type of property available; it would be hard to find a high initial yield on a prime shop for example.

4   MANAGEABILITY

Property scores low marks here. The ownership of property carries a mass of obligations and responsibilities. To some degree these can be sub-contracted, for example by a pension fund choosing to invest in an exempt unit trust, but the very process of sub-contracting deprives the owner of some of the advantages he would like from the fact of ownership. Management can also be sub-contracted to firms of property managers, but this is still likely to leave the owner with a range of obligations which he cannot depute without surrendering responsibility. In either case management will be expensive and the investor's income will be diluted. 'Management' is an important positive as well as negative issue for property, and is discussed in more detail later.

5   SPREADABILITY

Property is 'lumpy' and, therefore, not easily spreadable. Every property has a particular investment value (or more precisely a value spectrum or range). An investor cannot purchase, or sell, a part interest if the total value is too much for him because no satisfactory method has yet been proven for dividing ownership into parts. Property investment portfolios therefore tend to comprise indivisible units of high proportionate value when compared with an equity portfolio. Current attempts at 'unitisation' and 'securitisation' are addressing this problem and may well work, but at present all attempts at sharing are fraught either with problems concerning valuation, control, or liquidity.

6   RISK AND OPPORTUNITY

This need appears to be well met by property. Properties can offer a wide range of opportunities for enhanced return and also for diversifying risk, within the confines of a single market of course. There are not perhaps the diversity of ways of holding and trading equity stakes that occur within the stock market, with conversion rights, futures, options and so forth. These may appear eventually from securitisation. But despite that the property market offers the investment manager considerable choice.

V HOW ARE INVESTMENT DECISIONS REACHED?

Within the constraints described, property will provide a suitable equity investment to support a range of savings products or liabilities. However 'property' also offers a very wide range of opportunities, indeed superficially the widest of all ranges because each property is unique by location, by structure, by legal interest, etc. This section describes how an investment manager approaches this cornucopia, utilising research and information at a global and local level, and an appraisal of each individual opportunity, how he assesses the risks involved and how he views the enhancement of the reward by the use of gearing.

1 Research and information

Having decided to enter the waters of equity against the background already described, long-term savings institutions will be keen to understand and control the risks they are incurring. Their appreciation of the role which explicit and disciplined research can play in this has grown considerably over the last ten or fifteen years, but is perhaps only just starting to lap at the shores of property. For a long time institutions have collected intelligence or information about their property assets or potential assets, but much of this was sporadic or parochial in nature. Attempts to correlate the information collected, or even to record it in a disciplined manner, let alone to carry out more fundamental and conceptual research utilising what had been collected, were minimal. However the advent of computer technology plus a growing perception of a need has spawned an industry attempting to meet the need. At present the work is largely carried out either within the firms of property advisers such as chartered surveyors, estate agents, etc, or by a handful of specialists, but a growing number of institutions are now creating their own capacity.

The quality, the depth and the sources of this research and information is very varied, but its objective is to provide a guiding light in an uncertain world, with some attempt to understand the factors which will affect that uncertainty and the risks which they bring. It is also believed that better research better acted upon will bring competitive advantage. These are truisms, but what does 'research and information' (R & I) really mean? What does it cover?

The two words are used to emphasise that the subject covers everything from high-flown portfolio theory to the marshalling of simple facts or even opinions at the single asset level. But the trick is to synchronise the full range to produce well-focused and useful results. For descriptive purposes it is convenient to divide the range into four parts: fundamental, economic and financial, sector, and asset. In reality the parts are not, or should not be, in any way separate or there are dangers of non sequiturs arising.

1 FUNDAMENTAL R & I

This work spills over into and derives from the academic world. It attempts to explain and understand investment activities at a conceptual level; a particularly relevant example concerns portfolio management theory attempting to understand how portfolios, rather than individual assets, behave, how they should be constructed and managed. Most of the work is done at a high level, but generally utilises work originally based on the bond or equity markets because of the considerable sources of data in those markets. Some of this work is now being directed towards the property market, although at the time of writing its direct impact on property investment is probably still small.

2   ECONOMIC AND FINANCIAL R & I

Investors will seek to understand and forecast the global and national economic forces which will shape and influence the economic environment in which their asset must live. Such forces will have a vigorous impact on success or failure; views on inflation, economic growth, currency movements and interest rates, for example, will be crucial pieces of information. They will bring a capacity to make a coherent choice of which markets to invest in, both national (US v Germany v UK) and market type (shares, bonds, property, cash). The information will also carry messages down into the sector level; for example currency relativities appear to be a strong determinant in Oxford Street rents, levels of international trade may influence sectors of the City office market, or prospects for the competitiveness of British engineering may impinge on the industrial property market in the Midlands.

3   SECTOR R & I

Having formed a view of markets in absolute terms, the investor must understand whether there are local conditions within that market either in totality or at sector level, which may frustrate his expectations, or lead to them being exceeded. In the property sector such research is still in its infancy, one of the reasons being the paucity of recorded material, another being the difficulty of making judgments over the timespans implicit in property investment, and another, perhaps the reluctance of participants in the market to understand the necessity for such research.

4   ASSET R & I

Finally the investor will want information at the stock selection level. He will have articulated expectations from, say, shops, but he will need to know whether any particular local market can be expected to meet his expectations, or whether local causes of frustration exist. This area of R & I merges imperceptibly into physical and legal research of each individual asset and is, therefore, much more established in current property market expertise.

The sources of research are quite manifold. The investor's problem is to obtain material which may be commonly available, but utilise it in a way which brings him unique advantages. At all levels there is becoming available a growing platform of knowledge and forecast which is reasonably accessible to all who may enquire. Much of this is published. The material falls into three categories, indices of past performance, general market analysis and forecasts, and local or particular market analysis and forecasts.

The absence of a 'market index' to compare with the FT indices for the stock and government bond markets is a much commented upon feature of property. Two types of attempt have been made to fill the void. The first is a portfolio index in which an actual or theoretical portfolio, or group of portfolios, is valued regularly, usually quarterly, to produce a series of statistics of return; examples include those produced by Jones Lang Wootton, Weatherall Green & Smith and Richard Ellis. Generally each index covers a small range of properties, and reflects only those properties, and is in no way a market index. The second type attempts to aggregate as wide a range of actual properties as possible in order to approximate a market index. These cover larger groups of properties but the quality of valuation control is weaker. Examples include pension fund indices, Morgan Grenfell Laurie-Corporate Intelligence Group (£12.54bn as at 31 December 1986), the Wood Mackenzie Company (£5.213bn as at 31 March 1987) and the Investment Property Databank (estimated to be worth over £14bn as at 31 December 1987). The weakness of all these performance indices is the unavailability of the source data, which makes them of limited use to other researches.

General market information is now produced by most of the major firms of property professionals, and an increasing number of other advisers as well. They cover an ever widening range of subjects, as each product attempts to find a niche, and vary in depth and detail very considerably.

Local market analyses and forecasts usually focus on one town or area in an attempt to assess primarily the supply of and demand for property to occupy in those areas. They are produced by both local and national firms of estate agents.

Most institutions are willing to leave most of the research described to others, buying it in when needed. Their problem is to utilise that material, perhaps adding special perspectives, and to bring the results to bear upon their decisions. The larger institutions may well employ substantial in-house research capacity to fulfil this process but the smaller will have to rely upon a narrow range of personal judgments. Both may attempt, particularly the smaller fund, to commission exclusive research, asking some other body to undertake specific projects of utilisation. This has the clear disadvantage that its exclusivity is likely to have a short life. However, that may be a small disadvantage, as even original thought by a large institution is likely to escape quite quickly, even if only from the observations by others of its actions.

For these reasons, most individual research results in a short shelf-life. It must therefore be constantly reviewed, and it will be more valuable if it provides a proper and disciplined series of results. It needs to be dynamic in character, placing great emphasis on data, systems and models, rather than producing isolated, 'desert island' predictions, however correct those prove to be.

2   The appraisal

Calculation of the return required from or anticipated from a particular property, or indeed property generally, is probably one of the least sophisticated areas of activity. Historically, in the 1940s and 1950s when property was scarcely viewed as an equity at all, the return demanded was related directly to long-term gilts. A modest premium of 1 or 2% over gilts was demanded for the extra risk and trouble of property, and no account was taken at all of potential growth in rents. Indeed growth was often unattainable because leases granted were long, and contained no opportunities to review the rent. However, this was the genesis of the 'all risks' yield.

As inflation started to rise, investors demanded reviews in the rents, and the concept of growth emerged. At the same time what was then called 'the reverse yield gap' also emerged; because of the potential growth in rents, running yields fell below gilt yields. The table on p 55 below illustrates the turning point in the mid-1960s. At the time this was considered extraordinary, but it has, of course, continued to this day, to the extent that 'growth' dominates thinking about some areas of property investment, and the running yield on shops is more commonly compared, particularly in the prime market, with the dividend yield on equities.

However, this radical change was not accompanied by any equivalent change in valuation or appraisal techniques. The 'all risks' yield remained king. Equivalent or equated yields were invented to cover reversionary interests, but it was, for a long time, sacrilege to evaluate, or even consider, rental growth beyond to-day's full rental value. In the early 1970s various tables were produced to illustrate the rate of rental growth implicit in a property deal at a given running yield in the light of any chosen discount rate (ie, gilt rate plus a premium), but these were very simple constructions.

To add to the confusion in the early 1980s Norman Bowie and others pointed out that future rental growth was not only uneven and uncertain, but also seriously undermined by the obsolescence of physical structures.

Despite, or perhaps because of, these complications, the 'all risks' yield has continued to dominate thinking. It has the virtue of simplicity, and wide acceptance in a market place where the players must communicate with each other. The majority of property investors will express their willingness to trade in shops 'at 4%', or industrials 'at $7\frac{1}{2}$%' and these figures do carry meaning within the market place. However, investors are starting to develop a more explicit approach to the judgment of individual deals. DCF programmes are widely available for personal computers, and there is increasing intellectual academic debate about the issues. The difficulty tends to be that most attempts at explicit analytical techniques, because of the absence of adequate valid research, still

Initial Yields

Year	Shops	Gilts
1955	5.50	4.25
1956	5.50	4.75
1957	5.50	5.00
1958	5.50	5.00
1959	6.00	5.00
1960	5.50	5.25
1961	5.50	6.25
1962	5.50	6.25
1963	5.50	6.00
1964	5.50	5.50
1965	6.00	6.00
1966	6.00	6.50
1967	6.50	6.76
1968	7.00	8.00
1969	7.00	9.00
1970	7.50	9.00
1971	6.75	9.00
1972	6.00	9.00
1973	5.25	10.80
1974	7.50	14.80
1975	5.50	14.40
1976	6.00	14.40
1977	5.25	13.10
1978	4.25	12.40
1979	4.00	11.70
1980	4.00	14.10
1981	3.50	13.80
1982	3.50	13.80
1983	3.50	10.50
1984	3.50	10.30
1985	3.50	10.60
1986	4.00	8.90
1987	4.00	8.90
1988	4.00	9.30

Source: 1955–74 Allsop & Co
1975–88 Hillier Parker

leave huge areas to subjective judgment, and potential users are then put off, and revert to the 'all risks' yield which is at least familiar.

Most investor judgments continue to be made from a fairly simplistic, and thus manageable, basis. Market sectors (ie, bonds, stockmarkets, property, cash, etc) will be chosen from a view of competitors' positions, a reasonably thorough attempt to forecast returns over short periods (two years at the most), and considerably more subjective views of the longer term future. Within the property market, sector choices will be made upon views of portfolio balance and spread (eg, 40% shops, 40% office, 20% industrial) which will be derived again quite subjectively and with an eye to the competition. It will be a common perception that the setting of these parameters is crucial, particularly for the larger fund, because such portfolios take a long time to adjust, but the depth of thought in setting them will often not be great. Views will be derived quite subjectively, with an eye to the competition and heavily based upon historical perceptions, if only because the tools for forecasting are so inadequate. Clearly attempts will be made to assess future prospects, but these remain at present little more than crystal ball gazing beyond a two-year horizon.

At the individual asset level the appraisal techniques became more rigorous. Views will be formed of the local market within which the property sits. These views, which should, of course, reflect the relevant R & I, will derive strongly from personal observation; property fund managers feel a strong desire to see for themselves the assets they control or are thinking of acquiring. There is also an increasing supply of survey material available concerning the local economy, the supply of competing properties and so on. The physical structure of the building will also be quite rigorously assessed. Not only will its state of repair be measured but also its age, its effectiveness, perhaps even its likely economic life. Less frequently is its 'cost-in-use' (ie, an occupier's view) assessed.

The numerical conversion of this material is a great deal less rigorous. It will be most uncommon for more or less numerate adjustment to be made to the all risks yield for what has been observed. Explicit DCF modelling, although increasing, is by no means the common standard with the sole exception of development situations which are discussed below. The problems deriving from the use of DCF models have already been referred to, but if the model is to be utilised over any extended period quite heroic assumptions have to be made. It may be rightly argued that the need for heroic assumptions is as great or greater for an all risks yield evaluation, but at least such an evaluation is recognised for what it is. An attempt at more precise analysis may be rendered spurious, or even misleading, by the need to include subjective assumptions unless these are of only marginal significance. There is considerable argument about the elements a DCF valuation should contain and the following list is by no means definitive:

The target rate of return; the cash flow period; current rental details including net rent passing; rent reviews or reversion dates on leases, estimated rental values; rental growth; depreciation rates; annual running costs including expected inflation in expenditures; voids; cost, timing and effect on rent of refurbishment; purchase, review, letting and sale fees; investment yields; taxation applicable and grants receivable.

The period for such modelling is also uncertain. It might be for a known 'holding period', or for some known period by which the manager is to be judged; equally it might only cover a period to a particular rent review or a projected refurbishment. However, few analysts would be willing to attempt forecasts on the elements over any extended period and the most common compromise is to model over a short period, say five to ten years at most, and then revert to an 'all risks' yield.

The problems in this area remain under review, but most of the work remains insular to the property market. Little attempt is made to analyse or explain the cash and value flows in terms comparable to other equity (or even debt) securities.

It is easy to be critical of appraisal techniques used by investors, indeed it is unlikely that any wholly satisfactory techniques are achievable. The fact is that an investment decision concerning property involves making a large range of judgments over the relevant matters discussed in this section. Historically there has been a temptation to pass up most such judgments and make the decision on marginal criteria relating to the asset under consideration in isolation. Investing institutions have moved some way from this position and are increasingly aware of total portfolio considerations; this is evidenced by the considerable activity in buying and selling during the early and mid-1980s. At that time property was relatively unattractive; such activity must therefore be largely explained by attempts at fund adjustment. The decisions involved were therefore by no means exclusively marginal, but consistent with clearer targets or benchmarks for each fund. Naturally, such targets are rarely published, but their existence can be deduced from the known actions of many funds.

3 Risk

As has already been explained, all investors, but particularly those who choose equity investment, are concerned with risk, either to control it or to exploit it. But in property appraisal attempts at describing or measuring risk remain in their infancy compared with other markets. Modest essays at sensitivity and scenario analysis occur (again predominantly in development situations), but beyond this investors rarely go.

All participants recognise that they are incurring risks but their observation of that risk usually remains at the asset level, the risk that something particular does not occur or does occur. For example 'market risk' and 'asset risk' are now well established intellectual concepts of general application. The phrases would be widely identified in the property market, the former being seen as a product of the 'market' in which the asset stands and the latter as risk peculiar to the particular asset. Most property fund managers would view both these classes of risk as being largely physical (or at least observable) ones, related to changes in the economic background, changes in location, physical defects, bankrupt tenants, etc. They will seek to control these risks primarily at the physical level, by careful R & I at sector and asset level. A conversion of this observation of risk into the academic concepts of 'market risk' and 'specific risk' which can be controlled at other than the physical level is rare.

To take another example, there is little evidence either that timing is seen as an element for risk control. Again, most fund managers will clearly perceive that the timing of purchases will significantly effect their total return ('Empirical Support for the Importance of Timing: An analysis of Retail Property Investment Performance', M Blackwell of surveyors Gibson Eley – The Investment Analyst, January 1988) which is an advance over earlier beliefs that the quality of the property transcended all timing considerations. However, the timing of subsequent events, perhaps just as important as the purchase, are rarely considered. Two particular areas which are largely ignored are timing of rent reviews and timing of exit (or sale).

Looking at rent reviews first, whilst at a national market level changes in rent levels are generally fairly smooth as is indicated by published 'rent indices', at local level they move by fits and starts. But no public analysis of a fund is known which demonstrates any coherent and numerate attempt to control (or obtain added value) from this phenomenon, beyond, perhaps, attempts to complete proposed developments at a favourable stage.

Exit planning is equally rarely evident. The one exception to this is, again, developments where many funds will view completion of the development as one occasion to consider exit, reflecting the change from the high profitability of the development phase to the more modest profitability of subsequent ownership. But there is very little evidence that funds purchase the majority of properties with any considered view of a holding period. No doubt the reason for this is the difficulty of forecasting in any worthwhile sense over the periods it is normally felt necessary to hold properties for.

Because of the relatively undeveloped concept of risk, risk control is also fairly undeveloped. It will generally be limited to some attitude towards prime properties (which, as already described, are considered less risky), care over R & I and 'diversification'; the fact of diversification will be seen as reducing risk in absolute terms (further reference to diversification is made elsewhere in this chapter), and the comparison of how the diversification is achieved by different funds will be seen as controlling competitive risk.

Observation and control of risk in other investment markets is further advanced. For equities, in particular, a considerable literature has evolved from pioneering work by the American academic Harry Markowitz. The work suggests that investors are 'risk-averse', in that they will only accept higher risk on the expectation of greater returns, and then builds a theory of how individual securities are priced. For the major investor, risk must be seen in a portfolio context, and a workable theory must allow for this facet. The best known theory is the Capital Asset Pricing model but other theories, in particular Arbitrage Pricing Theory, are gaining a following.

The relative unsophistication of the property market is starting to be addressed. The role of research in property investment has assumed increasing importance in recent years, as evidenced by the growth of research departments in the larger surveying firms and institutions. Further, the need to consider property within the overall investment market is reflected by a greater willingness to apply discounted cash flow methods and techniques from portfolio theory to a property context. In anticipation of the unitised property market and in order to specialise in the more innovative methods of funding property developments, some firms and organisations have formed 'Financial Services' departments. Consequently training and education needs are changing, and this has led to the development of MSc degrees and diplomas in Property Investment and MBAs with a property investment component.

There is, therefore, a discernible trend towards increasing sophistication in the property market. However, a major task faces researchers and analysts in the future in applying new techniques to a property market which suffers from a lack of data and which, in many respects, remains highly secretive.

Whilst institutional investors are concerned about risk, and they may be more or less willing to take risk at an individual asset level, all are at great pains to ensure that they do not take it at fund level, ie, imperil in any way their fundamental viability. The normal tool of control is diversification or spread, and in the property world that spreading is usually limited to size (not more than x% in one property), use and location. Potentially there are a number of other types of spreading, eg, prime, secondary, tertiary, or lease term, but these are rarely ever recorded, yet alone utilised.

Institutions will also court risk to a modest degree. They will seek situations where, by the adoption of risk they can hope to attain enhanced return. Property development is the most common example, but the purchase of vacant property or specialist property is another, as is an atypical asset spread. In these situations the analysis of risk and reward is surprisingly unnumerate. As has been said, modest sensitivity and scenario analysis may be attempted, but the evaluation of those analyses remains highly subjective. It is probable that this derives from a historical perception (folklore?) that an important condition of success in the property market is 'feel'. In the property market, as all others, there will be many examples of successful players whose success has arrived from behaving untypically; such people are deemed to have had good 'feel'. That is unlikely. It is more likely that they were looking at the right things through luck or judgment, whereas everyone else was stuck with the wrong ones. The legend of 'feel' in the property market is enhanced by the inadequacies of its numerate description, the problems arising from the lengths of its cycles, the often illogical interference of the legislature, the strong elements of monopoly which remain within the property market, and perhaps also by the sheer physical impact on the environment by those who are 'successful'.

Institutions attempt to emulate that 'feel', and appear willing to run considerable risk in doing so, still with the caveat that the risk is run at the asset level and not the fund level.

At the individual property level institutions may well also become illogically risk-averse, precisely because properties are so conspicuous. A property fund manager may well feel himself considerably more exposed because one building representing 2% of his fund is unlet than with under-par rental growth at reviews, because a vacant building is clearly a visible 'failure'.

In summary, all institutions recognise that they are inevitably exposed to risk, all will have some view of the degree of risk they are willing to take, and all will consider that they have proper control over their risk. The quality of analysis is much more questionable.

4 Gearing

Perhaps the most potent tool of all for enhancing risk and return is gearing, the borrowing of money on fixed interest rate terms in order to finance an equity investment. As described later, 'fixed interest' can today take many forms, including being variable, linked for example to money market rates or the retail prices index. The key element though is that the rate of interest is *not* linked to the profitability of the investment. As a result the return on the equity of the investment after servicing the borrowing will be geared up (or down). A simple example:

Cost of venture	£100	Expected return	at 15% =£15	Actual return	£30
Borrowing	£70	Interest	at 10% = £7		£7
		Profit		£8	£23

With the return from the venture rising by 100%, the equity income has risen by 187.5%. Thus are fortunes built! The wealth created in private hands by means of a mortgage on a private house has been an excellent example, with widespread economic results. But the obverse is also true, and thus are bankrupts made. Gearing is therefore a dangerous tool, which can lead to negative values. With the clear ownership of even the most risky property asset it is virtually impossible to end up with a liability; the asset may be worthless, although even that is very rare for any extended period, or it may require further expenditure of bootless capital to salvage the asset but it will not carry a heavy financial liability. Gearing, whether by borrowing or the use of geared leasehold interests, can produce a liability implicit in the need to carry on servicing the borrowing or paying the ground rent whether or not there is any income at all from the investment.

It is therefore not surprising that long-term savings institutions are unwilling to gear their portfolios (indeed borrowing against assets is constrained by the

Insurance Companies Act 1982 and the Trustees Investment Act 1961). All investment portfolios in their hands are created to match a particular set of liabilities, as has already been described. The prime objective of a fund is to meet those liabilities with the *minimum of risk*. The 'minimum of risk' will vary between the products, but it has already been explained how risk averse the ultimate investors are. Because of the underlying liabilities, inescapable gearing introduces an element of risk which no fund manager or trustee can properly accept.

However, at the *asset* level gearing can be escapable provided that the asset is properly structured and is reasonably liquid. Thus institutions live happily with gearing in the hands of companies whose shares they hold because those shares are reasonably liquid, and they can thus hope to escape before the chopper falls, but more than that, the shares equally cannot become a liability because of the corporate structure.

VI THE MANAGEMENT OF ASSETS

A property portfolio will require a high degree of management, and it will require this at three levels. First, as with a share portfolio, it will require sector and timing management decisions surrounding a broad fund strategy. It will then require stock selection management; this will be more demanding than for a share portfolio because of the absence of a central market place and because of the technical difficulties surrounding the transfer of property interests. Then, at the third level, and beyond a share portfolio, the assets themselves must be managed. Each level of management requires different skills and must be viewed separately. The relative influence of each level of management upon performance can be debated, and some of the issues will emerge in what follows. Equally, the amount of management at each level can be governed to some degree, for instance by the choice of active trading as against a stable fund policy, or the choice of assets involving high or low levels of property management, but nevertheless each level is inescapable and relevant to performance.

1 Sector and timing management

A study of historical performance measures such as the HPMR/IC index demonstrates considerable divergence of performance between property market sectors over different time periods. For example central London offices have been particularly strong during 1987 and 1988, having been weak in the early 1980s. However, during those early 1980s retail property was particularly strong. If these divergencies could be harnessed, considerable added value would accrue to a portfolio. In attempting to harness them the working definition of 'sector' which is chosen will be important. A common view of a 'sector' will be offices, but it is clear that offices in the City of London have little in common with offices in Newcastle so far as investment characteristics are concerned. Equally, 'shops' might be another sector, and here there will be strong correlation between different geographical locations, although a few specialist areas, such as Oxford Street, may markedly differ. Thus the first role of management is to establish a clear geographical and physical view of 'sectors' relevant and available to the fund – a clear view of the hare. Utilising R & I, decisions must then be made upon entry and exit from those sectors to benefit from performance cycles; few funds will today feel able to echo the attitude of many traditional rural landowners that, over 2000 years, the cycles become less relevant! Although not for debate within this book, it is unlikely that this level of management can properly be carried out without reference to other investment markets, and the cyclical and timing opportunities and risks available within the property market must be assessed in parallel with equivalent opportunities and risks in those alternative markets.

2   Stock selection management

If sectors are coherently set, stock selection becomes less important and will be limited to identifying whether an asset has characteristics which will lead it to deviate from the sector either negatively (eg, its falling down), or positively (eg, a subsector has temporarily fallen behind a trend it should follow; such lagging is common in the property market because of unclear correlations and lags in information flows). Whilst this assertion would probably be accepted by many property fund managers, experience suggests that most still place stock selection above sector selection, and may thus deliberately or inadvertently corrupt a sector strategy. This apparent indiscipline will derive from the view that the property market is strongly opportunistic in character and that the taking of those opportunities is important; a view which is questionable. However, it does seem clear that the process of stock selection does require a keen and direct understanding of the rationale of sector selection so that the basis of the rationale is reflected in individual decisions. This can be difficult to achieve because of the complexity of the property market: for example, the importance of 'position' to occupiers, and the fine judgments which can influence position, or the value relevance of lease clauses, or the significance of structural or lay-out details, all make stock selection a highly complex task. The complexity will be magnified by the necessity to negotiate price and the changing perspective which will arise as price changes. This is an area of great difficulty. In principle a fund manager should be able to define the price he is willing to pay for an asset, given his sector and timing decision, and any assets available at that price should be bought as quickly as possible and without negotiation; in simplistic terms this is how transactions on the stock market occur. However a definition of price is extremely difficult for property because of the almost infinite number of issues which will affect it in relation to a particular property, and also because vendors expect to haggle over the price and quote accordingly. Management of stock selection therefore becomes of considerable importance, and its very process can corrupt or enhance sector selection.

3 Property management

This can vary considerably in degree, and a fund manager has a range of choices from properties which require a relatively low level of input (full repairing and insuring leases), to those with a very high input (eg, a shopping centre). The choice is not, however, entirely free because properties within the range may have quite divergent investment characteristics. Thus, in the example given, shopping centres are not a straight alternative to High Street shops; there is some correlation, but it is by no means clean. Equally, large multi-let offices in the City differ considerably from large single-let buildings; especially at the tenant level where they are in quite a different market.

Even at the simplest levels however, management decisions must be made to control the property and beyond that to extract from it the maximum of performance. The impact of such management upon performance is hard to measure objectively. It is clear that properties must be managed so that they are physically able to deliver the desired performance; rent reviews must be conducted if the rent is to rise, repairs must be executed if the structure is to stay sound, and so on. The quality of management surrounding such matters will impact upon value, but the significance will vary; in a strong vendor's market imperfections may be overlooked by purchasers, but in a buyer's market unskilled management may make an asset virtually unsaleable save at a prodigious discount. Beyond that, however, property assets carry considerable opportunity for enhancement. Such opportunities will range from the minor to the major, and will often be wholly outside the vision of the original appraisal, perhaps squeezing a bit more letable space by clearing a broom cupboard or updating some otherwise adverse lease covenants, to releasing value by co-operation with adjoining property. Such management can release considerable value.

The importance of all three levels of management has grown as a direct reflection partly of growing clarity in performance measurement facilities, throwing into relief what each individual asset is contributing to total fund performance, and partly from increased pressure for performance.

The significance of a changed and sharpened performance observation upon management standards is considerable. It is placing greater demands upon the surveying profession, its techniques and its standards of reporting; the screw will receive a further turn when management conduct becomes very public with unitised or securitised properties as, with such vehicles, the perceived quality of the managers may have some effect upon the unit price. Techniques learnt with such vehicles may become demanded practice for other properties. However, investors will rapidly recognise that high standards of management cost money. They will, therefore, demand greater accountability, and an even clearer market differentiation between 'management' and 'non-management' properties may emerge.

The property market itself has grown more complex and more fast-moving. A property portfolio must therefore be groomed and adjusted more frequently if it is to provide optimum results and it must therefore be managed actively, even if perhaps the concepts of management are not as clearly seen in the real world as has just been described.

4 Sources of management skills

The skills necessary to perform the management tasks are widely available in the market. Firms of surveyors, merchant banks and financial institutions offer various combinations of all three levels. The fund manager therefore has considerable choice. It is not appropriate here to discuss the quality of what is available, but some general comments can be made.

Many fund managers choose to put out property management. They do this because it calls for a wide range of technical and professional skills which may only be viable in-house for a very large portfolio. This would be increasingly true as the fund became more diversified and the demand for local or sector knowledge, quite apart from the fundamental skills, quickly becomes unmanageable. The problem to be overcome if only property management is put out is to ensure that the management is performed in true harmony with fund strategy; the property manager will no doubt be skilled in performing the tasks of management, but he will be faced with many choices, and the choice which is right for the fund must be made. At a simple and obvious level, if a property is programmed for sale it is rather better that it is not swathed with scaffolding for redecoration when purchasers view it. More complex, it is better not to be in dispute with the tenant over the rent at the time of sale, but what degree of compromise would be justified? The range of issues is infinite, but it is clear that proper control is difficult with the management separated and there is probably a performance cost, albeit one which the fund manager will be willing to pay, particularly if he doubts his own ability to fulfil the tasks with technical competence.

Stock selection management raises a number of issues. At its simplest, few fund managers are willing fully to pass to others responsibility for asset choice unless they are participating in a wider fund of some sort from which they can fairly readily exit, for example an exempt property unit trust. Whether this desire for 'hands-on' is really logical is questionable, but it undoubtedly arises from the physical nature of property and the belief referred to earlier, that 'feel' for the asset can add value; perhaps it also derives from a deep-rooted human relationship with 'land'. However, as with property management, considerable technical skills are called for in stock selection and therefore it is again quite common for fund managers to seek external advice and guidance. Managing stock selection is difficult on a do-it-yourself basis unless, again, you are managing funds of a considerable size. Use of external advisers brings the more than incidental advantage that such advisers can be chosen precisely for their presence as brokers in the buying and selling market place. Such advisers should be able to ensure that the fund is made aware of opportunities, albeit at a cost of total clarity about how such an adviser will manage the interface between a range of clients. Further because measurement of market value, compared with assessed value, plays such an important role it will also be of considerable value to utilise someone who can have a good view of that market value. Even for funds which choose to retain stock selection for themselves, there remains a crucial relationship with other players if only in the role of brokers.

Sector selection and timing management will rarely be placed outside. Managers may well seek considerable external advice, particularly those with limited or non-existent research facilities, but most will wish to retain full control of such crucial decisions. The sources and relevance of such advice have already been considered under the heading of research.

VII SPECIAL OPPORTUNITIES

1 Development

Development is viewed as being a very particular activity indeed; in many fund analyses it is placed as a class of asset in its own right. In part this separate classification will be because of the problem of valuation; it is very difficult to value a property during the course of development because the range of uncertainties is particularly large, uncertainties over whether it should be assumed that the building contract is continuing, or is terminated and has to be re-started, uncertainties arising from the flow of money on the building contract, uncertainties over eventual letting, uncertainty over how to treat any development profit and so on. For these reasons developments are usually included at the lower of cost or value, thus including no profit, and the figure is recognised as being highly imprecise.

But apart from the valuation issue, the separate classification also reflects a clear conceptual differentiation. It is widely accepted that development is a 'risk' business, by which it is meant that it carries risks and brings opportunities of a different degree and even nature to ordinary ownership and dealing in the investment market. First it is seen as an activity in which that risk can be amply rewarded; the number of property developers in large motor cars to whom fund managers have lent money is living proof of the rewards! To indulge in the process will normally be an attempt to retain some or all of that profit for the institution. This is referred to below.

Secondly, development enables an institution to control to some degree the quality and nature of its buildings. This can perhaps also be achieved by careful buying but, by undertaking the development himself, the fund manager can control the quality of building, and also the pattern of letting, to precisely his taste. He can also hope slightly to pre-empt the investment market by developing buildings for which he believes there will be a shortage of supply, thus ensuring that he is 'in the market' when the shortage impacts upon values.

Finally, the development process takes time. It is, therefore, as a general expansion of the previous point, a method of providing, at the time of your choosing, for future investment needs. If the need is not there, the finished product can always be sold. To some degree it can be used as a method of locking oneself into a particular value scenario which is perceived to be favourable, giving a flavour of 'futures' and even gearing without actual money risk.

However, development is seen as risky, and institutions will have different views on the degree of risk they can take. The buffer they use to control that risk will be a development partner, someone able and willing to absorb the risk which the institution will not take. This will usually be a property company, but exceptionally may be another institution or even a local authority. The range of solutions reached is nearly infinite, but a spectrum can be identified with four benchmarks.

1. The institution is site assembler and developer itself. It thus carries all the risk and takes all the reward. In principle they are well placed to take this role as they do not have to borrow and therefore can avoid any gearing risk. However, most are not equipped to fulfil the role technically, and have concern about their ability to control it.

2. The institution 'joint ventures' with a developer. In this scenario the institution carries broadly equal risk and takes broadly equal reward with the developer, but is comforted by his skills and his financial interest which is also at risk. In its purest sense this arrangement is not common, largely because the developer will not be able to provide his share of finance. The arrangement therefore tends to be corrupted to some degree with unequal inputs and unequal rewards.

3. The institution chooses to take a little risk, but leaves most with the developer. This is probably the most common scenario and has many variations. The usual format is that the institution provides all or nearly all of the capital required to execute the development. On completion and letting it will make further payments to the developer based upon a formula derived from the achieved rents. This is commonly achieved by 'slicing' the income. For example:

> Income up to 6% return on capital – 100% to institution
> Income from 6% to 7%   – 100% to developer
> Income from 7% to 8%   – 50/50 inst/developer
> Income from 8% to 9%   – 75/25 inst/developer
> Income over 9%   – 100% to institution

The income accruing to the developer will generally then be capitalised at an agreed rate (say $7\frac{1}{2}\%$ in the example) and that is used to calculate the payment the institution must make to the developer. Occasionally the developer may remain 'in', and the formula will define his future share of income. Clearly the formula is infinitely variable at the figure level. It may be varied with the developer leaving in some capital stake (eg, the site) throughout the development period, and even subsequently if he retains an interest.

All variations are merely attempts at apportioning the rewards to the taste of the parties, and to reflect the risks each is taking. Thus the institution will be able to raise its return a little, but at the price of leaving some of the return with the developer. As far as the institution is concerned the trick, of course, is to get the balance right and to choose a developer who *can* absorb the risk; the 1970s showed that many cannot, and the provider of the finance has to take it because he has no alternative.

4. The institution takes no development risk, but agrees to buy on completion. In this case the fund is doing little more than buying a future on the asset concerned. That future may be at a price fixed at the outset, or variable, depending upon the eventual letting outcome; only rarely will it depend upon the investment market condition at completion. Because it is offering the developer a guaranteed exit at a future date, the fund will hope to enjoy an enhanced return over buying a completed property in the market, but that is not for a development risk, it is only for a timing risk.

Apart from risk control, there is one other potential benefit of working with a developer; he may bring to you a particular site opportunity not otherwise available, or a development idea which is innovative. The site opportunity is very common. A major role for property companies is adventurous purchasing of sites often years before a development is feasible or obvious. They may acquire the whole site or just critical parts so that they control the situation. They are then able to offer the opportunity to an institution demanding an appropriate stake or role in the remainder of the development process. If the opportunity suits the institution it has no choice but to negotiate terms.

The introduction of innovation is also important to an institution. Buildings are continually evolving in their method of construction, in their design, their layout and even their use. This process of evolution has been particularly rapid in the last 40 years. Funding institutions are not normally equipped to lead in this process; a few have succeeded, but the majority are unlikely to employ staff or even professional advisers with the necessary innovative flair (or even cheek!). Innovation also involves added risk. Development companies are frequently the source of the ideas, and may well also be able to absorb some or all of the risk on one of the last three bases described above.

Given that development offers funding institutions a number of potential advantages, is their appetite likely to continue or to grow? There are three aspects to consider in answering this. First, having built up their portfolios during the last 30 years or so, institutions will already hold within those portfolios major development opportunities. Assuming that they have identified the opportunity (which is, of course, not always the case) they must decide whether and how to realise it. Attitude to risk, technical resources and cash availability will control their response. They may choose to sell the site to a developer at a price which, in their view, reflects a fair slice of the eventual profit. In the mid-1980s, when institutions were not committing significant new funds to property such sales were commonplace. Or they may choose to carry through the development themselves, providing their own finance and such technical and professional resources as they command, buying in the rest. Again, this is commonplace with the rebuilding of shop units, rebuilding and refurbishing office buildings, etc. Finally they may choose to take a partner. At present this is a great deal less common; one of the few recent examples is the new town centre shopping scheme for Ilford where the Prudential owned the key elements of a site, but rather than providing all the finance itself it chose to bring in the Norwich Union to provide most of the new money. The reasons for the rarity of such partnerships largely spring from the problems which surround all forms of sharing property (described under 'securitisation' below). The attractions of such partnerships are, in theory, considerable, allowing increased diversification and risk spreading. If a satisfactory form of securitisation is devised, it is likely to become widely used in this context. Given their existing holdings, the institutions are certain to play a growing development role at least in that regard.

Secondly, the risk they are willing to take, and thus the quality of a development they seek and the role they seek to play, will be dependent on issues outside the property industry. As has already been noted, they see development in part as an opportunity to enhance return in ways which give them a pleasant variety of options. Their desire to enhance returns will depend upon the competitive pressures put upon them by their own market place. In a world of growing consumerism, growing financial sophistication and growing globalisation it is reasonable to assume that competitive pressures will, if anything, increase. Again, therefore, the continued attraction of development is clear.

Finally, institutional appetite for development will be dependent upon the rate of change in occupier's demand for property, changes in location, type or quality. Development only brings enhanced returns if it is meeting new and higher value occupier's needs; the amount necessary to replace buildings which have physically, as opposed to functionally, decayed is not great. The remarkable rebuilding of the City of London in the late 1980s precisely exemplifies this; the buildings being replaced were mostly physically sound, but the occupiers of City offices demanded new types of building, and were willing and able to pay for them. The 1980s have seen similar changes across much of the investment spectrum – larger 'standard' shop units, out of town retailing, 'hi-tech' industrial buildings, re-sited warehouse demands linked to the motorways and other retail changes, and so on. Given the apparent energy of the British economy, it seems likely that the physical structures which support that economy will display similar 'energy', which implies continued changes in occupier demand. It is not for this book to attempt to forecast the duration of such economic activity, but in 1988 it appears likely to continue, albeit perhaps at a slackening pace. Institutional demand for development would follow a similar pattern, as they strive to take the opportunities, or struggle to maintain the physical status of their property portfolio.

Continued enthusiasm seems assured, but what role will the financial institutions attempt in the spectrum already described? In the post Second World War rebuild of British cities, institutions took the extreme 'no risk' line, providing finance but largely in debt, or near-debt form. As each subsequent cycle of development activity has emerged, they have been willing to take greater risks, reflecting the growing competitive pressures upon them. They are now supported by a large professional and technical resource in private practice which is designed to aid them. They still have considerable financial muscle, if not perhaps quite the cash flows of the 1970s. As described, they also have the motive. It is probable that they will seek now the extreme risk end of the spectrum wherever they can achieve it and, indeed, during the mid and late 1980s they have played a growing part as direct developers.

Three things will restrain them. First, they will be competing for sites with a very vigorous property company sector. The competition applies as much to the sites they already own as to new ones because any rational fund manager will be tempted by high offers for sites he owns which appear to give him all the development reward without the problems. Unless, therefore, funds can be as efficient as property companies at identifying optimum opportunities, they will be crowded out. In this competition, they have few advantages. They may already own all or part of the site, which is a strong advantage if they know what they are doing. But beyond that they compete on equal terms. The fact that they have cash available is no advantage provided that the overall investment manager is managing his resources properly, and seeking the optimum outlet. Their ability to be leaders in the development world will, therefore, depend upon their skills.

Secondly, their willingness to be leaders will be dependent upon the amount of new building they seek in relation to the resources they control. To control direct development properly requires good management skills. These may be hard to retain in an institutional environment in any quantity. If, therefore, the call is for new buildings and quickly, institutions will be willing to sacrifice some of the return to property companies in order to achieve early completion.

Thirdly, the part institutions play will depend upon the rate of true innovation which is occurring in the occupiers' market. As has been said already, institutions are not natural innovators in the property market who move in big strides. They are successful at 'industrialising' an established process and moving that process forward in small steps. They are not equipped to take the large step forward. Most innovations in recent years demonstrate this. The rebuilding of the City of London has been developer/occupier led, retail warehousing has equally been developer led, as have 'business parks' (interestingly in the latter case an institution, Electricity Supply Nominees, was a trail-blazer with Aztec West, just outside Bristol. However, it got its timing wrong and frightened a number of other possible players). If innovation continues institutions will probably provide the finance, but will choose the low-risk end of the spectrum.

In summary, therefore, continued institutional appetite for development and development risk appears likely. Their success and their relationship with the other players in the market will result from competition. Some institutions will continue to be relatively risk averse, at least in this area of their activities, but all will be attracted towards raising their profile.

2   Property companies

Property companies are corporate bodies who hold all or most of their assets in the form of property. The *nature* of the properties will vary greatly, some specialising in particular sectors of the market. Some will hold large portfolios of developed assets, others will almost entirely be developers or traders, selling on completed buildings.

The diversity is considerable but all ultimately represent some facet of 'property'. Around 135 are publicly quoted on the International Stock Exchange, and their shares are widely available. The investor in the share obtains his return by means of dividends and movement of the share price. Both these elements will ultimately derive from the property market, adjusted by the management skills of the company and its financial structure. The returns available can, therefore, be expected to have some relationship to the property market in which the company chooses to invest.

Shares are therefore seen as a surrogate for direct property to some degree and it must be the case that, over an extended period, there will be a close arithmetical correlation between the movement of property share prices and property values. The absolute relationship has tended to favour shares throughout the post-war period as might be expected in what has been predominantly a rising market, reflecting the effects of gearing, perhaps better stock selection, and perhaps also more dynamic property management.

Divergency between share price movements and property prices is also created by the incidence of tax. In broad terms a shareholder is double-taxed compared with a direct holder of property because the property company is a taxable body on income and capital gains, and the shareholder will again be taxed on dividends and realised gains in share prices. In the case of income the double taxation element will be substantially reduced for a corporate tax paying shareholder (although not for an exempt fund such as a pension fund), but capital gains (CGT) remain double-taxed and the share price will reflect some discount for the potential CGT liability within the company. The position has been improved for older property companies with the abolition of CGT on pre-1982 gains, by the Finance Act 1988 and by the indexation provisions contained in the Finance Act 1984.

Over shorter periods the share price will move differentially from the underlying direct asset, in part reflecting views of that underlying value but also reflecting changing views of gearing, CGT discount, management skill and so on, together with general stock market sentiment. It may also move as a bellwether for the direct property market and, as previously mentioned, it is possible that share prices will move, on occasion, as an accurate anticipation of the direct market. This can be explained partly because hard knowledge in the direct market is always postdated to some degree, but also because the stockmarket is made up of many players trying precisely to anticipate future events. Sometimes they get it right!

Property company shares offer the investor four particular features:

Management
Gearing
Liquidity
Other participants

1 MANAGEMENT

Property companies take from the investor all the special elements of asset and property management, leaving only those levels of management common to other shares. It is clear that property companies also offer a pretty wide range of management skills, from those who do not differ all that much from institutional skills, to the property equivalent of the pioneers. By developing a view of those skills investors can hope to back winners.

2 GEARING

They become winners at least in part because of their use of gearing. Attitudes to gearing have already been discussed, but property companies offer it at the asset level, and in a wide variety of shapes and forms. The level of gearing companies deemed appropriate varies considerably. For example, Land Securities has maintained a level of 10–15% as defined by debt/equity, whereas Brixton Estates runs gearing of around 60% of shareholders' funds. In addition to the level of debt in a company, the type of debt is interesting, in particular the proportion of fixed and variable rate debt and whether it is short or long in duration.

3 LIQUIDITY

There is a market in shares. It may occasionally be a thin market but, for most of the larger companies, it is there and the investor can deal at the margin, knowing exactly where he is. He knows when he has bought, he knows when he has sold, he knows the price he is dealing at and he knows the market value of his shares. Liquidity gives the investor an opportunity, if he can seize it, to enter a rising market (or exit a falling one) more quickly than direct property. The depth of liquidity may limit the opportunities to the margin, but the competitive advantage at the margin can still make a difference.

4   OTHER PARTICIPANTS

That liquidity exists primarily because there are other participants in the share market, particularly non-institutional participants; people with other views and priorities.

However, all these characteristics are common to all publicly quoted companies and the necessary sector and stock selection and trading skills lie in that market. For these reasons, property shares are nearly always held as part of an equity portfolio, not a property portfolio, and they are managed in the market-led style of equity shares and not the more asset-led style of direct property.

3   Overseas property

Reference has already been made to the use of 'spread' to control equity risk. One obvious avenue for spreading is into overseas markets and economies. The table below illustrates the net annual investment by pension funds and insurance companies in overseas markets from 1983 to late 1987.

Pension Funds Net Investment (£m)

		Overseas property	Overseas bonds	Overseas stock markets
1983		91	− 59	1,613
1984		164	200	230
1985		− 159	280	2,418
1986		− 20	17	2,594
1987	I	− 4	− 4	1,595
	II	− 13	10	328
	III	28	40	269

Insurance Companies Net Investment (£m)

1983		—	579	836
1984		—	327	257
1985		− 9	104	1,041
1986		− 5	447	884
1987	I	6	99	319
	II	0	75	365
	III	4	95	256

Source: Business Monitor MQ5

From this it will be seen that they have been disinvesting from overseas property, tending to realise portfolios built up in the late 1970s and early 1980s. Despite this recent disinvestment, overseas property is seen as a potential avenue for investment. Detailed motives and objectives for investing in such markets vary considerably, some viewing it as a diversification of a property portfolio, others as a diversification of a total equity portfolio into a separate asset class. This confusion is further compounded by differing attitudes on the currency risk involved; should this be taken with the property portfolio results, or isolated and treated as a separate issue? There is also further obscurity about the quality and degree of diversification actually being achieved. Clearly some diversification is being achieved simply because the portfolio has been extended, and it appears intuitively likely that an overseas property will perform differently from a British one, if only because it will be subject to different local letting and investment market conditions. However it is a good deal less clear whether there is any meaningful relationship between the two performances and therefore whether any disciplined diversification is being achieved or whether it is largely random. There is also little published evidence on how overseas property markets behave in relation to each other. Some track record of performance in a number of markets is being assembled by a number of property advisers, particularly some of the leading chartered surveyors who operate internationally, but certainly at the published level the time series are usually quite short, perhaps 10 or 12 years, reflecting the youth of performance measurement related to property.

As a result of all these uncertainties there is some doubt whether overseas portfolios within themselves are being built, or at present can be built, with any coherent view of diversification. This uncertainty, coupled with the obvious additional risks of investing in unfamiliar markets and differing legislatures, has meant that the number of funds who do invest in overseas properties is limited and almost certainly a great deal less than those who invest in overseas bond and stock markets.

However, whether or not they currently participate, most long-term savings institutions would view overseas property markets as a medium for spreading.

Understanding of the asset risks being taken on overseas markets has undoubtedly grown, often in the light of bitter experience. At the simplistic level, it used to be explained that the US market must be attractive because initial yields were so much higher than in British markets. It is probably now more widely understood why running yields were, and still are, higher. Equally there is greater understanding of the risks arising from the difficulties of management control.

Generally it could be said that the experience of British institutional investors in overseas property in the late 1970s and early 1980s has mirrored quite closely their similar experience in Europe in the 1960s. The mistakes have not been quite so great or quite so conspicuous in their detail, and it must be remembered that in both cases a few players achieved considerable successes, but overall their efforts have not added value commensurate with the risks which were taken. If that is right, it must call into question the suitability of overseas property assets for long-term savings institutions, anyway at present, or until they are presented to the investor in a form which more closely matches his needs. Perhaps they fit better into the ethic of property companies.

4   Securitisation

Adverse comments were made at the beginning of the chapter about the 'marketability' and 'spreadability' of property interests. This weakness springs inevitably, and probably unavoidably, from the feudal legal structures by which property is owned. Interests are always tiered, dominant and servient, and the passage of interests always carries with it a highly complex paraphernalia of physical and legal obligations which are surrounded with an ever growing tide of statutory and case law. Attempts have been made to develop 'side-by-side' leases, but all are flawed to some degree, if not at the time of drafting then by subsequent events. Thus emerges the rich world of 'marriage values'.

The underlying motivation to those attempting to create 'securitisation' has been two-fold. First to overcome this legal burden and to enable the birth of interests in property which are simple, small, equal and thus readily tradeable. The second purpose is more subtle. A property provides a flow of income and capital value within the land and the building itself, as well as outgoings and capital payments. At source these are wholly intertwined; the only attempts to untwine have been the ground lease and the mortgage. The former attempted to separate the income flow into two parts, one highly secure (usually without any obligations to repairs, etc) the other to a greater or less extent marginal carrying all the obligations. The latter separates the cash-flows into a debt security and a matching geared equity interest. These simple divisions were adequate for a long time. However, the needs of investors have become more complex, and other markets have started to offer a wider range of securities each with more closely defined characteristics. For example, debt securities offer a wide range of repayment patterns, equity and fixed interest become mixed with 'convertibles' and so on. The motive behind this second aspect of securitisation is to divide the cash flows of a property into such packages in order to appeal to different investors. Both seek also to make interests in each of the 'packages' readily tradeable.

Whilst much of this could probably have been achieved without the help of the authorities, the field became much more accessible when:

1. the government agreed to introduce s 76 into the Financial Services Act 1986 which offered an enabling framework to overcome many of the investor protection laws, and

2. the International Stock Exchange in London agreed in principle to quote single property vehicles, whether companies, trusts or other.

    At the time of writing various groups are working through the detail of proposed methods of securitisation, and attempting to influence the production of regulations by which any new market must be governed.

The process of creation has taken longer than expected, but throughout the period doubts have been expressed about the new market. Will there be any buyers? Will there be any liquidity? What relationship will the trading price bear to the value of the whole building? And so on.

It is not the role of this chapter to answer such questions, except perhaps the first. Will there be any buyers? There seems little reason to doubt that debt securities arising from the process will be intrinsically acceptable. The volume of demand will, of course, reflect the current attitude to debt securities, but the successful placing of the debt part of the securitisation of Billingsgate should be adequate evidence. But what of the equity interests? Inevitably any opinions expressed here must be just that.

We have already established the interest of long-term savings institutions in the equity of property. After a rough phase in the early and mid-1980s that interest is probably reviving. But the fundamental question is, will they exchange the control which ownership brings, with its flow of opportunities, for the weaker control but liquidity which securitisation offers, and what is their price for doing so? If their price is high, then the innovation will not work because no one will find it worth his while to securitise a property; it will be more profitable to sell as a whole.

The difficulty in answering the question arises because it is difficult to isolate the 'illiquidity premium' which institutions attach to their demands for a property return. There is evidence that there is such a premium because large investments in relation to their market appear to trade at a higher yield than smaller ones. But this difference can be accounted for by more than 'illiquidity'. Equally, anecdotal evidence suggests that, during the 1980s, investment managers have become increasingly irritated with the illiquidity of property compared with other assets, although this usually had more to do with their inability to sell it rather than to buy it.

If the institutions will, in effect 'buy' liquidity, will they use it? Will they buy stock and then sit on it, or will they trade? The increase in active management of institutional property portfolios suggests a move towards a willingness to trade, but that is not adequate. The answer will depend upon the purpose for which the assets are bought, and also the substance of the eventual market.

Taking those two points separately, it seems likely that some funds, particularly the smaller ones who otherwise find it difficult to hold property at all, will use securitised assets as their bedrock holding of property, and from those only modest trading can be expected. Other (and perhaps larger) funds will utilise securitised assets in two ways. First as a quick way into a market which is promising to perform well, being followed by the purchase of complete properties in the same market and the sale of the securitised assets. Secondly they may also seek to take an active trading role in the market. Such a role is commonplace in the stock and bond markets. The perceptions which lead to each trading deal are manifold, but they surround an underlying view of ultimate value; if the market appears to be 'cheap' one buys, and if 'dear' one sells taking account, of course, of dealing costs. Cheapness and dearness will derive from forecasts of future income flows (dividends in the case of equities) and the present value which the market will put upon those flows. Thus changes in interest rates will be relevant because it will change the discounting, changes in perceived risk will alter the 'risk premium' the market seeks (it can be argued the fall in the equity market in October 1987 was as much due to a change in the risk premium as to any measured reduction in future dividends). The relative value of opportunities in all appropriate investment markets will also be considered in an attempt to anticipate market sentiment towards the sector of asset being observed because this sentiment will influence the direction and rate of change in values in any market where prices are set at the trading margin. Finally present and future net earning capacity (net distributable profits in the case of shares) will be closely observed and items of news or rumour which are likely to affect that earning capacity will be highly relevant.

In the case of bond markets the income flows are substantially predictable (not wholly so because of the risk of default) so interest rates and market sentiment are the dominating influences. But because the dealing costs are low, and the market is 'substantial' (ie, it is often possible to deal in very large sums) the market trades over very short periods on very small divergences in value; it is by no means uncommon to buy a large line of stock in the morning and sell in the afternoon.

A willingness to deal actively, and the skills to do it, are thus well established. Whilst the elements in a securitised property market will be unique to it, they will contain similarities to both the stock and bond markets with a quantum of income predictability because of the length of leases leading to movements in the market price a little analogous to bonds and a quantum of uncertain future income flows deriving from property events leading to changing perceptions analogous to shares. It is therefore quite feasible that a securitised property market will give institutions an opportunity to trade, and they may well take that opportunity, perhaps hoping also to utilise knowledge which they can obtain from the complete assets which they hold.

The likelihood of this stance depends, also, upon the substance of the eventual market, in what quantities assets can be traded, what market makers spreads will be and by how much prices move in relation to the costs of dealing. The answers to these issues must again be speculative but some depth and volatility can be expected. There are many potential players in the market, many with quite long pockets and with differing perspectives. The property market is also as full of rumours as any other, and as full of differing opinions. Activity even for ungeared securitised assets is not unachievable, and this would be enhanced geometrically by geared assets.

It is by no means clear where a tradeable property asset will be held in institutional portfolios, the equity funds or the property funds. This to some degree depends upon the substance of the market, but given the likely nature of the products being created they may well be held in both. Both may hold them, for the inherent potential of the assets to further the objectives of the fund, and to match rival funds who also hold them; offensive and defensive reasons.

One thing which seems clear is that if these prophecies are in any way fulfilled securitisation points to considerable change in the way in which property is viewed as an equity asset, and the extent and depth of that change will depend upon how widespread the market becomes. In ten years it will be necessary to re-write most of this chapter!

VIII THE CHANGING STAGE FOR LONG-TERM SAVINGS INSTITUTIONS

So far in this chapter we have described the interface between long-term savings institutions and their provision of equity finance to property as if it were stable. That is not, of course, the case. Not only is the property market changing, so are the institutions themselves. Two major revolutions are occurring. The first is a reduction in inflation expectations. As we have seen, these expectations have been one of the major influences on institutional attitudes to the equity of property. Because it is by no means clear whether inflation is truly being conquered, or just checked a little, the future trend is particularly uncertain. The second revolution springs from the considerable changes which the 1980s have witnessed for the financial services industry, and therefore for the long-term savings institutions as major players in that industry.

It is beyond the scope of this book to discuss in any detail this process of change but the seminal events have been:

– the erosion of tax privileges for life assurance, principally the Finance Act 1984 which removed tax relief on premiums,

– the move towards 'portable pensions' commenced in the Finance Act 1987. That is to say the creation of a pension fund or reserve which is attached to an individual for his benefit rather than to a job,

– the introduction of considerable control over the way financial services are sold under the provisions of the Financial Services Act,

– the lifting of exchange control during 1979,

– the attempt to ensure the role of London as a major world financial centre by the events surrounding 'Big Bang' in October 1986.

The response of many institutions to the pressures and opportunities produced by these events may well have considerable impact on their relationship with, and activity in, the property market. Three are worth identifying, the effects on their products, their marketing and their areas of operation.

1 Products

Most of the events listed will, and indeed were intended to, increase both opportunities and competition. One likely response to both those stimuli is to define one's products more sharply. This enables a product to focus more obviously on an identifiable area of interest to one's customers. An example of this would be the introduction of 'currency funds' following the removal of exchange controls. These products were designed for investors who had become aware of the investment potential in these markets and were now free to invest in them. They were also aimed at those who had a need for currency protection, such as expatriates.

Defining products more sharply is also a good defensive tactic against competition. It enables a producer more clearly to differentiate his product from those of competitors and provided he reads the market correctly in his differentiation, and delivers the results of course, he may expect advantage.

These processes are already under way in the financial services industry. It is uncertain how far they will go, but the direction and the result is clear. A more defined product will require more defined investments to support it. The large pools of investment which at present form life assurance funds and large pension funds may tend to get broken down into more closely defined pools linked to particular products (or even particular investors as now occurs with PEP and may well occur for 'portable' pensions).

Because of its particular characteristics, in particular its size, its illiquidity and its valuation problems, property does not fit all that well into such a scene. This should not mean that it is intrinsically unsuitable, but rather that it will have to fight harder for inclusion, and it may well be fighting for a smaller place. No doubt ingenious solutions will be found, and securitisation is likely to be one of them but, despite the resurgence of interest in the equity of property in 1988, its future role in supporting long-term savings products is undoubtedly changing.

2 Marketing

The events referred to are not only changing what institutions seek to sell, but also how they sell them. Much of this change is not of direct relevance to property, but it has led to one major innovation, potentially of some consequence, their move into estate agency.

To a large degree the acquisition of estate agency chains is not relevant to this chapter as it is dominated by the residential market; that is their target. However the local knowledge contained within such a national network may be of considerable value in sector and asset research. Institutions will clearly respect the need to keep the affairs of each individual client confidential, in accordance with proper professional standards but the totality of the information may well carry important messages if only it can be assembled, read and interpreted.

In the acquisition of residential agencies, a number of institutions have also acquired considerable commercial resources as well. The use they will make of these is not yet clear. Will they attempt to preserve what they have got? Will they build on it and create national networks of commercial skills? Or will they float off in some way what they have bought? If they retain or build they will still have the same need to control professional confidentiality, but clearly this will be a further addition to their general and local knowledge base. It will also give them the opportunity for greater 'hands-on' local management at the asset level. They will have to control conflicts of interest to the satisfaction of all their clients and this will not be easy; it will be even harder to demonstrate to a hostile critic. However, it is not unachievable as is demonstrated by the merchant banks (usually!) in other markets and if it can be achieved they may see it as an opportunity to reduce some elements of risk at the asset level and to increase the range of property opportunities available. This is particularly relevant because it may widen the type of properties they consider suitable. Earlier in the chapter it was pointed out that 'prime' properties are not, by their nature, the best performers but the problems of controlling more diverse non-prime portfolios is greater. Perhaps the move into estate agency will provide an opportunity to reduce these problems.

It is interesting that several of the larger firms of chartered surveyors and property specialists have set up their own 'financial services' organisations, having identified that these changes have opened new opportunities. Whilst they are approaching the market from a different starting point, some fruitful competition and co-operation can be expected to emerge over time.

3 Areas of operation

The final result from these events which is directly relevant to the equity of property is the increasing 'globalisation' of financial services. The removal of exchange controls enabled long-term savings institutions to invest around the world, and investment in overseas property has been discussed. However, this is only part of the story. Institutions are now free (or reasonably free because each country offers local restrictions) to offer services around the globe. They can, therefore, look outwards and overseas 'institutions' may be expected to look at our market. 1992, the year when European barriers are due to fall, provides one particular example, but the trend is increasing across the world, perhaps reflecting the slow creation of a true 'world economy'. Those are issued beyond this book.

The globalisation of long-term savings institutions may bring two results which are relevant to this chapter.

At the simplest level, British institutions may provide a channel for overseas money into the equity of British property, either in the form of 'managers' of that money (if, for example, they received instructions to manage all or part of a foreign pension fund), or as partners (foreign investors are concerned about the risks they take in the British market – the obverse of earlier comments—and could be more comfortable with a local partner with whom they have wider business contacts even if those contacts are sometimes seen as rivals). Also the more adventurous overseas institutions may seek to establish a bridgehead in our markets. In either event, the sources of money interested in the equity of British property may well increase and perhaps, eventually, increase many times over.

The second impact could be to unleash a third attempt at overseas property investment, but this time supported by local business exposure and perhaps local liabilities.

The result of this activity could be to move property into being a more 'global' asset, held widely and traded widely. This would clearly be greatly assisted if quoted, tradeable forms of ownership, free from the complication of local property law, became widely available.

IX   CONCLUSION

In this chapter we have defined 'equity' and seen how property can fulfil that definition. We then identified the 'needs' of equity investors and studied what opportunities and problems property brings, utilising long-term savings institutions as our template. They are by no means the only source of equity, but at present they are the dominant ones. However, we have seen that the institutions are subject to strong pressures for change and many of those pressures do not favour a high property content, a situation which may be remedied by increased 'globalisation' of the market, if that can be achieved.

Perhaps this chapter raises too many 'ifs and buts', but inevitably the future is uncertain. However, there seems to be no reason to doubt that the ownership of property will continue to be a source of wealth. This will be so because, for as far ahead as we can see, property and buildings will be necessary for economic activity and location and quality (or perhaps appropriateness is a better word) will bring advantage to the occupiers. Whilst that continues the 'equity of property' will remain a source of interest to investors. The only matters open to question are how they choose to get at that equity.

Chapter 3

Debt Finance

Richard Wolfe

This chapter starts by describing the background within which bank lending to property has re-established itself as a major factor in the funding of commercial property development in the UK. It examines the key factors taken into consideration when a bank decides to fund either a new property development or refurbishment or to arrange a facility to fund existing income earning properties. Limited recourse financing is described and how a bank attempts to evaluate the risks undertaken. The need for syndication is discussed as are some of the more sophisticated bank funding products that are currently available to the large quoted property company. Finally, there is a basic description of how long-term mortgage finance is arranged.

The chapter concentrates mainly on the financing of property from a debt view point as opposed to general corporate funding.

I INTRODUCTION AND BACKGROUND

1 Recent growth in bank finance

The United Kingdom commercial banks have been financing property as a part of their everyday business for many years. A large proportion of the current outstanding bank debt is provided by the clearing banks on small to medium size properties at regional level throughout the country. Without very much in the way of specialist skills, this seems to work satisfactorily. It is only when the amount of finance required reaches a certain level that other sources of funding are sought as the clearing bank reaches its local internal limits and the level of risk increases, often beyond the resources of the bank in its ability to analyse the risk. The volume of development now occurring in the UK, as users of buildings demand a new generation of efficient and attractive space, has naturally brought into focus the question of how these developments will be financed. After the problems of the banking crisis in 1973/74 which led to a hiccup in the funding market for larger property projects, the institutions came into the picture. Of course they have always been involved in property over the years, especially prior to the difficulties of the early 1970s, but they did become the major force in property financing in those years that followed the crisis. These institutions (ie, pension funds and insurance companies) provided attractively priced 100% funding packages for property developments which they would forward commit to purchase at a discounted yield on completion. Although providing satisfactory returns during the period of high inflation in the 1970s, property's performance began to look quite pedestrian compared to the more sparkling returns offered by the equity markets, during the prolonged bull market and low inflationary environment of the mid 1980s.

Institutions shied away from investment in property during this period. Many pension funds preferred to stay out of the higher risk areas of pre-funding speculative developments, but retained an interest in purchasing completed fully let schemes. This situation then provided a large gap in funding for developments. Many banks had been providing secured facilities to property companies, funding for their property portfolios with a few, mainly US banks, actually making construction loans, having gained valuable experience in working out their bad debt portfolios in the 1970s. The banks, having gained in confidence and especially in experience, began to open a window for other banks to participate in larger development finance facilities. This enabled the newly interested banks to 'piggy back' off the expertise of the established real estate lenders and form their own specialist property financing units. Banks were employing property professionals and began to acquire the expertise necessary to be able to assess the risks and the qualities of the developments they were being asked to fund. This more professional approach enabled banks to realise that capital values and, in certain circumstances, rents could go down as well as up and that a rising trend in values was common but not inevitable. Developers began to realise that the rewards which they were achieving through the more speculative route of bank financing were often much greater than those achieved through the traditional institutional 100% pre-funded arrangements. They actually had to commit some cash in the form of equity, but the profit was often considerably greater because the institutions would purchase at a lower yield when the property was completed and fully let, thus creating a higher investment value and a larger profit margin for the developer.

At the present time (August 1988) there is approximately £19bn of bank debt in the property market. This rather begs the question of how this debt will be repaid. However, with the continuation of the current bear phase of the stock market (at least at the time of writing), an increasing commitment to property is being anticipated by the institutional investor, especially as many sectors of the property market have been producing greatly improved returns in recent times.

The advent of securitisation would seem to offer considerable potential for take-outs in the future. This subject is being dealt with elsewhere in this book, but it would seem that the various vehicles proposed, chiefly PINCs and SAPCOs, will probably take time to establish themselves. The naturally conservative investment institutions will want to follow their marketability and performance for a period before substantially committing themselves to this new market. But in the long term, we may see the investment base widened to the private investor and a very considerable source of take-out to bank funded property development finance permanently established.

2   Comparison with 1973/74

The concern about repayment of debt leads naturally on to comparisons with the property market slump and the secondary banking crisis in 1973/74. One can feel much more comfortable with the situation now for the following reasons:

1. Developers generally are very much stronger financially than they were in the 1973/74 property crash. At that time there were many 'one man' property companies with little worth and a lot of debt. Most of the leading developers today have sound balance sheets built up over the past four to five years of successful trading. Their net worths are strong, their cashflows satisfactory. Credit support given to limited recourse loans through partial principal and cost overrun guarantees can often give considerable comfort.

2. The leading banks have established experienced property units and no longer lend blindly with little research and knowledge of the market as they did before. Most of these leading banks have property experts in their teams and regularly go to the chartered surveying profession for independent valuations or appraisal reports on individual areas of the market. Although in actual terms £19bn of debt is a large amount, most of it is syndicated within the banking community with no particular bank appearing to be over committed to the market in its portfolio spread. Furthermore, most banks have fairly well diversified portfolios, and those newcomers who do not, have generally concentrated on economically strong areas of the market such as the South East, where tenant demand is consistently higher and investment interest consistently keener than other parts of the country. Some concern could be levelled at those banks which have committed their portfolios entirely to the City of London office market, where there is potential for over-heating following the recent sharp rise in rents and the advent of a possible over supply of space in the early 1990s. However such banks are probably fairly few in number.

3. One of the principal causes for the crisis in 1973/74 was the dramatic and unprecedented rise in interest rates, which virtually doubled to levels never seen before. Many developments became unfeasible at these new interest rate levels and many portfolios of properties could not provide rent sufficient to service the bank debt arranged to support them. The borrowers' resources

were insufficient to do that too. However, we now live in a time of volatile interest rates and although in recent years there seems to have been established a certain band in which interest rates fluctuate (7.5% to 14%) there seems little likelihood of a sharp doubling of rates from these levels again. Most of the sensible banks will have taken into account interest rate risk when constructing their own feasibility studies. If a project is very sensitive to an increase in interest rates of the magnitude experienced over the past five to six years, then it is obviously questionable whether the bank should be financing it anyway.

4. The general economy of the country looks much more sound than in 1973/74 and lenders can feel more comfortable to be lending against this background. Considerable development is taking place nationwide but there is ample evidence of continuing strong demand for space from users in most areas to support the building programme. The current growth of building activity is therefore, in the main, tenant-led. The only potentially overheated markets at the time of writing are probably the City of London office market and perhaps large out of town retail centres.

So it is against this background that we can look at the current generation of facilities being offered by banks to fund property. Bank financing is a perpetually changing subject and what is written below is the current state of play only. However, it can be guaranteed that it will continue to evolve in the future. The main considerations given below to property lending should nevertheless continue to be relevant into the future.

II PROJECT DEVELOPMENT FINANCE

1 Introduction

The increase in new commercial development that took place in the mid 1980s, and which happened contemporaneously with a diminishing profile from the traditional institutional funder, brought secured bank finance sharply back into focus.

The latest breed of developers, delighted with the success of their initial developments, saw excellent opportunities ahead to the end of the decade as virtually all sectors of the commercial property market seemed ripe for development. The internal resources and balance sheets of these developers were clearly going to inhibit their abilities to take on as many projects as they would like. Therefore, a new system of limited recourse/off-balance sheet financing was introduced by the leading property bank lenders. Banks were prepared to take on this type of financing as their growing sophistication in the property market had led them to the obvious conclusion that it was the property being developed which would be the principal source of repayment of the debt. In the past, bankers had rather considered property financing as a loan to a developer secured on the project being developed. The primary source of repayment appeared to be the borrower supported by the property. Bankers realised in the light of their painful experiences in the 1973/74 crash that the right property at the right value provided better security than the covenant of the borrowing company, however strong it may appear to be.

Clearly, with the smaller developer, if the property could not be let when completed, then it was going to be very difficult to refinance it or indeed sell it. Much more research was undertaken, through the bank's in-house property experts and through external appraisals and valuations prepared by the leading firms of chartered surveyors, into the viability of the underlying development scheme. So the emphasis was shifted from a loan facility being viewed simply as a secured banking transaction more to a thorough understanding of the property risks being undertaken.

Once convinced that the likely outcome of the development was going to be a successful one, the bank lender would then seek to structure a loan based on a percentage of value, typically between 65–70%, and to undertake to the borrower that it would only seek repayment from the refinancing or sale of the development and not from the borrower. The bank would expect to see between 10–20% of the development costs (which was normally the difference between the loan amount and the anticipated total cost of completing the project), invested by the borrower *ab initio* as equity. The developer furthermore would contribute any additional costs incurred in excess of the loan amount, in order that the development might be completed and let up prior to refinancing.

The amount of equity required to be injected by the developer would very much depend on the level of the underlying risk. Clearly a pre-let development has considerably less risk attached to it than a speculative one, a pre-sold development even less. However, it is usually prudent to expect the developer initially to contribute between 10–20% of the total anticipated costs.

The bank lender therefore believes that the 30%/35% difference between completed value and the total loan amount should provide a sufficient cushion against the vagaries of investment yields or rent or interest rate fluctuations.

2 Typical structure

Thus we have the structure of a typical limited recourse bank construction loan. This basic principle has been accepted by all the main property lending banks. The banks will lend a hard core of the total development costs without recourse to the developer but committing the borrower, or third party if the developer is not strong enough, to contribute all the other costs. If a project is planned to be developed with an estimated total value of £10m, but costing £8m, a bank funding

70% of the value expects to put in place the following arrangement:

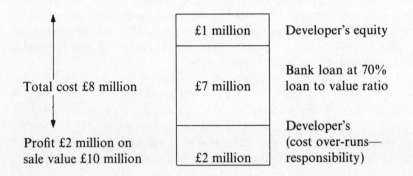

	£1 million	Developer's equity
Total cost £8 million	£7 million	Bank loan at 70% loan to value ratio
Profit £2 million on sale value £10 million	£2 million	Developer's (cost over-runs— responsibility)

It is basically prudent to insist that the developer injects its equity at the front end even if it has considerable corporate strength. It tends to focus the developer's attention on progressing and successfully completing the project. In some cases, with a strong developer, the banker may be prepared to allow it to put up a portion of the equity initially whilst guaranteeing to put the balance in at the end of the development, after the bank facility has been exhausted. That is a sort of 'sandwich' facility. Care must be taken here to structure a sensible banking arrangement with at least some equity being injected *ab initio*. This is because the loan is of a non-recourse nature. For example, if the bank has lent the initial costs up to 90% and expectations that the development will prove to be a profitable venture have substantially diminished, the developer could decide to walk away from the project before it is committed to contribute its own resources as agreed. The bank would then have the responsibility of building out the development and would, in fact, itself become the developer. This is an extremely unlikely outcome however, although similar types of financing arrangements put in place in 1973/74 experienced just such an outcome.

3   How much to lend?

When deciding the loan amount, it is essential to have closely analysed the total cost of development, including a sensible contingency for increased construction costs. A contingency may be typically 3% to 5%, although on a difficult project such as a tricky refurbishment, a higher contingency may be required. A typical feasibility study is shown as an example in Appendix I at the back of the book. It can be seen that the costs break down into certain basic areas:

1. Site purchase and associated costs.

2. Construction and associated costs.

3. Financing costs.

4. Professional fees.

Selling fees can be included or simply deducted from sales proceeds.

It is essential that steps are taken to ensure that these costs are not allowed to escalate too greatly. This of course is difficult as very few developments go exactly to plan. It may be necessary at some stage in the development programme to improve the specifications of the building because of changing tenant demand. Interest rates may increase, the cost of building materials may increase and so on. Some of the dangers of increased costs can be mitigated however, by taking sensible precautions. The cost of acquiring the site has usually already been established and is a fixed amount. The architect's, quantity surveyor's and engineer's fees are usually fixed at the outset, although the engineer's fees could increase in certain circumstances. Agents' letting and selling fees are usually predictable as well. The principal danger areas for increased costs are construction and financing.

It would be wise generally to insist that the developer obtains a fixed price contract from a reputable construction company. If small contractors are employed a full investigation of their financial resources and track record in building similar projects should be made. If satisfied, then a performance bond could be obtained[1]. However, in most sizeable building contracts (say above £2m), it is advisable to insist on one of the large national contractors. If a subsidiary wins the contract, it is important that the parent company gives a guarantee. A fixed price contract is not exactly what it says, as the price can be allowed to increase to cover inflationary pressures on both building materials and labour costs. A bank will often be under pressure to accept a management fee contract with the hopes that the contractor appointed will arrange to have the building completed on a cheaper basis. Care should be exercised by analysing the background to the situation before accepting one of these contracts. The main aim is to try to establish at the outset the maximum total cost of the development. A fixed price contract helps in this respect.

Often terms have been agreed verbally with the contractor but the contract has not been signed. The bank should try to ensure that the developer gives the bank's lawyer a copy of the signed contract highlighting all the amendments if a JCT model contract is used.

The other significant area of potential cost over-runs is in interest costs. The

---

1 A performance bond is a contractual commitment given by a bank on behalf of the contractor, usually in an amount of 10–20% of the contract amount, given to the bank financing the development. These are not true guarantees but contractual commitments by the bank to pay a certain sum of money in a specified event (ie, failure satisfactorily to complete the contract). The bank issuing such a performance bond or guarantee will wish to take a counter indemnity from the customer, the contractor. Once an unconditional bond or guarantee has been given by a bank, that bank will be liable to pay on demand the sum of money for which the bond is given and will only escape if it can demonstrate fraud or that the liability for which the demand is made is outside the terms of the bond. The fact that the contractor denies it has broken its contract will be of no avail if the bank has guaranteed to pay on first demand.

dramatic doubling of interest rates in 1973/74 was one of the major causes of the property crisis at that time.

Often when a developer comes to see his banker with a feasibility study of the development he requires to be financed, he typically puts the interest cost in at current rates plus what he feels is the right margin. This can be a problem if interest rates are at the bottom of their cycle (in recent years short-term rates have fluctuated between 7.5% and 14%). The likelihood is that they will rise and fall during the life of the loan, so it is appropriate to test the sensitivity of the appraisal to a range of possible interest rates. If the development still looks viable then the banker can safely continue with its intention to fund. It is very difficult to minimise interest rate exposure on a development loan, but some approaches are set out below.

4   Mitigating cost over-runs

If rates are at the lower end of the scale it can be possible to fix in the hard costs (ie, the site and initial acquisition costs) for a longer period or indeed the entire period of the loan at a fixed rate.

Usually development costs are drawn down as and when they occur and will have to be funded at the rate applying at the drawdown stage. Again, when a further hard core of borrowings have been accumulated a further long interest period can be fixed if the prevailing rates are attractive. On very large projects of £50m or more it may be possible to arrange a series of forward interest rate swaps to be fitted in with the anticipated drawdown schedule to fix the interest cost at the outset. It is necessary to have drawdowns of at least a minimum of £2 to £3m to enable this type of arrangement to take place. The sterling swap market, at the time of writing, cannot cope with amounts below this level.

Another potentially difficult area in analysing costs is the void period. That is the period of time it takes to let the building from practical completion. Most prudent feasibilities are prepared on the basis that it takes in the region of six months to let the building.

In the case of shopping centres, where immediate tenant demand may be stronger, it is not unusual to assume a three month void. It is prudent to work on at least a six month void as, even if letting goes well, it is not unusual to see a rent free period of six months given as an inducement to an incoming tenant.

So we have discussed the various ways of mitigating cost overruns and emphasised the importance of analysing the anticipated and realistic total costs of development. Very few developments complete at cost or below cost. Very often savings can be made in one area only to be balanced by cost overruns in another. Basically the rule must be 'banker beware'. Sensible financial contingencies must be included in any appraisal.

5   Appraising the sale value

Next, we must focus in on the sale value. Some banks have their own 'in-house' valuer, others prefer to use external firms of chartered surveyors. Either method is satisfactory, although there are points in favour of and against each:

Points For and Against 'In-House' Valuer

For	Against
Faster	May not have day-to-day experience of the particular area of the market under scrutiny. This tends to result in over conservative value (possible clash with client).
Cheaper	
The valuer is part of the bank's lending team and can often provide valuable initial input affecting pricing and structuring of loans and identifying risk. Also readily available for comment on legal matters including lease terms, etc.	

Points For and Against External Valuer

For	Against
Can in certain circumstances be liable for the valuation figure.	More expensive (could be a problem if fees have to be paid before borrower is committed and subsequently walks away).
Should have good exposure to the particular part of the market being appraised. Care should be exercised to appoint a valuer with the appropriate strengths.	Often slow to obtain value. This can lead to uncertainty as to whether or not the development is viable or if the loan amount is sufficient for the development requirements. May not necessarily understand the exact financial requirements and problems of the loan transaction.

NB In the case of a loan syndication, it would be necessary to commission an external valuation as other, participant banks, will not rely on the lead bank's internal valuation.

Typically, as a rule of thumb, a development should produce a profit of about 20% on cost. In certain circumstances one can feel comfortable to see this margin reduced to 15%, especially if there is a strong possibility of inflation in rents during the building period. The developer's speed in letting and selling is important. Extreme caution should be exercised in funding schemes where the profit margin is below 15%. Increased costs can very quickly eat into the profit.

When calculating the loan amount, consideration should also be given to the likely form of take-out or repayment of the facility. If the investment market in the property being financed is uncertain or it is the developer's intention to retain ownership of the building once completed and let, then a refinancing is going to be required either from the bank or a longer term mortgage lender. In either case it will be necessary to focus on the developer's ability to service the interest costs. This is not going to be a problem if the developer is financially strong and capable of servicing the likely debt service shortfall between rental income received from the building and interest costs. However, there can be a problem in the case of a financially weak developer or a smaller, growth-orientated developer where cash flow has to be channelled into new projects.

The difficulty arises from the fact that income yields on buildings in this country tend to be below medium- to long-term interest interest rates. Yields on prime buildings may very well range between 4.5% and 8%, whilst interest rates fluctuate between 7.5% to 14%. Normally, the yield on cost will be higher and as the bank will be lending, say, 80% to 90% of cost, the yield on the loan should be at a higher level but may still not totally service the interest costs. In the case of a retail development scheme, where yields are typically the lowest, it is not unusual to see a yield of say 7% on the loan amount at completion.

In instances where the developer's future cash flow is uncertain and the expected yield on the final loan is insufficient to service the debt, then the bank may wish to scale down its loan amount in order to try to avert the possible embarrassment of a default later on.

Often, developers like to have the ability to extend the development loan beyond practical completion until the first rent reviews, which usually take place five years after the commencement of the lease. The interest rate risk can be reduced here by agreeing (if interest rates are at the lower end of the scale), to arrange a forward interest rate swap at the outset of the transaction or later, (during the course of construction), to fix the cost of borrowing for the hold period prior to rent review and sale. The cost usually involves an annual premium; this may prove worthwhile if interest rates are expected to increase substantially towards the end of the construction and letting period.

6   Security

Obviously this is an extremely important subject. Care must be taken to cover every conceivable potential difficulty when negotiating the loan documentation. It is recommended that the developer should be encouraged to establish a wholly owned subsidiary to own the development to be financed. Often developers will want to do this for their own corporate purposes. However, the provisions of the recent Insolvency Act 1986 require that for the mortgagee bank to have clear, unfettered rights of security in the event of default, it is necessary for the bank to hold a first floating charge over the borrowing company as well as a first fixed charge over the site and development. An administrative receiver appointed under the terms of a floating charge owned by another creditor can severely inhibit the owner of a first fixed charge's ability to exercise its rights and remedies if the borrower gets into difficulties. Furthermore, if the borrower gets into difficulties and applies to the court to appoint an administrator[2], the court would have to give notice to the holder of a floating charge. The holder of the floating charge can pre-empt the appointment of an administrator by utilising its ability to appoint an administrative receiver[3]. It is imperative that lenders take proper legal advice in the matter of loan documentation and security and if 'in-house' legal counsel is not familiar with secured property lending, then external lawyers with good conveyancing and banking expertise must be consulted.

Adequate insurance cover for the building must be arranged at the outset and the bank's interest noted on the policy document. Should the developer fail

2 An Administrator is a new officer created under the Insolvency Act 1986 and is neither a Receiver nor an Administrative Receiver. The appointment is by order of the court upon the petition of the company itself or a director or any creditor. The purpose is to give a company in financial difficulties a period of grace in which to re-organise its affairs without the risk of a winding-up petition being presented by the holder of a charge appointing a Receiver. The court may make an order if it can be convinced that such an order would allow the company or a part of it to survive as a going concern in the event that it is temporarily unable to pay its debts, or if it will achieve a more advantageous realisation of the company's assets than would be effected on a winding up.

3 An Administrative Receiver is another new officer created by the Act and any Receiver appointed by the holder of a floating charge (without reference to the court) and will be an Administrative Receiver subject to certain requirements being satisfied. The floating charge must relate to the whole (or substantially the whole) of a company's property. Reference to the Act itself or a lawyer, is recommended if further enlightenment is required. The importance of the ability to appoint an Administrative Receiver is that the appointer may pre-empt the appointment of an Administrator. (See footnote 2 above.)

This is because an Administrator cannot be appointed without first giving notice to the holders of a floating charge. The floating charge holders then have five days to take any action such as the appointment of their own Administrative Receiver to protect their security interests. However the court is obliged to reject an application for the appointment of an Administrator if an Administrative Receiver has already been appointed unless the appointer (eg, the Bank) has consented or there is a defect in the security which the Administrator would be unable to pursue. This is important as an Administrator is given comprehensive powers to manage the affairs of the company including its property as agent for the company. The Administrator can deal with property that is subject to a first fixed charge, as if it were not so subject. Furthermore, the holders of a first fixed charge's powers are considerably curtailed as is its ability to sell the charged property or even complete its construction and its ability to appropriate any rental income would be suspended whilst the Administrator has jurisdiction over the assets of the company. Nevertheless things do not look as bleak for the lender or holder of a first fixed charge as some would lead us to believe as an Administrator dealing with an asset subject to a first fixed charge must obtain the court's permission to sell it. This will only be given if the proceeds are paid to the holder of the first charge and if these are less than the amount which the court believes would be realised in an open market sale, the Administrator must make up the deficiency. Furthermore the holder of the first charge is still entitled to receive rental income from the property even if this is temporarily detained by an Administrator.

during the course of construction of the development, the bank will wish to reserve the right to continue to build out the project or to sell it as it is. It is usually more beneficial to build out than to sell, as a half-completed building has fairly limited appeal in the market place unless extremely well located. In the circumstances, it is usually advisable to take a legal assignment of the building contract. This means that the bank is tied into the construction contract and that if the developer fails during the construction period, the bank can step into the shoes of the developer and require the contractor to continue to build the development under instructions from the bank. Even though no guarantee is usually given by the bank that it will exercise its rights, it is a great comfort to the contractor, as he may be concerned about the developer's ability to meet progress payments, or indeed his ability to continue to make any payments if he goes into receivership or liquidation. The contractor has the comfort of knowing that the bank is there to meet payments throughout the loan facilities and may elect to continue thereafter in the event of default. It would be an extremely expensive business for the mortgagee bank in possession of a half-completed building to appoint a new contractor to build out the project, should the previous contractor walk off site.

It can be advisable to take an authority from the borrower which requires the future rental income to be paid directly to the bank. Collecting the rents, or having them paid into an account at the bank, can be an onerous task and problems can arise should the bank become classified as a mortgagee in possession, which carries demanding responsibilities. However, it is recommended that an undated authority relating to the future payment of the rental income stream is signed when the documentation is completed and then held in reserve in case of need. The borrower can then collect the future rental income uninhibited by the bank, but should a default occur, the bank can simply date the assignment and activate the charge.

Care should be taken properly to register all charges within the specified time limits. It is assumed that the reader is are already fully conversant with these basic technical matters.

In the event that a pre-sale of the development is arranged during the course of construction, it is advisable to arrange a legal assignment of the benefit of the sale contract.

Cost overrun guarantees from the borrower's parent company or from a third party (which may be required to be secured if the guarantor is not of sufficient covenant), must be taken. Such guarantees should cover all costs associated with the development, including interest charges. It is very important that the guarantor is fully informed of the extent of its contingent liability. Ideally, it is recommended that such guarantees should not be restricted as to time or amount.

It can be acceptable for a developer's equity contribution to the project to be in the form of a bank guarantee. Such a guarantee must be unconditional and, depending upon the bank concerned, can usually be considered to be as good as cash. It is also occasionally necessary to take other acceptable security to cover the principal amount of the loan if the basic security does not give a sufficient cover initially to secure the loan satisfactorily. If the value of the basic security increases during the loan period it may then be considered possible to release the extra cover obtained.

In brief, the main security which needs to be taken at the outset of a development loan is as follows:

1. First legal charge over the site and building.

2. First floating charge over the other assets of the borrower.

3. Legal assignment of the building contract (if the contractor is of insufficient strength a performance bond may be required to be taken).

4. A cost overrun guarantee from the ultimate parent or other acceptable group company (companies) or a third party.

5. Any other appropriate guarantees.

6. Satisfactory insurance cover for the development with the bank's interest noted.

7. In the case of a 'one man developer' or a developer that places considerable reliance on one individual to make the scheme work, it can be advisable to insist that the borrower take out a key man insurance policy with the bank's interest noted thereon.

8. Furthermore, it is wise to obtain duty of care letters or agreements from the professionals employed on the development. These letters are inevitably given to the developer as employer. However, as the bank is now a major part of the development team (and in the case of default might even become the developer), it is essential that the professionals should have a duty of care to the bank. These professionals typically comprise the following:

> Architect
> Quantity Surveyor
> Engineer
> Mechanical and Electrical Consultant

7 Pricing

In pricing the loan facility the banker must exercise its own discretion, based on its own experience but understanding completely the risks being taken. All too often, bankers fall into the usual trap of being influenced by events taking place in the ordinary corporate finance markets where lending rates to the leading medium and large sized corporations have reached ridiculously low levels. However, the risks involved in property financing are quite different. If the borrower is a strong entity and is borrowing on balance sheet on either a secured or an unsecured basis, the pricing would obviously have to reflect the rates at which the borrower is able to raise funds generally in the inter-bank market.

Quite often, the development funding is arranged on a limited recourse basis irrespective of the developer's financial strength. Nevertheless, bankers must not be seduced into funding projects at fine rates against general assurances that the developer would never allow the bank to lose money should difficulties arise. The fact is that the documentation will probably give the developer the power to walk away if the going gets rough. The bank is in fact putting up risk money and should be rewarded accordingly. Furthermore, the continued monitoring of a construction loan costs time and money which also should be paid for. Basic pricing on a construction facility usually involves the following elements:

1. *Arrangement Fee*

   This covers the cost of all the preliminary investigations and internal reports and approvals and, in the case of an in-house valuer, its valuation fee. There is also an element of extra reward for risk being taken on the project. In the case of a syndicated loan (see below), in certain circumstances, part of this fee can be distributed among the syndicate banks as a participation fee.

2. *Management Fee*

   This covers the on-going costs of monitoring the project and is usually payable on an annual or semi-annual basis.

3. *Commitment Fee*

   This is usually a small fee which recompenses the bank for making the commitment and is charged on the amount of the facility that remains unutilised from time to time. The facility amount will be drawn down in stages over the life of the loan. This fee reimburses the bank as it has the obligation to provide the facility amount and cannot utilise these funds for other lending opportunities.

4. *Interest Margin*

   This is the margin above the cost of funds that is charged to pay the bank for its risks in lending the project funds. It should be remembered that the loan is drawn down in stages and (in my view) the bank does not earn sufficiently on this part of the facility charges. The average amount undrawn during the life of the loan is about 50% of the facility amount. Reserve asset costs (to satisfy The Bank of England's risk/asset weighting ratio), will also be charged, typically amounting to about 1/16% to 1/8%.

   It can be possible for the ongoing success of the project to be reflected in a reducing margin. The lending bank will want to make its own calculations on risk/reward for speculative development loans but it is possible to consider some reduction in the margin once the development has been 100% pre-let or pre-sold.

5. *Repayment/Cancellation Penalty Fee*

This is usually chargeable if the facility is not drawn down or is pre-paid within, say, six months of loan signing. This reimburses the bank for making the commitment and taking the risk but not achieving the correct earnings.

There can also be other charges made. Some banks prefer to charge part of the arrangement fee once the borrower has accepted the offer of finance but before the loan agreement is signed, whereupon the balance is payable. This reimburses the bank for all its efforts should the borrower fail to go through with the transaction.

External valuation fees will be for the account of the borrower, as will the bank's legal fees. However, some banks prefer to assimilate these and charge a larger arrangement fee. In the case of a syndicated loan even more attention will be paid by the bank to the management or agent's fee, as the bank has considerably more work to do in keeping the various syndicate members appraised of the progress of the development and in dealing with day-to-day problems.

I have steadfastly avoided putting the actual figures behind the various charges. That is for the individual bank to decide. It can be considered imprudent to charge an interest margin much below 1% on a limited recourse loan where the bank is looking entirely to the project to repay its loan. More often the margin on a sound commercial scheme with a good developer, supported by a quality professional team would be between 1% and 2% depending on the risks, state of pre-letting or pre-sale. Banks will have their own policies on fees.

8   Equity participating loans

It is not unusual for certain, more experienced banks to commit a larger proportion of the development costs than is usually lent in similar circumstances. This may be because of the bank's in-depth understanding of the risks involved and of its pre-conviction of a likely successful outcome. Whatever the reasons for taking this extra risk, which may mean funding 100% of the development costs or at least a higher than usual loan to value ratio, the bank is really contributing equity funding to the development which should receive an equity reward. This reward can be taken either as a percentage share of the profit, or as an extra fee usually charged once the development is successfully completed, let and sold. The amount of this extra risk and the appropriate reward is a matter for negotiation between developer and banker. It is recommended that only experienced banks in the property market consider establishing such an arrangement. It is also worth noting that there can be special tax considerations affecting the borrower which will have a bearing on the subject.

9   Summmary – the banker's view

To sum up, the banker will want to study closely the risks he is taking when undertaking a property development loan. The bank will probably be providing up to 90% (if not more) of the development costs, often on a very speculative basis initially. If all goes well, the developer will normally receive a very handsome profit, often amounting to a sum many times greater than the equity it has put into the project at the outset. The banker, at best, usually receives a return that is only between 1% and 3% of its funding commitment. This would seem to be an inequitable sharing of the profit outcome. The banker is a very real and important part of the development team providing the funding without which the development would not have taken place. The bank must thoroughly understand the development process and be flexible enough to react swiftly to changed conditions on the development. However well planned, it is rare for a project to go exactly to plan. For example, there may be a strong anchor tenant who requires special additional facilities; there may be site problems when the ground is broken; underground services may need replacing, even new planning conditions could arise. The banker must be part of the development team and must have an adequate monitoring system and perspective of the project in order to be able to react positively.

III   THE MECHANICS OF SYNDICATED PROJECT FINANCE

1   Background

Over recent years many banks have become interested in being involved in property financing. These banks can be divided into two basic categories; those that wish to be involved in depth on an ongoing basis and those banks that wish more to participate in syndicated loans arranged by other banks. The former category of banks will have established teams of experienced personnel both on the banking and property sides. The latter category will perhaps commit only one or two people to writing new business, or will include property lending as part of their corporate finance or project finance divisions. They may be unwilling to commit the time, money and personnel necessary to establish an independent property lending division. These latter banks will normally finance smaller projects themselves, whilst looking to participate in larger project development funding arranged by banks in the first category, whose abilities they respect and can rely on for projects that they would like to fund. They will have to convince themselves as to the feasibility of the project and the credit risk and other considerations regarding the borrower. There is no recourse for a syndicate member to the lead bank once a commitment has been made, save in respect of a manifest misrepresentation of facts. However, there is a disclaimer written at the bottom of information packages supplied by a lead bank.

2 The role of the lead bank

The larger and well established property lending banks are well known to the property community generally and developers requiring bank finance for the larger developments will usually approach one of these banks to arrange a funding package. Once the bank has been convinced as to the reliability of the project, a financing structure will be arranged. This will take into account its knowledge of what the general banking community will find acceptable as regards risk, reward, types of project, geographical area and so on. If a mutually acceptable structure is agreed and the lead bank has obtained internal approval either to underwrite the whole facility required or a portion of it, undertaking to syndicate the loan amount on a 'best effort' basis, then an external valuation from an acceptable firm of chartered surveyors would have to be commissioned. In the establishment of an acceptable loan to value ratio, participating banks in a syndicated loan will require an external valuation. Once the value has been established, the lead bank will work with the borrower in drawing up a presentation document or documents giving information on all aspects of the property, the borrower (including financial information) and the team behind the development.

This document will be circulated to certain banks who have expressed interest, after initial approaches by the lead bank have been made. It is often advisable to keep syndicates as small as possible, only involving banks which have a full understanding of the area of the market they are entering and the risks involved. A flexible attitude should be maintained by those banks during the course of the project as it is undesirable that cries of default are made every time there is a small cost overrun or other difficulty encountered in the development process. Clearly, banks have to keep strict control over the loan conditions and the way the loan funds are being utilised, but it must be realised that developments very rarely go exactly to plan. Care should be exercised then by the arranging bank to form a syndicate of banks that will feel comfortable with the development and developer during the course of the project. The lead bank will usually need to take a major participation in the loan. Both the participating banks and the borrower will feel more comfortable if the lead bank is committing as much as any of the other lenders to the syndicated loan facility.

Once the necessary acceptances have been received, subject to documentation, from enough banks to cover the required funding amount, then the syndication can be closed off. The next stage is to proceed to the establishment of the loan and security documentation.

3 Managing the syndicate – the agent bank

The lead bank, as agent for the banks comprising the syndicate, should be given sufficient autonomy and flexibility to be able to monitor and service the underlying development on behalf of the banks as far as is reasonably possible.

Those international banks which are participating should have sufficient delegated powers in their London offices to be able to cope with typical minor decisions that have to be made from time to time during the natural course of the development, should the lead bank not be given sufficient authority to make decisions on behalf of the syndicate banks.

It is preferable that unanimous decisions are not always required in the documentation on relatively minor matters, because delay in obtaining the necessary consents can have a serious impact on the development programme. Slow or difficult participating banks can cause considerable irritation to the borrower and lead banker, which can sometimes create a bad atmosphere between the development funders.

It is recommended that the lead bank has the autonomy to make decisions and to remain liable to the participating banks. Many of the problems in the 1973/74 crash arose from syndications where each participant had a vote and unanimous decisions from all syndicate members was required. This 'committee' system was invariably slow and unwieldy, leading to many decisions being influenced by smaller participants adopting an unreasonably negative attitude to try to induce the larger participants to take them out of a difficult or problem loan.

4 The importance of the syndication market

The growth of a large number of strong property lenders in the banking community with a sound and sensible attitude towards property lending is (in my view) a welcome change. Banks should try not to take such a capricious attitude towards this section of the market and should realise that the development of new and efficient commercial buildings has been an important part of the economic life of this country for many hundreds of years and will continue to be so into the future. If such banks continue to make it their business to understand and stay with the market, working through peaks and troughs, then they will find that they have created a profitable and exciting business.

The establishment of a sound bank syndication market will help greatly to finance the larger commercial real estate transactions that are arising all over the country. It is important that developers have an alternative source of funding to the somewhat mercurial appetites and sometimes stultifying funding arrangements offered by the institutional investors. Syndication can also serve the continuing needs of the large customer. Banks have internal limits and syndication is the best way to continue to serve the client's needs, whilst working within internal limits. Thus it is possible to retain a continuing and successful banking relationship.

IV INVESTMENT PORTFOLIO FUNDING

1 General comments

This is a fairly straightforward subject and most of the important considerations are more or less axiomatic. Many property companies, including the latest *regular inspections — management.*

generation of developers, are creating investment portfolios of good quality commercial properties, the income from which will provide a solid base of revenue in future years. This provides a very useful cushion during those periods when development activity slows down. Portfolio financing, of course, is a much more secure form of funding than development finance but the lending banker should remain vigilant and monitor the underlying properties thoroughly.

At the outset of the negotiations with the borrower, the bank will wish to commission a valuation in order to fix the basic parameters for establishing a loan amount. Due diligence should be exercised by the bank in order to satisfy itself that the quality of covenant of the tenants occupying the building or buildings to be financed are acceptable. This is because the bank is probably going to be relying on the tenants' continuing ability to pay rent in order to service the interest on the loan being arranged.

Properties should be visited regularly to make sure that they are being maintained to an acceptable standard, both as regards the tenants' accommodation and common areas. If things go awry with the loan facility the bank may find that it is in possession of the buildings comprising the security and looking for a sale. Clearly, well maintained buildings with good tenants are more likely to find an interested purchaser and a better price than ill kept ones. The bank needs to make sure that the developer is exercising a high standard of management over the properties that are subject to the bank's charge.

Regular valuations, at least on an annual basis, should be made during the life of the loan in order to ensure that there has been no deterioration in security value. As will be discussed below, certain security and income covenants will have to be maintained. The borrower must undertake to inform the bank of the increases in rents at the time of review and of any assignments of leases or sub-letting that takes place. In any event the bank will make sure in its documentation that no assignments or sub-letting, can take place without its prior consent.

2 How much to lend?

Typically, most banks have certain rules of thumb to be applied to property portfolio financing. The most common covenant they apply is the security to loan cover requirement which is usually 150%. Various other multipliers are used ranging from 133% to 175%, or even higher on occasion. The bank should be flexible in establishing the security cover parameters and should focus its attention on the credit strength of the borrower and its ability to service the interest expense on the loan during the life of the facility. If the borrower is financially strong, with a satisfactory cash flow and is borrowing on balance sheet with full recourse, then clearly the loan has a 'belt and braces' quality to it and the lender may wish to relax its security ratio.

However, if the borrower's future cash flow is uncertain or the loan is of a limited recourse nature, then a much more important yardstick to concentrate on is the rental/debt service ratio. This ratio requires the rental income, at all times, to be able to service a certain percentage of, (or cover by a certain margin), the continuing interest cost of servicing the loan. If the income yield on the portfolio is low, there could well be debt servicing problems arising in the future. The rental income/interest cover ratio is as important as the capital value/loan ratio. If the income cover is good then the bank can probably afford to sacrifice some of the security cover requirement from say 150% down to 130% to 140%, provided the properties being financed are reasonably saleable.

Care should be exercised at the outset of the loan (and will no doubt be considered in the initial valuation) as to the marketability of the underlying security. If the buildings are old and in need of modernisation, or if leases only have a shortish period to run, the banker must consider whether the security is acceptable. In two or three years' time the physical condition and nature of the security may have declined further and values also. In this situation a larger margin of capital cover will be required in order to protect the bank in a forced sale. Well maintained, 'state of the art' buildings with good tenants and with a long period of the lease still to run, may justify a lower security ratio. Other factors affecting the loan to value calculation are the quality of the building and the ability to relet it, should the existing leases expire or something happen to the tenant. If the building is in a good location there may be considerable growth potential in the site value.

Furthermore, as regards quality of the capital value risk, the bank should always insist on buildings that are acceptable to the investment community generally and that are let on conventional 25 year 'institutional leases'. Upward only rent reviews every five years with full repairing and insuring covenants would need to be part of the terms of such leases.

To sum up, the loan amount should be established by taking due notice of the borrower's financial strength, the quality and marketability of the security and the rental income/debt service cover. Deficit financing can be considered if the borrower is strong and has a good cash flow, providing rent reviews are about to occur within the following one to two years. Here the projected rent on review would need to service the debt outstanding thereafter.

3   Security

Most of the considerations discussed in connection with development loans above, apply here also. A first fixed and floating charge will need to be taken over the assets of the borrowing company, so again it may be necessary to establish a special subsidiary created to hold the properties being financed. The facility given to this new company can then be guaranteed by the parent company. Full insurance cover must be maintained on the buildings with the bank's interest noted. Care should be taken to ensure that the insurance premiums are paid on time. In this respect some sort of tickler or reminder system must be maintained. Again, it may be necessary to take an undated assignment of the rental income to avoid the management headache of having rents paid direct to the bank from a multiplicity of tenants with the bank being responsible for maintaining the proper collection of the rents, servicing the interest and payment away of surfeit funds to the borrower. With an efficient and financially sound borrower, it is not normally necessary to take these precautionary measures, as the bank can usually rely on the borrower's ability to service the interest costs as and when necessary.

4 Financial covenants

This has been previously touched on above. A security cover ratio will have to be fixed at the outset and must be maintained throughout the loan. Should the value of the security fall during the currency of the loan facility then either further security must be provided or a reduction of the loan must take place, so that the ratio again is complied with. If this does not happen within a certain grace period then the loan would go into default.

The rental/interest cover ratio must also be fixed and maintained throughout the life of the loan. Careful monitoring should highlight any reductions in rent due to tardiness in paying or bankruptcy of a tenant. Generally, during the life of an investment loan, these covenants tend to improve. Capital values (usually) rise from year to year, aided by the rental income flow which would normally rise at the regular reviews. Because of this situation, it is not unusual for a borrower to request an increase in the loan amount during the life of the facility, in order to maximise its borrowing potential if the ratios have materially increased. Other financial covenants relating to the borrower's balance sheet and revenue accounts may also need to be considered.

5 Loan period

Typically, the life of these loans extends up to five to seven years.

6 Pricing

As for development loans, pricing is at the discretion of the individual bank lender. Generally, a front end fee is charged of between $\frac{1}{2}$% and 1%. Fees on investment loans tend to be lower than those charged on a development loan. The interest margin will reflect the lending risk.

V MULTI-OPTION FACILITIES

1 Background

A multi-option facility is a very specialised facility only available to the large national and multinational corporate entities. However, a few of the larger property companies are obviously of sufficient financial strength to avail themselves of the more sophisticated methods of borrowing in the Euromarket.

Hence, for the purpose of this book, it is relevant to include such facilities, albeit briefly. This type of facility is generally unsecured, although there are instances where certain medium sized property companies have raised such borrowings on a secured basis. These facilities have tended to be rather on the small side for this market.

The Multi-Option Facility (MOF) is the latest stage of evolution in the general corporate finance market for bank funding. It arises out of the trend towards securitisation of debt. After the syndicated credit market breathed its last, five or six years ago (there are signs though that it may resurrect again), the Revolving Underwriting Facility, or RUF, effectively replaced it in recognition of the fact that the market regarded paper as an acceptable alternative to making simple advances.

Subsequently, there has been a tendency by bank depositors to disintermediate banks as a result of the deterioration in the credit standing of many of the banks. This enabled sufficient volumes of paper to be distributed through the RUF arrangements to establish a permanent European market for short-term debt obligations known as the commercial paper market. This trend originated in the domestic US markets.

The Euro commercial paper market grew rapidly with the result that borrowers saw a dramatic reduction in their costs of raising short term finance through these markets. However, in short, various capital requirements imposed by central banking authorities resulted in the paper element of a transaction being divorced from the obligation to lend money and hence the Multi-Option Facility was born.

2   Structure

In essence, a MOF involves a group of bankers providing a large corporate entity with a commitment to provide cash advances at a predetermined margin for a certain period. Attached to that group is a group of uncommitted tender panel banks which can bid to provide short term advances or acceptance credits at perhaps a margin below that under the committed line if it suits them to do so. If the borrower is unable to raise funds at a satisfactory rate through the uncommitted tender panel then it can utilise the committed line at the fixed margin rates. In addition, there is as a further uncommitted line made available from financial institutions to provide the borrower with commercial paper programmes in whatever currency it needs as and when available.

In this way, by separating a committed term facility from a more opportunistic uncommitted arrangement of borrowing alternatives, a borrower is able to take advantage of the benefits that may arise from time to time on a short-term basis, whilst retaining the longer term commitment from a syndicate of banks committed to provide funds as and when necessary.

Fundamentally, the banks guarantee a maximum interest margin payable by the borrower. This effectively provides the borrower with more options than a standard revolving underwriting facility. Under the RUF arrangement a borrower has to approach an underwriting panel and if the amount or rate is not forthcoming then there is an option to approach a committed stand-by syndicate. With a MOF there can be a variety of currencies available and the borrower can elect which option he wishes to pursue, with no obligation to approach the tender panel initially. Therefore, the RUF/MOF facility is a very flexible revolving arrangement.

Typically, a MOF comprises:

a. A two to five year commitment to provide a stand-by line for a fixed amount in the form of a revolving credit facility underwritten by a group of international banks and arranged by a lead bank.

b. A tender panel facility with options for the issuance of short-term bearer securities such as Euronotes, drawing of short-term multi currency advances or issuance of sterling acceptance credits or US dollar bills of exchange, etc. These tender panels have the ability of providing the borrower with lowest cost funds in a variety of different instruments.

c. If the borrower is likely to be drawing funds in a variety of currencies, it is usual for there to be a 'swingline' facility available in order to provide funds on a same day basis for use when switching between domestic and Euromarkets.

The lead bank usually acts as tender agent and operates the mechanics of the bidding procedure.

3 Pricing

The pricing structure is usually as follows:

1. *Facility Fee*

   A facility fee or underwriting fee is paid to the committed banks whether the facility is utilised or not.

2. *Margin*

   This is expressed as the margin over LIBOR at which the committed banks will make advances to the borrower.

3. *Utilisation Fee*

   This fee is paid in addition to the margin, depending on the level of utilisation required by the borrower. Typically no utilisation fee will be payable on the first 50% of drawings under the committed facility, but a fee may be added to the margin if drawings exceed this percentage.

4. *Arrangement Fee*

This is payable to the lead bank for arranging the facility.

In the context of this book, an examination of the MOF technique can only be brief. As stated earlier, only the largest property companies are able to utilise this rather select form of short-term debt financing and, generally, most debt arranged to finance property does not come from this area.

VI LONG-TERM DEBT

1 The mortgage debenture market

A mortgage debenture is essentially a loan where the banker's role is substituted by a group of investors. The loan is of a long term nature, often between 15 and 35 years and is secured on the property or properties being financed. The borrower simply mortgages the property to a trustee who holds it on behalf of the lenders (investors); the beneficial ownership, as with ordinary secured bank loans, is retained by the mortgagor.

The investors, as quasi-mortgagees, are entitled to receive interest payments over the life of the mortgage and to the return of the principal, at redemption. If the borrower fails to pay the interest or principal, or breaks any of the covenants contained in the debenture agreement, the investors have rights enabling them to take over the property and dispose of it to recoup their investment. On 31 December 1987 The Stock Exchange estimated that there was outstanding approximately £7 billion worth of quoted corporate debt comprising mortgage debentures, debentures and unsecured loan stocks.

2 Who makes the loans?

Quoted corporate debt is usually purchased by institutional investors, particularly pension funds, life insurance and general insurance companies who require long-term assets to match their long-term liabilities. The diminishing supply of gilt-edged securities emphasises the growing need for such alternate forms of investment. The majority of the larger institutions have within their organisation specialists in bonds and property and are therefore well equipped to make decisions on the different types of property backed investments.

3 Usual terms of a sterling denominated mortgage debenture

1 LOAN AMOUNT

This is determined by the capital and income covenants required by the investors. Most loan amounts are for a maximum of 60–66% of the value of the property securing the loan. Such value must be independently determined by an acceptable firm of chartered surveyors on behalf of the investors. The prospective interest payable on the loan or bond (often called the 'coupon'), must be covered by the current rental income stream from the properties by a multiple of a least $1\frac{1}{8}$ to $1\frac{1}{4}$ times. This cover must be maintained throughout the life of the loan. The interest rate or coupon is usually at a fixed rate. These terms can be made more flexible; for example, the coupon can be stepped over the life of the bond. This can be very useful if the property being financed has only just been completed and let. It is quite likely in these circumstances that the initial yield from the property would be insufficient to cover the long-term interest rate for the issue. In this instance the coupon can be increased at regular intervals throughout the bond to match the rent reviews. Overall, the investor would receive a return that may be slightly better than the straight fixed coupon bond. It is also possible in certain instances to increase the capital raised where income cover is generous.

Marketability is an important factor in attracting an institutional investor, ie, the ability for an investor to buy and sell a security quickly and in large amounts. This requires an efficient market-making system, but traders will only take substantial positions in stocks for which there is a sufficiently large range of institutional holders willing to buy and/or sell.

2 THE TERM

Most institutional investors prefer a term of 20 to 35 years for a mortgage debenture bond, although it is possible to achieve 15 years on occasions. It is very common to have a single redemption date although it is not unusual to give the borrower the option to redeem the bond on any day during a four or five year period. It is also possible to amortise the bond over a period. Generally, however, investors prefer a single redemption date; earlier repayment provisions at the option of the borrower severely restrict the marketability of a bond.

3 INTEREST RATE AND YIELD

Interest on a mortgage debenture is payable semi-annually at a fixed rate. Investors look to the overall return, known as the gross redemption yield, which they will receive over the life of the bond.

The Gross Redemption Yield (GRY) takes into account not only the interest payments and the price of the bond, but the final redemption proceeds. Hence, GRY is defined as that rate of interest at which the total discounted values of future payments of income and capital equate to the current price.

When pricing a new issue, the issuing house or stockbroker will decide on a GRY which will be acceptable to investors, given the credit risks and characterisation of the bond. In this respect, existing comparable issues with similar loan amounts, maturities and security are considered, as are gilt edged risks of a similar maturity and coupon. The result is that, in practice, the proposed GRY or effectively the pricing of the bond reflects the GRY of a comparable gilt plus a margin known as the 'issue margin'.

Institutional investors consider gilt edged stocks to be the best credit risk available. Because of this, gilts command the highest prices and the lowest yields within the domestic sterling market. It has been the present government's policy progressively to reduce the Public Sector Borrowing Requirement and therefore a diminishing supply of gilt edged stocks are being issued on to the market. Good quality corporate bonds and mortgage debenture stocks are seen as an alternative investment, but investors require higher returns than gilts to compensate for relatively poorer marketability and increased credit risk.

It is possible to issue the bond either on a conventional basis at a price close to par, or on a deep discount basis where the coupon is set at a rate below the long-term rate. It can be possible for the coupon to be zero. In these instances the loan amount is reduced and the investor receives proceeds after the redemption date equal to the par value of the nominal amount of the bond. The overall return to the investor would be comparable to a conventional issue. However, in practice, the GRY may be slightly higher to compensate the investor for the absence of any income during the period of the loan.

Let us take as an example a hypothetical £21m, 20 year quoted debenture issue. If the issue margin is 150 basis points and the semi-annual GRY on the appropriate comparable gilt edged stock is 9%, producing an issue yield of 10.5%, this can translate into the following alternative terms:

Issue price %	Issue proceeds	Semi-annual coupon %	Redemption proceeds %	GRY %
£12.912	£2,711,520	0	£100	10.5
£54.383	£11,420,430	5	£100	10.5
£75.118	£15,774,780	7.5	£100	10.5
£100.000	£21,000,000	10.5	£100	10.5
£104.148	£21,871,080	11	£100	10.5

It can also translate into the following stepped coupon bond:

Issue price %	Coupon structure		Redemption proceeds %	GRY %
£100	Years 1–5	5%	£100	10.5
	Years 6–10	7%		
	Years 11–15	10%		
	Years 16–20	23.3%		

Issue price %	Coupon structure		Redemption proceeds %	GRY %
£90	Years 1–5	5%	£100	10.5
	Years 6–10	7%		
	Years 11–15	10%		
	Years 16–20	17.216%		

It is of course possible to issue bonds on an unsecured basis and also in large amounts in Eurosterling. However, Eurosterling is only available to the largest property companies.

4 ISSUE PRICE

The coupon and issue price are agreed after the issue yield has been fixed and the stock can be issued at a discount or premium to par to give either a lower or higher coupon.

If the issue price is lower than par by a certain percentage, which at the time of writing is 15%, or if the issue price is a discount that is equal to 0.5% for each year of the bond's life, it becomes a deep discount bond for tax purposes. This has certain advantages for the borrower and the lender depending on their own tax status. In essence, if the issue is classified as a deep discount bond, the notional interest (ie, GRY) rather than the actual interest payable is then tax deductible to the issuer. The difference between the GRY and the actual coupon, which is rolled up over the life of the security and repaid at redemption, is taxed as income in the hands of the investor but only when the bond is redeemed. The asymmetry of tax treatment between issuer and investor can provide an attractive cash flow benefit to the issuer of a deep discount bond.

5 SECURITY

In general terms, there are three forms of security; mortgage debentures, debentures and unsecured loan stocks. The most secure is a mortgage debenture where the security would comprise a first legal charge given by the borrowing company, (and if necessary its subsidiaries supported by guarantees), over specified properties, augmented by floating charges also given by the borrower and any of its subsidiaries over all of the properties being financed. The trust deed constituting a mortgage debenture will usually allow substitution of properties with the consent of the trustee, provided the stated capital and income covenants are satisfied.

For a debenture, the borrower gives as security a floating charge over all or virtually all of its assets. An administrative receiver, on behalf of the holder of a debenture, can enter into possession of the assets charged if the borrower fails to meet the terms of the agreement. But until this happens the borrower, unlike the mortgagor in the case of a mortgage debenture, can change the form of the assets subject to the charge.

The situation of an unsecured loan stock is axiomatic. Clearly, this sort of instrument is only issued by the largest property companies.

6   QUOTATION

Under The Stock Exchange listing regulations it is possible to quote a corporate loan even if the issuer's shares remain privately held. The principal advantages to such an issuer are publicity and a slightly lower issue yield for the mortgage debenture because of the greater perceived liquidity or marketability of the stock.

An accountant's report on the revenue accounts and balance sheets for the previous five years is also required. In addition full details of the properties securing the issue are needed, together with an independent valuation by a firm of chartered surveyors, and certain other information on the borrower and its directors. It is worth noting that The Stock Exchange will now permit the quotation of a single property company.

Unquoted mortgage debentures are capable of being placed with a small group of institutional investors. Nevertheless, the information to be made available and the terms of the trust deed would be more or less the same as required for a quoted stock.

Quoted bonds are usually underwritten by the issuing house, (typically a merchant bank or merchant banking subsidiary of a joint stock bank), so that the proceeds of sale are guaranteed to the issuer, thus protecting it from negative investor reaction or market conditions on the day of issue. Unquoted stocks are generally placed on a best endeavours basis by the issuing house.

VII   HEDGING

The subject of hedging is becoming of increasing importance when considering debt finance for property. This is especially so for investment portfolio funding. In the United Kingdom we have all come to terms with the fact that we live in times of perpetually fluctuating interest rates. It seems that the law of gravity works in reverse—what goes down, must go up again. It is therefore important when entering into long or medium term financing arrangements to consider hedging debt costs, especially if upward changes in interest rates are likely to have an adverse effect on the viability of the underlying transaction, ie, the profitability of a development or the ability to service interest from rental income, in the case of an investment portfolio funding.

1 Interest rate swap

Typically, increases in interest costs do not have a significant impact on a development's feasibility during the construction phase. Lower utilisation of the loan facility during the initial monthly drawdown stage reduces the impact of interest rate increases on the development's profitability. However when the development is completed and the amount outstanding on the loan is approaching its upper limit, interest rate increases really begin to bite, especially if the building is only partly let or even unlet. Earlier in this chapter, I suggested the possibility of arranging a forward interest rate swap to mitigate the potentially crippling effect of rising interest rates at the end of the construction period. The swap would take effect once completion of the development can be anticipated and would continue thereafter for a pre-agreed period of time. This period would allow for letting and selling or re-financing of the building.

A swap in this form could be especially useful if low interest rates are prevailing early on in the construction phase. An extra fee would be payable as this is a forward transaction. A more comprehensive hedging of interest rate exposure is difficult for development loans as drawdown amounts are often too small to forward swap in the market. I have touched upon this earlier in the chapter in discussing interim construction loans.

Hedging of interest rate exposure on funding investment portfolios is relatively more straightforward. An interest rate swap can be arranged through the funding bank, or indeed another bank, in order that the borrower, which is being funded on a variable rate basis, may swap its floating rate obligation with another borrower which has access to fixed rate debt but requires cheaply priced floating rate debt. The bank acts as an intermediary between the two borrowers. It enters into two separate agreements and effectively takes the risk of default by one party. For arranging the swap and taking the credit risk, the bank charges a fee which is usually added on to the fixed interest rate. Swaps are always best described schematically.

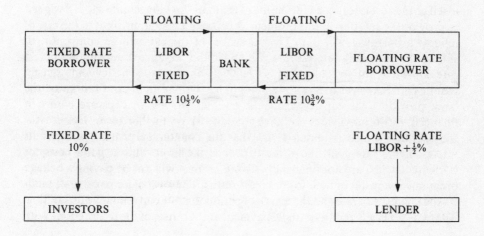

As can be seen, the result is an exchange of interest payment obligations. Effectively the floating rate borrower is paying a fixed rate of $10\frac{3}{4}\%$ and receiving floating LIBOR. The transaction is with the bank and the floating rate borrower is unaware of the transaction on the other side. Typically the fixed rate borrower is a financially strong entity with a high credit rating enabling it to access the bond markets for fixed rate debt. It requires floating rate debt and therefore will exchange a part of its fixed rate funding for the floating rate obligations of the other Borrower.

It will receive a higher fixed rate via the bank from the floating rate borrower which it will pass onto the investors whilst utilising the extra margin, in this case $\frac{1}{2}\%$ to reduce its floating rate costs. It will effectively be paying LIBOR minus $\frac{1}{2}\%$. This means that the floating rate borrower will be paying an acceptable fixed interest rate that it would be unable to access itself and can pass on the LIBOR rate received from the bank to the lender and include its $\frac{1}{2}\%$ margin.

It must be understood that an interest rate swap transaction is fundamentally separate from the underlying loan that it is initially hedging. This means that the prepayment of the loan does not necessarily mean that the interest rate swap has to be unwound prior to its expiry. This could result in a loss, or indeed a gain, depending on how interest rates were standing at the time of cancelling. The swap transaction can remain in place and other floating rate debt in the borrower's portfolio can be hedged by the same swap transaction. However, if the credit risk on the swap has been secured on the underlying property, which would have been sold or refinanced, further security may have to be provided.

2   Interest rate cap

Property investing developers are usually born optimists and are often reluctant to fix an interest rate on their obligations, believing that rates will fall during the life of the loan. They feel that further benefits from reducing interest rates will be lost if an interest rate is fixed for the life of the loan. An interest rate cap is designed to provide the solution to this problem. A cap sets a maximum limit to the rate of interest a borrower will pay. The purchaser of the cap will be compensated, should the prevailing interest rate rise above the pre-agreed maximum interest rate, known as the strike level. It is effectively an insurance policy and as such, requires the borrower to pay a premium or fee. Unlike an interest rate swap, the bank providing the cap (typically the counter parties for caps are banks or financial institutions), does not have a credit risk on the borrower. Indeed, it is the borrower which is taking a risk that the counter party bank will pay its interest if the rate goes above the cap or strike level. This is good news for borrowers which are not financially strong, as they will not be paying a heavier premium as a result of their lower credit status. The level of fee payable depends on the interest cap rate and the length of period that the cap remains outstanding. The fee is generally paid as a single payment at the outset of the transaction. With this hedging technique a borrower receives all the benefits of falling rate, whilst limiting its exposure to rising interest rates for a 'one off' fee. Should the holder of a cap wish to terminate early, the contract may be sold back to the grantor or counter party, thus allowing the holder to recover some of the initial costs of the transaction. Alternatively, the contract can be offset by taking an opposite position in a floor on identical terms (see below).

3 Floors/collars

An interest rate floor is the opposite of a cap. Here, a minimum interest rate is agreed, but in this case the bank pays the borrower a premium. Even if interest rates fall below the floor rate the borrower pays only the agreed minimum interest rate. A further option is an interest rate collar, which is a combination of both a cap and a floor. It specifies a minimum and maximum interest rate band.

This can be popular for a borrower as the fee received on the floor mitigates the fee payable on a cap. The collar therefore sets a band within which interest rates may fluctuate, but limits the upward and downward movement of rates. This gives the borrower a limited flexibility whilst capping its maximum interest rate exposure.

In summary, wise borrowers wishing to control their exposure to fluctuating interest rates will take advantage of some of these recently established hedging techniques. Interest rate swaps and caps are a particularly worthwhile method of avoiding potential difficulties in the cost equation when considering debt finance for property.

VIII SUMMARY

To conclude, I would like to express my hope that debt will take a more permanent role in the finance of property in the future. In the past, providers of debt finance have been somewhat capricious in their commitment to property generally. However, the recent surge in development activity, much of which has been financed by bank debt, has resulted in many banks establishing experienced property lending teams which they will not wish to disband if the market quietens down. Development activity may begin to slow down in the early 1990s but there will be plenty of new challenges for financiers as more innovative methods of funding are arranged for the large, completed development schemes which will need to be refinanced at that stage. Banks can take comfort from the fact that land is in short supply in the UK. Historically, values and rents have increased reasonably consistently, despite the occasional economic crisis. Good understandings have been built between property companies and their bankers which hopefully will grow further in the future. The experience that bankers have had in areas such as the third world only serves to emphasise the relative attractions of property as a secure financing market for banks. However bankers must learn from the tough experiences they have had in the past to develop the necessary skills and expertise which will enable them to offer a better service to their clients in the future, whilst establishing a rewarding business for themselves. Above all, they must not panic when the going gets rough.

Chapter 4

The Accounting Issues

Michael Peat

This chapter is principally concerned with off-balance sheet financing and with the more recent development of off-profit and loss account financing. The chapter explains why off-balance sheet financing may be an attractive option in some circumstances and the regulatory environment in which the acceptability of off-balance sheet schemes must be judged, as well as why such schemes have become more common in recent years. The chapter goes on to discuss several property related off-balance sheet financing arrangements. It then describes ED 42 which when published as an Accounting Standard should, together with the proposed revised Companies Act definition of subsidiary, require finance raised under sole purpose off-balance sheet arrangements to be brought on-balance sheet. The chapter concludes with a discussion of the off-profit and loss account accounting opportunities seen in instruments such as deep discount debentures, redeemable convertible loan stock and redeemable equity warrants.

1 INTRODUCTION

This chapter is principally concerned with off-balance sheet financing and with the more recent development of off-profit and loss account financing. It explains what these terms mean and gives examples of techniques used. The emergence of these techniques reflects the importance of accounts as a basis for investment and lending decisions, as well as the fact that accounting is as much an art as a science.

1.1 Financial ratios

Published accounts form an important part of the decision making information for actual and potential investors and lenders. The following simple example, which compares financial information for two illustrative companies, demonstrates how the means of financing a business may influence investment and lending decisions.

	Company A £m	Company B £m
Balance sheet		
Net operating assets	100	100
Financed by:		
Debt	10	80
Shareholders' funds	90	20
	100	100
Profit and loss account		
Operating profit	15.0	15.0
Less interest payable	(1.0)	(8.0)
Profit before tax	14.0	7.0
Tax	(4.9)	(2.5)
Profit attributable to shareholders	9.1	4.5

Companies A and B are identical except for the manner in which their operations are financed.

Two key financial ratios may be calculated from the above:

(i) the gearing (or leverage) ratio –
     this relates borrowings/debt to shareholders' funds; it can be expressed by quantifying debt either as a percentage of net operating assets or of shareholders' funds; as a percentage of net operating assets A's gearing would be 10% and B's 80%; as a percentage of shareholders' funds A's gearing would be 11% and B's 400%; expressing gearing as a percentage of shareholders' funds is the more common usage (gearing may be referred to as the debt to equity ratio if expressed in this way);

(ii) interest cover –

     this expresses the profit available to pay interest (normally profit before interest and tax) as a multiple of the net interest (or finance) charge; A's interest cover is 15 times and B's 1.88 times.

The gearing ratio is used to compare levels of debt between companies or between stages of development of a single company. Interest cover indicates the safety margin before profits become inadequate to cover the interest charge.

Both gearing and interest cover are used extensively by lenders to determine whether a company's borrowings are at a reasonable level and whether it is prudent to lend more[1]. Investors (and analysts) are of course also concerned with a company's capacity to absorb a downturn in profits without having to sell assets in possibly unfavourable market conditions, and use these ratios in this context. In addition, the share price of many companies depends to an extent, particularly in a bull market, on the market's anticipation of future deals. If the market believes that a company's gearing is such that it has little prospect of raising further debt and thus is unlikely to be able to finance expansion without recourse to its shareholders, the company's share price may be depressed. While B above shows a better return on shareholders' funds (22.5% compared with 10.1% for A) its share price might be marked down compared with A's not only because its risk profile is higher but also because its scope for expansion (without raising more equity) is more limited[2].

To develop the example it is now assumed that A has an opportunity to undertake a development which involves expenditure of £40m, and that it can meet £5m of this from its own resources, with the balance being provided by debt finance. The impact which this would be expected to have on A's balance sheet is as follows:

	Without project £m	With project £m
Net operating assets	100	135
Financed by:		
Debt	10	45
Shareholders' funds	90	90
	100	135

The gearing ratio (as a percentage of shareholders' funds) increases to 50%. The directors might consider that this would have a depressing effect on the share price as well as restricting their flexibility to respond to future opportunities. It might therefore be decided to circumvent the problem by structuring the project so that the company can secure the profit without having to record the assets, or more importantly the finance, in its balance sheet. Much of the rest of this chapter

---

1 In practice this is complicated by the fact that differing levels of gearing are considered appropriate for different assets.
2 Gearing assumes greater importance when equity finance is more difficult or expensive to raise, as has been the case since October 1987.

is concerned with ways in which this objective could be (or could have been) achieved; however, before discussing off-balance sheet financing techniques it may be useful to describe briefly the regulatory environment in which they must sink or swim and to explain why they have become more common in recent years.

1.2   The regulatory environment

Clearly companies are not free simply to present their accounts as they see fit and there are now several sources of regulations with which statutory accounts are required to comply. Firstly, the Companies Act prescribes in broad outline the principles which should be followed in preparing statutory accounts (the most important of which is that the accounts must show a true and fair view) and also sets out detailed disclosure requirements. Secondly, the accounting profession publishes regulations, known as Statements of Standard Accounting Practice (SSAPs), which cover both accounting and disclosure matters. Finally, if a company is listed (either on the main market or on the Unlisted Securities Market) The Stock Exchange also specifies certain mandatory disclosure requirements.

The auditor is required to make an independent examination of the company's accounts and to report formally to its shareholders whether the accounts show a true and fair view and are properly prepared in accordance with the Companies Act. Auditors are also under a professional obligation to ensure that the accounts comply with SSAPs. If the auditor considers that the accounts do not show a true and fair view, or fail to comply in a material respect with the Companies Act or an SSAP, he must state that fact in his report unless, exceptionally, he concurs with a departure from an SSAP. This is a serious step which is seldom taken in practice. If an auditor proposes to qualify his report in this way he would generally discuss the matter with the directors who will often agree to adjust the accounts so that the qualification is not necessary. In addition, the auditor will usually alert the directors to any failure to observe the relevant requirements of The Stock Exchange.

As referred to above, the auditor's statutory duty requires him to exercise independence in considering whether a given accounting treatment is acceptable. His responsibility is increased by the need not only to ensure that a particular set of accounts is presented in an appropriate manner but also to safeguard the currency of accounts for the long term. As regards the latter, it may be that a treatment adopted in a particular set of accounts is defensible in the company's own circumstances yet would be a departure from the accepted convention or an untenable precedent, and therefore unacceptable in a broader context.

1.3   The emergence of off-balance sheet financing

The temptation for companies to seek to finance projects off-balance sheet has been referred to above. However, off-balance sheet financing has become relatively common only in the past few years and the reasons for this are worth considering.

Traditionally property has been financed largely by equity, often from pension funds and other institutional investors, principally as a reflection of the historically long-term nature of the investment and the fact that the unrealised capital yield is not shown in the profit and loss account while the cost of debt (ie, interest) is. However, property portfolios are now worked harder to match the return provided by competing investment media and the gearing and tax advantages of debt finance are accordingly exploited more fully. In addition, the growing number of smaller developers, who may believe that their talent and professionalism enable them to earn a better return than the more traditional developers but who often have more limited equity resources, have become increasing consumers of debt finance.

The banks have also played their part. Until the 1970s the image of the conservative banker may have had more than an element of truth. In general, bankers regarded their primary duty as that of safeguarding the bank's assets and thus would lend only on the safest terms, with the kinds of loans made showing little change over many years. In the 1970s there was an influx of funds, largely from OPEC countries, and banks faced up to the need to invest these on competitive terms. This, together with other developments such as the globalisation of the banking industry, led to increased competition between banks to identify profitable lending opportunities and required them to adopt a more flexible and innovative approach towards borrowers. Clearly the developing needs of the property sector were one of the prime markets for the banks in this respect.

As competition intensified in the 1980s the sophistication of financing arrangements continued to increase. Banks had been used to managing their own balance sheets for supervisory purposes for some time, and it was a comparatively small step to suggest to their borrowers ways in which these off-balance sheet techniques could be introduced to the transactions being considered. In other words, the emergence and growth of off-balance sheet financing was largely a matter of 'supplier push' rather than 'demand pull'.

A subsidiary element contributing to the emergence of off-balance sheet financing was the approach towards accounting conventions in general and SSAPs in particular. In the UK (unlike some other countries such as the United States) accounting standards have never been intended to be applied mechanically to every circumstance. Rather they seek to set out the broad principles which are to be applied in drawing up accounts. This is generally fairly well understood and is made clear by the Explanatory Forward to SSAPs. There has, however, been a recent trend for this broad approach to be ignored and for banks and others to pursue accounting treatments which appear to be consistent with the letter of accounting standards, even if they are at variance with their spirit or are otherwise unrepresentative of best accounting practice.

2   EXAMPLES OF OFF-BALANCE SHEET FINANCING

In the following paragraphs some of the arrangements which have been used to finance property off-balance sheet are described and the accounting implications discussed. Current accounting and company law developments may, however, entail important accounting implications for several of the arrangements referred to. These developments are explained in section 3 of this chapter.

2.1   Controlled non-subsidiary

If a property developer sets up a largely debt financed subsidiary company to undertake a particular project this would have no significant accounting advantages because, in addition to a company's own balance sheet, a consolidated balance sheet, prepared on the basis that the company and its subsidiaries form a single economic entity, must be published. Most readers of accounts base their analysis of financial position on the consolidated accounts, rather than on the company's own accounts, as the former best reflect economic substance.

One of the most common off-balance sheet financing arrangements is for a company to be formed in such a way so that it is not technically a subsidiary of its 'parent' within the meaning of s 736 of the Companies Act 1985 and yet is in substance little different. For example, by law a company is a subsidiary of another if the latter is a member and controls the composition of its board of directors. If the latter has the right to appoint no more than half the board but its directors each have two votes while the other directors each have one, it will not control the composition of the board (and therefore the former company will not be a subsidiary) although in effect it will exercise almost total control. Similarly, a company is a subsidiary of another if the latter holds more than half of its equity share capital in terms of nominal value. The technique in this respect is for a company to own shares which represent no more than half of the nominal value of the share capital, but which give a right to, say, 99% of the company's profits. The company would not technically be a subsidiary even though its 'parent' enjoyed 99% of its profits and, as referred to above, effectively controlled the board. Further discussion of this kind of structure, often referred to as the 'diamond structure', and an explanation of how loopholes in the Companies Act definition of a subsidiary are taken advantage of, are set out in Appendix 1 to this chapter.

The difficulty these arrangements present for auditors is acute. Generally it will be fairly clear that the company (or controlled non-subsidiary) is not in law a subsidiary. The problem then arises as to how the effective, but not legal, subsidiary should be dealt with in the consolidated accounts. Prior to the publication in March 1988 of the draft SSAP on Accounting for Special Purpose Transactions (ED 42), it had been considered by some accountants that it was not permissible to consolidate a company which was not a legal subsidiary.

The Accounting Issues   119

Accordingly all that could be done was to insist on supplementary disclosure of the assets and liabilities of the 'non-subsidiary'. This would generally be by way of a note to the accounts. However, if the effect on the accounts of not consolidating the non-subsidiary was particularly material, it might be necessary to present 'pro forma' figures in addition to the basic accounts; that is to give the figures that would have been presented had the non-subsidiary been consolidated.

There are, however, good grounds for doubting whether disclosure can be an adequate solution to the problem posed by controlled non-subsidiaries. It is entirely proper (and the universal practice) for accounts to include notes which expand on the information given in the main financial statements or provide further supplementary information. It is another matter, however, for notes to present a view different or contradictory, rather than supplementary, to the main financial statements. To illustrate: a balance sheet might show creditors of £100m, with a note analysing this between bank borrowings and trade creditors; however, it would not be permissible for the note to state that the figure of £100m does not include all the creditors of the group. Thus those accountants who take the view that the borrowings of a controlled non-subsidiary are equivalent to borrowings of the group cannot easily be content with disclosure by way of note.

Reservations may also be expressed as regards the use of pro forma figures. Inevitably presenting two sets of figures rather than one is confusing and poses the question 'which is right?'.

2.2   Sale and leaseback

Sale and leaseback is an old established technique whereby a property user (for example a retailer) raises funds from its property portfolio, and perhaps makes a profit on the sale, without having to sacrifice the use of the property.

As long as both the sale and the leaseback are at fair market values accounting for the transaction is straightforward as summarised below:

○ the property would disappear from the balance sheet,

○ the sale proceeds (net of costs and tax) would be included as cash or a debtor in the balance sheet,

○ a profit (or loss) would be recognised equivalent to the difference between the net sale proceeds and the previous carrying value of the property, and

○ rent payable would be charged over the term of the lease.

Increasingly, however, the terms of sale and leasebacks are more complex and, in such circumstances, the above accounting may not be justified. Variations in sale and leaseback arrangements include, in particular, put and call options whereby the seller has the right to buy back the property at a pre-determined price (thereby preserving an interest in the capital growth) and the lender has a put option to require the seller to repurchase at the same price (thereby protecting the lender from capital losses)[3].

Accounting for leases is dealt with in SSAP 21. This draws a fundamental distinction between a finance lease and an operating lease. A finance lease is defined as 'a lease that transfers substantially all the risks and rewards of ownership of an asset to the lessee'. Any other lease is an operating lease. In the case of leases of property this means that a lease is likely to be an operating lease if, as is normally the case, the lease provides that rentals will be set to prevailing market levels at reasonably frequent intervals and the title to the property reverts to the landlord at the end of the lease. The effect of these provisions is that the landlord retains the benefit of increases in both rental and capital values[4]. If, however, the leaseback is a finance lease, SSAP 21 requires the lease to be 'capitalised' by the lessee, that is the property asset is included in the balance sheet at its fair value and the obligation to pay rentals included as a liability of a similar amount. The rental payments when made are apportioned between an amount which represents the reduction of the liability (ie, capital repayments) and the balance which is accounted for as a finance (or interest) charge; in addition, any profit or loss on sale is deferred and recognised over the lease term. In practice there is a simpler method of accounting for the balance sheet side which reflects the substance of the transaction as fairly (perhaps more so), which is simply to record the sale proceeds as a liability. This results in the carrying value of the asset being left undisturbed.

It follows from the foregoing that the categorisation of the leaseback as a finance lease or an operating lease determines whether the asset, and more importantly the related financing, can be taken off-balance sheet. This is discussed further in Appendix 2 to this chapter; however, in practice the decision is often difficult except where there is a standard lease which is clearly an operating lease, as explained above. The initial presumption with respect to other sale and leaseback arrangements will normally be that they are finance leases, on the basis that in a sale and leaseback the seller/lessee starts with the property and continues to have uninterrupted use of it.

2.3   Lease and finance leaseback

The lease and finance leaseback, a sale and leaseback variant, is a useful means of structuring the finance of a property which is going to be used in the business of the developer. For example, a manufacturer acquires the freehold of a site on

---

3   Option arrangements are described in more detail in section 2.5 below.

4   The landlord not only has these rewards, but also has the risk that the capital value might fall or not increase by the amount required to give him his assumed return when the lease was negotiated. As regards rental values he normally does not take the risk of a fall since most leases provide for rent reviews to be upwards only, but the increase on review may be less than assumed.

which he proposes to build a warehouse for his own use. The finance agreement between the manufacturer and the bank might be structured as follows:

○ the manufacturer grants the bank a lease for (say) 25 years for no premium and at a peppercorn rent;

○ the bank enters into a contract with a builder to build the warehouse (the builder and the warehouse design are specified by the manufacturer); and

○ the bank enters into a leaseback with the manufacturer for a term of 25 years. No premium is payable under the lease. The rentals are calculated to reimburse the bank for the development expenditure plus interest.

The lease and finance leaseback differs from the sale and leaseback in that it is rarely entered into in order to obtain an accounting advantage. In a transaction of this sort, the normal rules of SSAP 21 would clearly require the property and the obligation to pay for it to be reflected in the manufacturer's balance sheet. This sort of transaction is much more commonly motivated by tax considerations, in particular the desire for the bank to be able to obtain the benefit of capital allowances. This benefit (ie, reducing the bank's tax) will be shared with the manufacturer as it will be reflected in the rentals payable under the leaseback.

2.4 Sale and repurchase

Another form of transaction similar to sale and leaseback is the sale and repurchase arrangement. This normally comprises two agreements, one for the sale and one for the repurchase, which are entered into simultaneously. The price payable to repurchase will generally be the same as sale price plus an amount which is in effect interest. The intended effect of this arrangement is that the seller's balance sheet after the sale and prior to the repurchase includes the cash received (the sales proceeds) but neither the property nor the obligation to repay the cash (ie, the debt is taken off-balance sheet).

It is, however, unlikely that a company's auditors would accept that the property and obligation to repay the cash should be excluded from the balance sheet, even prior to the developments discussed in section 3 below, because the seller/repurchaser retains substantially all the beneficial interest in the property.

A slightly more sophisticated sale and repurchase arrangement is, however, commonly used by housebuilders to finance showhouses and has been successful in taking the finance off-balance sheet; an example is as follows.

The builder sells the completed showhouses to a financier which grants the builder the right to use the houses for a fee, usually equal to interest on the funds advanced by the financier. The builder undertakes to sell the show houses (to members of the public) as agent of the financier, retaining from the sale proceeds as an agency fee the excess of the sale proceeds over the amount due to the financier.

The commercial effect is that the builder is in exactly the same position as if he had borrowed the funds and given his showhouses as security. The resemblance to the straightforward sale and repurchase agreement is obvious, with the critical difference that the houses once sold will, in all probability, never revert to the builder nor will he have to make good any shortfall in the sale proceeds. Although the builder will invariably guarantee to the financier that the houses will be sold within a certain period of time, and that he will make good any unforeseen shortfall in the sale proceeds, in practice the time period and values will be chosen so that he is most unlikely to be called upon to do so.

There is a further attraction of such arrangements in that it is sometimes suggested that the builder may legitimately report a profit in the period in which he enters into the sale agreement, and need not postpone recognition of the profit until the houses are sold to members of the public. This treatment is, however, by no means universally accepted.

2.5 Options

Property transactions frequently involve the grant of options to purchase a property (or the shares of the company which owns the property). The accounting profession has not, to date, prescribed rules to be applied in accounting for, and the disclosure of, options.

Options are often used as an alternative to secured borrowings and to create off-balance sheet financing structures (as referred to under section 2.2, sale and leaseback, above). For example, an investor wishes to acquire a property primarily with a view to its long-term capital appreciation. The property is currently worth £10m and will be financed by £1m from the investor's own resources and by bank borrowings of £9m. If it were inconvenient for the investor to include these amounts in its balance sheet it could, in principle, arrange for the bank to pay £10m for the property and then pay the bank £1m for an option to acquire the property at some future time for a predetermined price. The predetermined price would take account of the initial purchase price and the bank's interest and other costs less rent received. Bankers are, of course, prudent people and in case the value of the property declined, the bank would probably take an option under which it could require the investor to acquire the property for the same amount.

The effect of such an arrangement is that the investor is in a position little different from owning the property outright, as either the investor will exercise its option to acquire the property (if it is worth more than the predetermined price) or the bank will exercise its option if it is worth less. There would therefore be a strong case for saying that the property's beneficial ownership is acquired by the investor when the options are granted. However, under current accounting conventions all that might be shown in the investor's accounts is an investment in the amount paid for the option, ie, £1m, with disclosure of the contingent obligation under the put option.

2.6 Joint ventures

Property developments are frequently undertaken through joint ventures. This has the commercial advantages of spreading the risks between the participants and permitting the project to benefit from the participants' aggregate expertise and control of possibly scarce resources. The joint venture will usually be constituted as a separate company.

Joint ventures are normally reflected in the accounts of the individual investors under the equity method of accounting by recording the investment in the balance sheet as an asset, stated at the cost of the investment plus the investor's share of profits earned to date. The consequence of this approach is that if the joint venture company has borrowings neither they nor the related property interests will appear in the balance sheets of the participants. For example, Rosehaugh and Stanhope Properties PLC have a joint interest in a company called Rosehaugh Stanhope Developments (Holdings) PLC (RSD) which is developing the Broadgate complex in the City of London. Both Rosehaugh and Stanhope have prepared accounts to 30 June 1987 and, quite properly, make extensive disclosure of RSD's affairs and their involvement in it. Rosehaugh's debt included in its consolidated balance sheet amounts to approximately £71m and Stanhope's to approximately £8.5m. At the same date RSD's debt amounted to £183m. Even if this amount is divided between the parties, it is clear that the borrowings included in the consolidated balance sheets of Rosehaugh and Stanhope understate the true levels of the groups' indebtedness and, of equal or greater importance, a major part of the groups' business is not fully reflected in their balance sheets.

No criticism of Rosehaugh or Stanhope is intended by the above. Both have followed existing accounting conventions and have made detailed disclosure of the treatment adopted and of the effect of so doing. The point at issue is whether existing conventions are appropriate; in other words, do they result in an investor's balance sheet which fairly reflects its operating and financial position?

2.7 Non-recourse debt

The characteristic of non-recourse debt is that the lender's rights are restricted to the particular asset which is pledged as security. Thus if a development has been financed on a non-recourse basis and proves to be unsuccessful the developer may decline to repay the debt and the lender will only have recourse to such proceeds as he can secure by selling or taking on the development.

It has often been suggested, normally by bankers, that non-recourse debt may, in presenting the balance sheet, be netted against the asset it is financing. This largely reflects bankers' and lenders' primary interest in balance sheets, which is to determine whether there are sufficient assets available to repay existing and future debt. If this approach is followed, debt which only relates to one asset and the related asset are irrelevant and would be netted off. However, as discussed in section 3, the purpose of accounts extends beyond credit and liquidity assessment and netting off non-recourse debt is not generally an acceptable approach.

3   ED 42 – ACCOUNTING FOR SPECIAL PURPOSE TRANSACTIONS

3.1   Legal form and commercial substance

As discussed in the preceding section, the majority of off-balance sheet financing techniques exploit situations where the strict legal form of a transaction is at variance with its commercial substance. Until recently it was often maintained that the accountant or auditor was powerless to insist that the transaction should be accounted for other than in accordance with its legal form unless there was clear authority (such as a requirement of company law or an SSAP) for doing so. Accordingly, all that could be done was to disclose the assets and liabilities held 'off-balance sheet' in the notes to the accounts. The disadvantages of presenting important and perhaps contradictory information in the notes to accounts are referred to in section 2.1 above.

The accounting profession's proposed solution is set out in ED 42 – Accounting for Special Purpose Transactions. This is an Exposure Draft of an Accounting Standard or SSAP. As the term 'Exposure Draft' suggests, it is a draft document issued for comment. It is likely, given the complexity of the subject, that the SSAP when issued will differ in certain respects from the Exposure Draft.

There are, in simple terms, two possible approaches to the problem of accounting for special purpose (or off-balance sheet) transactions, which may be referred to as specific and general. Under a specific approach accounting standards would address each of the several kinds of transaction separately and specify the appropriate accounting treatment. There are, however, several problems with this approach. Firstly, as referred to in section 1.3, there is a tradition in the UK that accounting standards are broad statements of principle rather than detailed sets of rules. This characteristic might be compromised if a large number of complex standards were to be promulgated in a short period of time. Secondly, the kinds of transactions concerned are numerous (the arrangements described above are merely examples chosen for their relevance to property finance) and it would involve a very extensive commitment for the Accounting Standards Committee to take on the necessary number of projects. Finally, this is a field of constant change and innovation; it seems inevitable that once standards had been set for certain kinds of transactions, new types would be developed.

For these reasons, the Exposure Draft adopts a general approach to the problem of off-balance sheet financing and seeks to give guidance as to the way in which all kinds of transactions should be accounted for. It does, however, illustrate the application of its principles by reference to specific kinds of transactions and in addition deals specifically with the 'controlled non-subsidiary'.

The basic requirement set out in the Exposure Draft is that transactions should be accounted for in accordance with their economic substance, having regard to their effect on the enterprise's assets and liabilities. This is a carefully formulated requirement which is distinguished from the statement that substance should take precedence over form or, as it is sometimes put, that economic substance should take precedence over legal form. The Exposure Draft notes that many off-balance sheet schemes have relied on narrow interpretations of the effects of individual transactions, concentrating on aspects such as transfer of title or the particular legal structure adopted, without regard to the effect of the arrangement as a whole. In other words, the legal form if taken as a whole (ie, if a series of transactions are taken together) is not necessarily at variance with the economic substance.

The concepts of 'assets' and 'liabilities' are central to the Exposure Draft. Assets are described as 'probable future economic benefits controlled by and accruing to an enterprise as a result of past transactions or events', whilst liabilities are described as 'probable future sacrifices of economic benefits'. These concepts are not intended to be equivalent to the legal concepts of ownership and obligation.

3.2 Implications for specific kinds of transactions
How then does ED 42 propose that the arrangements discussed in section 2 should be accounted for?

3.2.1 CONTROLLED NON-SUBSIDIARY
ED 42 pays particular attention to the controlled non-subsidiary. It defines a controlled non-subsidiary as 'a company, trust or other vehicle which, though not fulfilling the Companies Act definition of a subsidiary, is directly or indirectly controlled by and a source of benefits or risks for the reporting enterprise or its subsidiaries that are in substance no different from those that would arise were the vehicle a subsidiary'. The Exposure Draft, if adopted as an SSAP, would require that such an entity is normally accounted for in the same way as if it were a subsidiary.

3.2.2 SALE AND LEASEBACK
As noted above, sale and leasebacks are required (by SSAP 21) to be accounted for essentially as borrowing transactions when the leaseback is a finance lease. ED 42 expands on this requirement by making it clear that the terms of the arrangement as a whole must be considered in order to determine the appropriate accounting treatment; it is not sufficient simply to look at the lease in isolation. This would prevent the accounting treatment which has sometimes been adopted recently whereby a sale and leaseback transaction has been carried out by means of a debt financed vehicle in which the seller/lessee has an equity interest, in order to permit him to retain the benefit of future capital appreciation.

3.2.3 LEASE AND FINANCE LEASEBACK
As referred to above, lease and finance leaseback are generally tax rather than off-balance sheet financing driven transactions and would normally fall outside the scope of ED 42.

3.2.4.   SALE AND REPURCHASE

The insistence of ED 42 that a series of related transactions is looked at as a whole makes it clear that sale and repurchase transactions of the kind referred to above should be accounted for as borrowings.

3.2.5   OPTIONS

The Explanatory Note prefacing ED 42 contains a particularly careful discussion of the role of options. It proposes, if exercise of an option is considered probable, that the transaction or arrangement should be accounted for on the basis that the option will be exercised. 'Probable' in this case should be construed fairly narrowly; it does not mean simply that it seems likely that the option will be exercised but rather that the transaction is arranged so that it is highly unlikely that the option will not be exercised. As referred to previously, this would be the case where there are two options, one giving the right to buy and one giving the other party the right to sell, so that it must be in the interests of one of the parties to exercise.

3.2.6   JOINT VENTURES

As long as a joint venture entails a genuine sharing of risk and reward in the stated proportions, ED 42 will not require a participant who has an interest of 50% or less to disclose separately its share of the joint venture's assets and borrowings in its balance sheet.

3.2.7   NON-RECOURSE DEBT

As regards non-recourse debt, ED 42 specifically states that once analysis of a transaction or arrangement shows that an enterprise has an asset and a liability, then it is not appropriate to offset them. As mentioned in section 2.7, if accounts are viewed solely as a basis for lending decisions there may be a basis for netting off non-recourse debt. However, accounts serve purposes other than indicating assets available to support and repay debt. If, for example, a shareholder cannot ascertain the assets at a company's disposal to generate income (because they have been netted against debt) a true and fair view of the company's affairs may not be presented. Accordingly all material assets and liabilities should be categorised separately in the balance sheet, as they represent either the prospect of future economic benefit (in the case of assets) or constitute liabilities which the company will have to meet (in the case of debt) and should not be netted off.

3.3   Implementation of the Seventh Directive

The controlled non-subsidiary has also attracted the attention of the Department of Trade and Industry, which has stated that it is unacceptable for the definition of a subsidiary to be evaded so that the assets and liabilities of companies need not be shown on their 'parent's' consolidated balance sheet, despite the fact that the 'parent' has effective control of the company. The growth in concern about this practice has coincided with the need for legislation to implement the Seventh EEC Directive on company law which deals with group accounts; the

Department have announced that they intend to avail themselves of this opportunity to take legislative action on the problem.

The Department have stated that the forthcoming legislation will make several changes in the existing definitions. For example, it will specifically address contingent voting rights and situations where a shareholder cannot appoint the majority of directors, but can appoint those who have a majority of votes which may be cast at board meetings.

These proposals would in themselves render ineffective the arrangements outlined in section 2.1 above and Appendix 1. However, the Department have also announced that a new, additional, definition of a subsidiary will be introduced. Under this definition, S will be a subsidiary of H if H holds a 'participating interest' in S *and* either H exercises a dominant influence over S or S and H are managed on a unified basis. There will be a presumption of a 'participating interest' when it amounts to more than 20% of share capital, but the legislation will not contain any interpretation of the terms 'dominant influence' or 'managed on a unified basis'.

The Department have also stated that the forthcoming legislation will clarify the effect of the requirement that the 'true and fair view' is paramount. In particular it will be made clear that the accounting rules of the Companies Act may be departed from in order to achieve a true and fair view even where additional disclosure might arguably be sufficient to enable the accounts to show a true and fair view.

The statement mentions two areas where, in the Department's view, it would be appropriate for further guidance to be given by means of accounting standards. These are:

o the interpretation of the new definition of a subsidiary; and
o the circumstances in which it may be appropriate for consolidated accounts to include the amounts of assets and liabilities and profits and losses of a non-subsidiary in exactly the same manner as a subsidiary.

Whilst it is, perhaps, unwise to speculate on the effect of future legislation, particularly in advance of the parliamentary bill, it would appear that the promised measures will make it both much more difficult to form controlled non-subsidiaries and to avoid consolidation of such companies. The effectiveness of the new legislation will, however, depend to a large extent on the response of the accounting profession to the challenge of developing and implementing standards in this area.

4 OFF-PROFIT AND LOSS ACCOUNT FINANCING

4.1 Introduction

The previous sections have focused on off-balance sheet financing; however, there is a more recent development, referred to as off-profit and loss account financing, which should also be mentioned.

Charging operating costs directly to shareholders rather than charging them in the profit and loss account has been practised in a relatively minor way for a number of years. For example, directors and employees may be remunerated by means of share options. The cost when the share options are exercised (ie, the difference between the exercise price and the market price) is not charged in the profit and loss account (although earnings per share will be affected) but directly to shareholders in the form of dilution of their equity interest in the company. Similarly convertible loan stock has been common for many years, whereby a lower interest rate is secured (and therefore charged in the profit and loss account) by giving the holder the right to convert into equity at a fixed price in the future. Some of the techniques used in the recent growth of off-profit and loss account financing are described below.

4.2   Deep discount debentures

One of the principal features of financing property development is the time lag between the initial investment in the property and the generation of cash through sale or letting. A traditional loan which requires regular payments, at least of interest, throughout the loan period therefore gives rise to a cash flow mismatch. This can be overcome or minimised by effectively deferring the payment of interest by using deep discount debentures. Their characteristic is that the interest coupon is lower than an economic rate, but the bond is issued at a discount to compensate. For example, instead of issuing a five year £100m bond at 9% a borrower might issue a deep discount bond with a nominal value (ie, repayment value) of £142m, an issue price of £100m and interest at 2%. The extra £7m cost represents additional interest resulting from the deferral of part of the annual interest payment (ie the reduction from 9% to 2%).

A variant of the above is the stepped interest bond. Under this arrangement the interest payable is initially set at a low rate, say 2%, with interest payable in respect of the later periods at a higher rate, say, 25%.

From a financial perspective the legal descriptions attached to the various payments made to the lender are irrelevant. In order to assess the cost of the loan all that need be known is the amount and date of each payment; whether it is documented as being principal, discount or interest for a particular period is irrelevant. For example, it is clear as far as the above is concerned that the deep discount really represents rolled up interest and that, in the case of the stepped interest bonds, some of the interest paid later in the loan period relates to earlier periods.

In order to account for these loans in an appropriate way it is necessary to calculate the overall effective rate of interest and impute interest on this basis. This will result in a fair presentation of the real interest cost relating to each period. A worked example of a stepped interest arrangement is presented in Appendix 3 to this chapter. Unfortunately there is as yet no mandatory requirement for this method of accounting to be applied in practice, although the Technical Committee of the Institute of Chartered Accountants in England and

Wales (the Technical Committee) has issued a discussion document which recommends it.

It will be noted that the accounting treatment proposed above tends to accelerate the recognition of interest (for deep-discount or stepped interest loans). As already mentioned, property developments generally tend to take some time before they generate income. It is therefore sometimes suggested, where loans of this kind are used to finance property developments, that this accounting treatment fails to match revenue and expense (as required by the 'accruals' concept).

This argument is, it is suggested, based on a simplified view of the accruals concept. The first essential of the accruals concept is that income and expenditure are recognised as they are earned and incurred rather than when they are received and paid. In the case of interest expense, it is clear that it accrues at a constant rate on the amount outstanding. The matching component of the accruals concept can be dealt with by capitalising that part of the interest expense which relates directly to property developments rather than charging it to the profit and loss account.

4.3 Share premium account

One of the factors which complicates accounting for deep discount debentures is the law relating to the share premium account. Companies are generally required to credit to the share premium account the amount by which the proceeds of an issue of shares exceeds the nominal value of the shares issued. The uses of the share premium account are restricted by law, but there are certain purposes for which it is expressly permitted to be used (s 130, Companies Act 1985). One of the permitted uses is to write-off the costs of issues of shares or debentures, including 'commissions paid or discounts allowed on debentures'. It is difficult to believe that a deep discount debenture was contemplated when the legislation was drafted, however the view generally adopted in practice is that it is legally permissible to write-off the deep discount against the share premium account. Generally this would be expected to be achieved by amortising the discount through the profit and loss account (as notional interest) and then transferring (by way of a movement on reserves) an amount from share premium account to retained profits.

4.4 Redeemable convertibles

A variant of the traditional convertible loan stock referred to above is the redeemable convertible loan stock. A number have been issued recently by companies like P & O, Argyll, Asda, Burton, Dee, Hillsdown, LIG, Next, Smith & Nephew and Tesco. The interest coupon (typically 4 to 5%) is lower than for a conventional convertible, with the holder being compensated by the inclusion of a redemption option. If the share price does not increase sufficiently to make conversion worthwhile the holder may opt for redemption at a premium over the issue price, which means that he is effectively guaranteed an annual return of, say, 9%. This premium is generally described in the issue documents as 'supplementary interest' and the annual interest yield on this basis is specified. If however the conversion option is exercised then the potential redemption feature becomes irrelevant.

The major accounting issue is whether the potential redemption premium should be accrued and charged in the profit and loss account as interest over the period to the date when it may be exercised or whether the possibility of redemption taking place should, if it is considered unlikely to crystallise in practice, merely be noted as a contingency.

The basic argument for accrual is that in substance the redemption premium is rolled-up supplementary interest and is effectively borne by the issuing company whichever option is chosen by the holder of the convertible. If the holder chooses redemption then the premium is borne directly as a cash payment. However, if the holder chooses conversion the premium is still borne indirectly in that it represents the effective consideration for the issue of the shares, on the basis that if the company did not have the conversion commitment to honour it could have issued a similar number of shares for cash at the normal discount to the market price at the time (which would almost certainly be a higher price than the conversion price).

The commercial decision of the holder of the convertible whether to opt for conversion or redemption will naturally take into account the redemption premium; only if conversion offers a more beneficial result will he forego the redemption option; the original issue price will play no part in his calculations.

The basic argument for non-accrual is that redemption is a fall-back feature (to protect the holder) that is unlikely to crystallise in practice and therefore is no more than a contingency to be referred to in the notes to the accounts. It is suggested that providing for interest that will probably never have to be paid is not appropriate and that the contingency should be reviewed at each accounting date on its merits. If poor share price performance has significantly increased the likelihood of the redemption option being exercised then under this approach a provision would be set up at that time.

No definitive guidance is presently provided by the accounting profession. However, preliminary guidance is given in a Technical Committee release (TR 677) issued in November 1987. This favours the first approach referred to above and suggests that the potential redemption premium should be accrued and charged to the profit and loss account.

4.5   Convertible preference shares

Most convertible issues have been in the form of bonds, but a more recent variation, exemplified by the United Biscuits issue as part of the financing for its

£335m acquisition of Ross Young's in April 1988, is the issue of convertible preference shares with a redemption premium option. There is a strong case for saying that the principles discussed above should apply in the same way and consequently that systematic accrual should be made through the profit and loss account for the potential redemption premium, however remote its potential crystallisation appears to be.

4.6 Debt with equity warrants

Another method of reducing the cost of debt charged in the profit and loss account is for debt to be issued simultaneously with equity warrants (eg, as issued by Thorn EMI and Rowntree). Equity warrants give the holders the right to subscribe for shares at a price which is usually fixed at the outset. The warrants may also be redeemable; in other words the amount paid for the warrant is repayable if the warrant is not exercised (eg, as issued by Wates City of London Properties). Although the warrants and the debt will usually be issued simultaneously, they are traded separately so that the holder can sell one and retain the other. The objective of issues of this kind is, as for convertible debt, to secure a lower interest rate for the debt than if it were issued on its own.

Although there is little authorative guidance in this area, most accountants would agree that the proceeds must be allocated between the debt and the warrant, based on the best estimates available, and accounted for separately. The warrant proceeds are generally taken directly to a capital reserve rather than being recognised as profit. Where the warrant is redeemable the accounting should be similar to that suggested in TR 677 for redeemable convertible loan stock.

5 CONCLUSION

With the publication of ED 42 and the expected tightening of the Companies Act definition of subsidiary the counter offensive against off-balance sheet financing and other similar techniques has begun. The issues are complex, as ever the 'innocent' may be affected as much as the 'guilty', and there are many views to be reconciled. However, the importance of protecting the integrity of accounts so that they reflect economic reality rather than merely empty legalistic form is widely accepted and, even before ED 42 becomes an Accounting Standard and the revised definition of subsidiary becomes law, there is already a perceptible, although by no means universal, hardening of attitudes against arrangements the sole or main purpose of which is to distort balance sheet or profit and loss account presentation. It is to be hoped that good and expeditious progress towards finalising the Accounting Standard and the revised definition of subsidiary is made and that these will serve as a basis for a more rapid response on the part of the accounting profession when similar accounting issues come to the fore in the future.

Appendix 1

STRUCTURES FOR 'CONTROLLED NON-SUBSIDIARIES'

The definition of a subsidiary is set out in s 736 of the Companies Act 1985. This provides that a company (S) is a subsidiary of another (H) if (and only if):

 (i) H is a member of S and controls the composition of the board of directors, or

(ii) H holds more than half in nominal value of the equity share capital in S.

In addition S will be a subsidiary of H if S is a subsidiary of another subsidiary of H.

The diagram below shows a share structure of the type widely employed in practice to circumvent this definition:

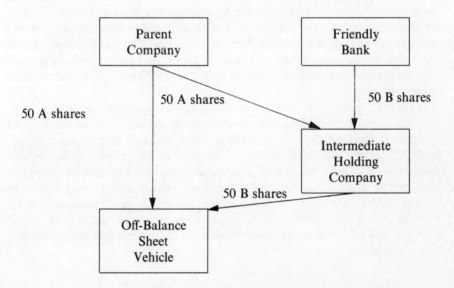

This structure is often described as the 'diamond structure'.

The A shares and B shares each have the same number of votes except on a vote to appoint directors. The holders of the A shares have the right to appoint three directors without reference to the holders of the B shares; similarly the B shareholders have the right to appoint three directors without reference to the holders of the A shares. However, at board meetings of the off-balance sheet vehicle (the quorum for which requires the presence of an 'A' director) the 'A' directors each have six votes whilst the 'B' directors have one each. Rights to dividends and return of capital on a winding up may be split so that the 'A' shareholders received 99% and the 'B' shareholders receive 1%.

Clearly the parent effectively can dictate board policy of the off-balance sheet vehicle and will receive 99.99% of its profits. Hence the vehicle is in substance no different from being its subsidiary. However, the vehicle does not fall within the definition set out above.

The parent does not strictly have the right to control the composition of the board of directors. The parent may appoint only half the board of the vehicle and half the board of the intermediate holding company. The fact that the directors appointed by the parent carry a majority of the votes which may be cast at board meetings is not addressed in current legislation.

The second half of the definition is also avoided by careful attention to the meaning of the phrase 'nominal value of the equity share capital'. Both A and B shares fall within the definition of 'equity share capital' given in the Companies Act. 'Equity share capital' is defined in s 744 of the Act as the issued share capital of a company 'excluding any part of that capital which, neither as respects dividends nor as respects capital, carries any right to participate beyond a specified amount in a distribution'. The phrase 'a specified amount' means an amount which is expressed as a ceiling, for example 6% of the amount paid up on the shares. In this example, the amount of the dividend to which both the A and B shares are entitled is unlimited. Although it is clear that the dividend right of the A shares is far greater than that of the B shares, the definition of a subsidiary requires that the measure of the relative weight of the shares is to be their nominal value.

It will be noted that the above structure is relatively complex, and that, as far as the Companies Act definition of a subsidiary is concerned, a similar result could be achieved for example by having the B shares in the off-balance sheet vehicle held directly by the bank. However, in practice structures similar to that illustrated above are used, primarily for taxation reasons. For example, it may be necessary to ensure that the off-balance sheet vehicle and its parent may be treated as falling within the same group for group relief purposes or for corporation tax on capital gains, or it may be necessary to minimise the stamp duty payable on transfers of property between the parent and the off-balance sheet vehicle.

Appendix 2

THE CLASSIFICATION OF LEASES OF PROPERTY UNDER SSAP 21

SSAP 21

SSAP 21 defines a finance lease as 'a lease that transfers substantially all the risks and rewards of ownership of an asset to the lessee'. All other leases are operating leases.

Guidance notes on SSAP 21

Further guidance on the classification of leases of land and buildings is given in the Accounting Standards Committee's Guidance Notes on SSAP 21 at paragraphs 139–144. It is made clear that leases of land and buildings are to be accounted for using the same criteria as other assets. It is specifically observed that:

'Many leases of land and buildings are for only a small part of the useful life of the building and the lessee does not obtain the economic benefits of ownership arising, for example, from any increase in value. Moreover, since the leases usually provide for regular rent reviews, the rent payable is regularly brought up to market rates and the lease thereby has the characteristics not of a financing arrangement but of the provision of a service. Most leases involving land and buildings would therefore be classified as operating leases.' (Paragraph 140.)

Exceptions to this generalisation are mentioned in the Guidance Notes including leases of specialised or short-lived buildings and leases resulting from sale and leasebacks (Paragraph 141).

It is stated in the Guidance Notes that the existence of rent reviews may cause the principal rewards of ownership to revert to the lessor and thus rebut the presumption as to the nature of the lease resulting from application of the '90% test' (Paragraph 142).

The '90% test'

The '90% test' is a mechanical method designed to assist the determination of whether a lease is a finance lease or an operating lease. SSAP 21 describes the test as follows:

'It should be presumed that . . . [a lease is a finance lease] if at the inception of the lease the present value of the minimum lease payments, including any initial payment, amounts to substantially all (normally 90% or more) of the fair value of the leased asset. The present value should be calculated by using the interest rate implicit in the lease (Paragraph 15). This is qualified by stating that the presumption created by this test can be rebutted in exceptional circumstances' (Paragraph 16).

The workings of the '90% test' can be illustrated by means of a simple example. The following assumptions are made:

Fair value of property at inception of lease	£100
Lease term	20 years
Rent (annually in arrear)	£6
Fair value of property at end of lease	£100

This lease has an implicit interest rate of 6% pa. Discounted at this rate, the present value of the rentals is £69. On the basis of the '90% test', therefore, this lease would be classified as an operating lease. Comparing the present value of the rentals to 90% of the fair value is equivalent to comparing the present value of the assumed fair value of the property at the end of the lease (£31 in this example) to 10% of the fair value at its inception.

It can be shown that this result would only be altered by quite significant changes in the assumptions. For example, the annual rental must be increased to more than £12 or, of the rental stays at £6, the fair value of the property at the end of the lease reduced to less than £18 before the '90% test' would suggest that the lease is a finance lease. As regards the period of the lease, the lease would be classified as a finance lease under the '90% test' if the period were longer than 40 years.

It should be noted that the results of the '90% test' are unaffected by the existence of rent reviews provided that, as is commonly the case, they provide only for rents to be increased and not for any decrease. If rentals could decrease, this would increase the likelihood that the lease is classed as an operating lease.

Where the lessee participates in the residual value this may have the effect of changing the result of the '90% test' and hence the classification of the lease under SSAP 21.

As a general rule, the '90% test' will virtually always suggest that a relatively short lease of property is an operating lease where the lessor has the right to the whole of the residual value and a finance lease where the lessee is interested in substantially all of the residual value. 'Relatively short' for this purpose should be taken as less than 30 years or so when the other factors are similar to those illustrated above.

Other considerations

As stated above, the result of the '90% test' can be rebutted in exceptional circumstances. In particular where there are regular rent reviews and the lessor has the right to receive and retain the increase in rentals (ie, most normal property leases), the lease would generally be regarded as an operating lease even if the '90% test' suggests it is a finance lease.

It is suggested that where leases result from a sale and leaseback, as the seller/lessee continues to enjoy the use of the asset it should be presumed that the transaction is primarily of a financing nature, rather than a property transaction and hence that the leaseback is a finance lease unless the contrary can be clearly demonstrated. It should, however, be appreciated that many sale and leasebacks do nevertheless result in operating leases.

Special care must be taken in the case of leases between related parties. In particular, it is suggested that, in assessing whether a lease transfers the risks and rewards of ownership of the asset to the lessee, all circumstances connected with the lease, including any interest of the lessee in the lessor, should be taken account of.

Appendix 3

ACCOUNTING FOR DEEP DISCOUNT LOAN WITH STEPPED INTEREST

Assumptions:

Amount received on issue	£100
Coupon payable	
End years 1–5	£1
End years 6–10	£5
End years 11–15	£25
Repayment	End year 16 at £275
Redemption yield (calculated from above assumptions)	10.92%

Year	Outstanding at beginning of year £	Profit and loss account charge £	Cash paid £	Outstanding at end of year £
1	100.0	10.9	(1.0)	109.9
2	109.9	12.0	(1.0)	120.9
3	120.9	13.2	(1.0)	133.1
4	133.1	14.5	(1.0)	146.6
5	146.6	16.0	(1.0)	161.6
6	161.6	17.7	(5.0)	174.3
7	174.3	19.0	(5.0)	188.3
8	188.3	20.6	(5.0)	203.9
9	203.9	22.3	(5.0)	221.2
10	221.2	24.1	(5.0)	240.3
11	240.3	26.2	(25.0)	241.5
12	241.5	26.4	(25.0)	242.9
13	242.9	26.5	(25.0)	244.4
14	244.4	26.7	(25.0)	246.1
15	246.1	26.9	(25.0)	248.0
16	248.0	27.0	(275.0)	—
		330.0	(430.0)	

Chapter 5

The Mechanics of Joint Ventures

David Bramson

In recent years, the joint venture has become increasingly popular in property financing, particularly in development funding. This chapter reviews its importance and examines its many forms. A comparison is made between the joint venture company and the joint venture partnership, particularly in terms of their relative tax treatment.

Problems and pitfalls in negotiating shareholding structures, control and management and the alternative approaches to profit distribution and the transfer of interest are reviewed in detail, as well as the other key considerations in drafting the document.

Finally, I reflect on the likely importance of the joint venture in the future and the degree to which its popularity is symptomatic of a rising property market.

I   INTRODUCTION

This chapter analyses the structures which are available under English law to enable two or more parties to participate in the profits gained from the development of property. The two principal vehicles on which any participation is based will be either a limited liability company or a partnership.

The factors determining the choice of structure will be subjective to the participants or the particular development and need to be addressed afresh for each venture. These factors may be summarised under the following headings:

1. The taxation position of the participants.

2. The timescale for the development and its disposal.

3. The number of participants.

4. The method of financing the development.

The basic choice to be made on a joint venture is for the participants to determine how their respective taxation positions may be affected by the purpose of the venture and the type of vehicle to be utilised. It is assumed that for the purposes of this chapter the joint venture proposed is for trading purposes so that the participants co-operate together to carry out the development, let it and sell to a third party for a profit.

The first question to be asked is whether the participant is exempt from paying tax (ie, is it a charity or a pension fund). If it is, it will be prohibited from trading and therefore cannot directly be involved as a developer without risking its tax exempt status. This will limit the vehicle which can be used to a limited company (or as a limited partner in a limited partnership). If the participant is an investor in a limited liability company which is incorporated for the purpose of trading this will *not* jeopardise the tax status of the tax exempt investor; but it will bring about group relief or consortium relief.

Where the joint venture is an individual the most tax efficient vehicle is likely to be one which is 'tax transparent' to enable him to take advantage of any tax losses or allowances against income from other sources.

It is possible for both tax exempt organisations and tax payers to be involved as investors through the same vehicle.

Any joint venture vehicle is likely to be useful only in the short term. Joint ventures therefore tend to be for carrying out developments within a limited time frame. On completion of the development either the property will be sold or one of the parties to the joint venture will acquire it.

Although any number of parties can be involved in a joint venture it is best to keep the numbers to a minimum. The practical difficulties of ensuring that the parties are kept informed and consulted are such that there must always be a limited number of participants.

Where a potential development has been identified it is often the case that one party does not have all the resources necessary to make the project succeed. In this case he will offer a share of the profits of the project to others who can bring their own skills or financial backing to the partnership. Arrangements where landowners, property developers, financiers and building contractors combine to carry through a project are not unusual and generally every joint venture will consist of two or more individuals or companies who will be able to procure that the development takes place.

A 'joint venture' is not a term of art. It is a general description of a 'partnership' where persons combine to undertake a project and to share in its success. The structure may take the form of a partnership but it is more likely to be a limited company or other arrangement.

II THE LIMITED COMPANY

1 Structure

If a limited company can be used as the umbrella for a joint venture this has considerable advantages. The structure of a limited company is known and well understood by the parties and their advisers and can be utilised to provide a wide range of debt and equity interests. It is a useful format where there are a number of shareholders. By creating different classes of shares one can both provide different rights for different shareholders and also different tranches of profits in which they share.

A company is the only joint venture arrangement available in England and Wales which is a separate legal person. A definite advantage of this is the ability of the shareholders to limit their liability to the amount of capital which they have subscribed or agreed to subscribe to the company. Even if the project is a disaster the shareholder can know precisely the amount of his liability when he agrees to take up his shares. This does not mean that the shareholders cannot agree to provide further capital should this be needed but the conditions on which that finance will be provided and how, if at all, it will be secured will be part of a shareholder's agreement entered into when the project is initiated.

Although shareholders have limited liability, the position of the directors of a limited liability company may be different and directors or 'shadow directors' may have personal liability if the company loses money by reason of their act of default.

2 Taxation

The reason why a limited company is not always used for joint ventures tends to be one of taxation. Although there are certain tax benefits there can be disadvantages too.

If the company is a subsidiary of one of the participants, group relief will be available. Even if it is not a subsidiary, consortium relief can be obtained by company shareholders who hold more than 75% of the shares. The advantage of group relief may be counter-balanced by the disadvantage of having to group the liabilities of the subsidiary company within the accounts of the parent. The accounting standards require that if one company 'controls' another the accounts have to be consolidated. The definition of control is very wide and will require consolidation of the accounts with the accounts of that principal shareholder in a deadlock company where the nominee director of one corporate participant has the casting vote.

Until recently, limited companies which wished to carry out developments without the borrowing in relation to the developments being shown on their balance sheet were able to do so because the accounting standards used strict definitions for ascertaining those borrowings which had to be taken into account when preparing a company's accounts and this assisted the creation of off balance sheet transactions. If the 'parent' did not have more than 50% of the shares (although it might be entitled to considerably more than 50% of the profits of the transaction) and did not have a casting vote in the case of a deadlock, the borrowing by the joint venture company would not have to be consolidated with the other liabilities of the 'parent'. The Accounting Standards Committee of the

Institute of Chartered Accountants has publicised its exposure draft 42 which indicates how it intends to tighten up its requirements for consolidation.

If the draft is acceptable the profession will adopt a practice of presuming that:

'a controlled non-subsidiary' will be treated as if it were a real subsidiary in the company's accounts. A controlled non-subsidiary is a company trust or other vehicle which is directly or indirectly controlled by and a source of benefits or risks that are in substance no different from those that would arise were the vehicle a subsidiary.

As can be seen this proposal applies to any vehicle, not just limited companies, but it is intended to be carefully applied and should not adversely affect the accounting treatment of commercial joint ventures where there is no element of ultimate control. The Department of Trade and Industry is likely to leave the auditors of the company to decide what 'dominant influence' means.

A joint venture company can accommodate a position where an investor wishes to trade in property but does not wish to be treated by the Inland Revenue as a 'trader'. For example, the trustees of pension funds are rightly concerned not to be deemed to be trading in property and taxed accordingly. However, if trustees acquire shares in a company which trades but hold those shares as an investment, there will be no such risk. Although the risk of trading is not there, there are other tax disadvantages. Because of the way ACT is calculated, a tax of 13.3% on the income which passes through the company will be suffered by the company even though the shareholder can reclaim ACT. The double incidence of tax on the profit earned from selling the property should not be a problem. Profits on the sale of the completed development will be trading profits not capital gains and will be distributed by means of a dividend. Again because the company is trading in land and buildings, capital allowances will not be a factor.

If the shares are held by a taxpayer as an investment, and no group or consortium relief is available, any losses incurred will be capital losses and cannot be set off against income. This compares adversely with the partnership structure.

3 VAT

From 1 April 1988 all developers of commercial land (as opposed to land for residential development) will be advised to register for VAT. Land construction costs and new buildings will be subject to VAT at the standard rate and rent under leases may be exempt or, at the option of the landlord, be subject to VAT also. As far as can be ascertained from the consultations to date with the authorities it is likely that most landlords will charge VAT and the ultimate purchasers of investment property from developers are likely to register VAT also. Over a relatively short period the commercial property sector is likely to opt for registration for VAT. The only real losers will be financial institutions like banks and life assurance companies who acquire or lease properties for their own use and cannot recover VAT as they do not charge VAT on the products and services which they supply.

4   Adaptability of company structure

A major benefit from the use of the limited company structure which is not tax-related is the ability for it to grow into an investment vehicle which can be marketed in its own right.

Even if when the company is formed, it is for one development to be carried out by the company on behalf of the original shareholders the intentions for the company may change. If the development is successful, the same company could be utilised to carry out further developments and new shareholders could be introduced. If this happens, the company could achieve a size and track record which would enable it to be floated on a recognised stock exchange. This would be a natural if optimistic progression which would not be readily achievable with any other structure.

5   Limited recourse borrowing

Any lender to the joint venture would be comfortable with the company structure which would enable him to obtain straight forward security by means of a legal charge over the property being developed and a debenture over any other assets of the company. In the case of a company formed for the purpose of one project the lender would normally require shareholders' guarantees, in appropriate circumstances non-recourse or limited recourse finance may be available.

Although the expressions 'non-recourse' and 'limited recourse' are commonly used there is no generally accepted definition. The concept of non-recourse lending is that the lender only looks to the security of the assets charged to pay back the loan if the project founders. In a development it is unlikely that any project loan is truly non-recourse. The lender will invariably require covenants by a person of substance to provide for cost overruns in order to guarantee that the development is physically completed if not let and sold. Even if the lender accepts a covenant to repay a loan from the borrower, which may be a £100 company, this may be described as non-recourse, but this is not legally so. If the borrower fails to repay at the prescribed date it will be in default and if it is a member of a group of companies this could cause a default under another loan taken out by another member of the group from a third party where there is deemed to be a default under a cross default provision. Cross default clauses are common and the only way the parent company may be able to prevent the whole borrowing structure of the group being put in jeopardy may be to redeem the 'non-recourse' loan. If the group includes a publicly quoted company the position is worse because the failure to support a subsidiary may put The Stock Exchange listing at risk. Even without the sanction of The Stock Exchange there is a very strong moral pressure to repay loans in order to avoid any possible stigma. The stigma will be there even where the interest rate may have reflected the inherent risks and notwithstanding the non-recourse nature of the loan. The only real non-recourse loans are where if events occur or time elapses there is an enforceable agreement that the lender *only* looks to its security and is not able to argue that a default has occurred.

The concept of limited recourse lending is one which requires limited guarantees to provide finance but with the lender agreeing to take on the risk of the loan not being repaid once those guarantees have been exhausted.

III   PARTNERSHIP AND JOINT VENTURES

On the face of it, the advantages of a limited company so far out-weigh the disadvantages that it is surprising that any other structures exist. However, other structures do have their advantages, particularly those of tax.

1   Limited partnership

If the joint venture arrangement is a partnership, this will be tax transparent as far as the partners are concerned and will enable the partners to carry forward any tax losses against income arising from the same trade or set the losses off against other income arising in the same year. However, save in the case of a limited partnership the partners are jointly and severally liable to third parties for any partnership losses. A partner can be liable for the other's income tax but not its corporation tax. As between the partners they can agree to indemnify themselves in such proportions as they may determine but the value of this indemnity is dependent upon the financial strength of the party giving it. It is possible to have a limited partnership where the liability of individual partners is limited. There must however be at least one general partner with unlimited liability for the project as a whole. In addition, the limited liability partners must not take part in the management of the partnership. If they do they lose their limited liability. Although limited liability partners may not act as managers they are entitled to make fundamental decisions without losing their protection. The limited partners can therefore decide to end the partnership, expel the general partner or take other action which goes to the root of the partnership's activity.

There is no reason why the general partner cannot be a limited company, thus effectively giving all partners the benefit of limiting their respective liabilities.

2   Maximum number of partners

Although it is unlikely to be a problem in property joint ventures one cannot have more than 20 partners in a partnership. Because the partnership is not a legal person the title to the property has to be held by the partners on behalf of the partnership under a trust for sale and only four of the partners can be registered as proprietors of the land. If there are more than four partners the title owners will hold it on behalf of the other partners also. The concept of the trust for sale is that the individual partners do not have a legal interest in the property but only in the proceeds of sale of that property. In the event of a dispute between the parties the property will have to be sold and the proceeds divided between the partners.

A partnership does not have the same stringent requirements as to formalities as a limited liability company but is subject to the Limited Partnerships Act 1907 which does provide an element of control. However, properly run partnerships will have similar checks and balances between the partners as exist under company law in practice.

3 Joint venture or partnership?

The parties will often attempt to create a joint venture which does not have the disadvantages of partnership liability. Whilst joint ventures are theoretically possible, they may be difficult to achieve in practice. The joint venture will be created by an agreement between the parties and even though this may specifically negate any intention of creating a partnership the facts may dictate the contrary. The basic test of a partnership is that it is a venture in the nature of a trade intended to make profits and where profits are to be shared between the parties. It does not matter that losses may be shared in different proportions or even that one party may have no responsibility at all for losses. It is always open to an aggrieved creditor of the joint venture to sue the joint venturer with the deepest pockets and allege a partnership. It is then for the person sued to show that the joint venture agreement did not create a partnership. If he fails to do so he will have to rely on the indemnity in the agreement from the other party or parties.

One way of overcoming a partner's liability in practice is for the partner to be a wholly owned subsidiary of the joint venturer with a nominal capital base. In these circumstances if the partner is sued the real participant will not be liable so long as that company was not purely the participant's nominee.

IV PARTICIPATION LENDING AND FORWARD FUNDING

The joint ventures mentioned so far tend to be true joint ventures insofar as the partners are embarking on the development activity each having substantially similar bargaining power even though they may have different areas of interest or expertise in the development process. Mention should be made of two other methods of financing development which although they are akin to joint ventures are not true joint ventures because of the disparity of the parties' negotiating positions. These are participation lending and development funding.

1 Participation lending

In participation lending, the lender providing finance in a traditional way will also take a share of the equity in the scheme. This will be because the lender is taking more risk than is traditionally the case or is trimming its interest requirement. It is not unusual for a lender to take a share of the profit where it is funding a speculative development or is lending more than approximately 70% of the cost or where the borrower's ability to repay is in question.

In addition to the usual mortgage and loan agreement the lender will also require a profit participation agreement. The loan documentation must be drawn from the borrower's point of view in such a way as to ensure that the profit participation is deemed to be part of the consideration for the loan. If the documentation is not properly drawn the result can be to have the profit payment disallowed against the borrower's tax. From the lender's point of view the profit payment must be seen to be reasonable and not disallowable as a penalty and must not be considered by the courts as an unfair fetter on the borrower's right to repay the loan. Unfortunately, the law of mortgages has evolved over several hundred years and for most of that time the need to protect the borrower against the rapacious lender was paramount. It is unlikely when commercial terms of a borrowing are negotiated between two well advised parties the courts will intervene and the lender be found to be guilty of undue influence. But in these days of increasing litigation and the substantial figures involved, the documentation should be prepared in such a way as to give the least possible argument to enable one party to delay or defeat the other's rights.

2   Forward funding

An ultimate purchaser of a completed development may assist the developer by providing interim finance to enable the development to be completed; in this case the purchaser will acquire the site at the inception of the development which will both give him security and restrict the stamp duty payable on the transaction to the amount paid for the site at the date of acquisition rather than the whole development cost including the site acquisition payment and building costs and developer's profit. Under the development agreement the developer will carry out the development and on its successful completion and letting will be paid the developer's profit.

The development finance will be funded at a lower rate than the developer could fund the development costs from other sources but as a quid pro quo the purchaser will buy at a price which reflects a higher yield than the purchaser would obtain on the acquisition of the completed development in the open market.

V   PARTICIPANTS' AGREEMENT

Every type of joint development will require a participants' agreement which controls the rights and remedies of the parties. In addition the arrangements governing the activities of a joint company will be covered by its Articles of Association.

In any joint venture arrangement it is important to differentiate the functions of each of the parties and also to establish the difference between day-to-day management and control.

To take the example of the project management of the development, it is relatively easy to see the difference between policy decisions and management responsibility. In practice it can be more difficult to define them. The developer partner is likely to be appointed project manager or at least have the responsibility for project co-ordination. This causes no problem when it is necessary to monitor the development but different considerations arise if the design of the development is to be varied or if any of the consultants are to be replaced. Similarly if parties are charged with obtaining finance or the letting or sale of the development, it is unlikely that the remaining parties to the joint development who have substantial financial interests to protect, will be prepared to be bound by one partner's decision on fundamental aspects.

It is therefore essential to identify the areas where the individual parties require to be consulted and those where their approval is required. If these are defined in the original Partnership Agreement there will be less room for disagreement subsequently. A sensible arrangement for companies' joint ventures and partnerships is for there to be two levels at which decisions are made. There can be an executive board to which management decisions are referred. The constitution of this board would be representatives of all participants with a simple majority needed to pass a resolution. Where any decision has a material effect on cost or value, this would be passed to a partnership committee where the participants vote in accordance with their entitlement to profit. However, some decisions may be so fundamental that any party should have the right of veto. In many cases, all decisions other than those which are purely management need to be referred to the participants any one of whom may have a veto.

It should be emphasised that there must be sufficient goodwill at the initial stages for the parties to believe that they can work together and will rely on each other's judgment. The checks and balances contained in the agreement should only be used as a last resort.

If any party has a veto, this will cause a deadlock which could result in the project grinding to a halt. It may be possible to have an independent chairman who has the confidence of the parties and who is given a casting vote to break a deadlock. If this course is not adopted there is always the possibility of referring disputes to an independent person to act as an expert or an arbitrator when the dispute arises. This is not desirable. First, it will inevitably cause delay. Secondly, the person appointed to adjudicate is likely to be a professional nominee and therefore not really equipped to make commercial decisions. Thirdly, any decisions made by the independent person are likely to be conservative and to adopt the most cautious approach. It is an abrogation of responsibility for the parties to give the difficult decisions to a third party who does not have a financial involvement. Therefore, in the absence of an independent chairman acceptable to all parties, the participants must be prepared to argue out their respective positions in order to achieve the objective of the development.

VI DISENGAGEMENT

If all else fails and one party will not see reason, the only way to break the deadlock is to unravel the joint venture. There are a number of ways to bring a joint venture to an end before its due date, but none of them is entirely happy where the disengagement takes place because the parties have fallen out. Although the structures of joint venture may differ it is likely that the procedures for unravelling them will follow a pattern.

Whatever the reality of the situation it is always open for a party wishing to acquire the other's shares to engineer a dispute. This is the problem inherent in any acquisition of interests in a joint venture, whether it is a corporate share acquisition or the acquisition of an interest under a partnership.

To take the simple example, where there are only two participants, there could be provision in the agreement for either party who wishes to proceed on certain lines against the wishes of the other to buy out the other's share at a valuation. The formula for the valuation could be agreed now or it could be left to settlement by an independent expert (or in the case of a joint venture company its auditors) at the time the shares are to be acquired. However, it is unlikely that any formula agreed now would be suitable in all circumstances and, in any event, there will always be the difficulty of valuing the work in progress when a development has not been completed, or where lettings are on the horizon but have not been consumated.

In a case where the participants are equal or almost equal parties, the method which seems to achieve the most equitable result is known by various names including 'the Texas Option'. If there is a deadlock, either party may offer to purchase the other's interest within a given time scale and at a figure quoted by the offeror. The offeree then has the option within the time scale of either accepting the offeror's offer or of buying the offeror's interest at the same price. If the interests are not equal the price must be calculated on a pro rata basis. Whilst this may not be scientific, it does mean that the person who makes the offer must attribute a value to the other's interest which he would be prepared to accept for his own. The arrangement could still be abused because a deadlock can be engineered at a time when one party knows that the other is not in a position to fund the acquisition of any further interest.

The whole area of control and what happens if deadlock is reached is fraught with traps for the unwary. In the case of participation lending or development funding, the party who has put up the finance will require a much greater degree of control and will not be prepared to enter into any arrangement which could see its interest being devalued. Similarly if the joint venture includes the landowner, he will not accept any method of determining a dispute which could effectively see the compulsory acquisition of his land by his erstwhile partner. In these circumstances, any untangling process would have to enable the landowner to re-acquire his interest.

Where one partner owns the bulk of the venture, the minority shareholder may be given the right to sell his minority interest to the majority owner, at stated dates or on events occurring, at a price which gives him the appropriate percentage value of the whole project. In this way he will not suffer the discount on value by reason of the sale of a minority stake.

VII   ULTIMATE CONTROL

In the true joint venture the rights of the parties to contribute to the development process will be positive. In the case of profit participation lending and forward funding the rights are likely to be negative. The controls which the lender or purchaser will exercise are those of veto. If the development does not proceed in accordance with the financier's requirements he will wish to disengage himself from his arrangements with the developer but he will also need to ensure that he can recover the money which he has advanced.

The lender will have his rights under the mortgage to appoint a receiver and manager or to exercise his power of sale. In either event, the developer will be at the mercy of the courts exercising their equitable jurisdiction to give relief.

The position under forward funding is not so clear. Generally the purchaser, having acquired the land, will grant a licence to the developer to carry out the development. If the development does not proceed in accordance with the terms of the agreement, the purchaser will reserve to himself the right of terminating the licence. In this case the court may have no inherent jurisdiction. It will be a matter of contract as to whether the developer has any right to argue against his licence being determined. It is therefore essential that the developer protects himself to ensure that he can only be ejected from the development site in the event of a material breach of his obligations. The developer's advisers should seek to ensure that in the event of their client being ejected from the site, he has a right of recourse to the court. Unless such a right is built into the documents it will be very difficult to convince the court that they should interfere in the bargain struck by the parties. If the breach is not a fundamental one, an alternative would be for the purchaser to have a power of attorney, granted by the developer, to enable the purchaser to complete the development and to recover the cost of so doing as a deduction from the profit from the development which would otherwise have been shared with the developer. In this way, the purchaser would be able to procure that the development is completed under its control, but some profit payment for the developer could be retained if this is appropriate.

VIII   MARKETABILITY OF INTERESTS

It will be clear from the position so far that the interests of the participants in a joint venture are not going to be readily marketable before the development is complete and let. This in turn means that the joint venturers have nothing which would be acceptable as security to their banks or other lenders. This is clearly a disadvantage and one of the reasons why many companies will not consider joint ventures.

Even if an interest under a joint venture were marketable, the other participants would not be prepared to permit the sales of participants' interests to take place, save at their discretion. The importance of the identity of each participant is fundamental, having regard to the joint decisions which have to be made and the possibility for being obstructive. Generally, the only disposal of an interest in a joint venture which would be permitted without consent is one to a company within the same group as the original participant. Even then there would need to be a warranty that, following such disposal, the transferee would remain a member of the same group as the original participator. If this did not happen, following the transfer the original participator could dispose of its shares in the transferee and the remaining joint venturer would have no ground for complaint.

If the requirement of transferability is important, the only safe way for all participants to permit this is by means of a procedure such as the Texas Option, outlined above. Rights of first refusal granted to existing joint venturers would not be an answer, because if the joint venturers were unable to take up these rights they could still be faced with a partner who was not acceptable to them. Any veto on the identity of a transferee would not be acceptable to an original participant who required the right to sell, as this right could be nugatory. It could only be exercised at the whim of the party with the veto. At least with the Texas Option, any partner knows that at the end of the day he may be able to dispose of his interest, either to his existing partners, or by acquiring their interests and thereafter being in a position to dispose of such interests as he considered fit.

IX   DESIGN AND BUILDING CONTROLS

Reference was made above to the difference between management and control and the need to define these differences, having regard to the particular project. Where any participant has a limited right of control, the parameters of his authority must be defined clearly. These will depend upon his area of expertise, but a crucial concern will be control over the building process.

Because of the potential liability for design and construction, any changes to the professional team should be the subject matter of participants' approval as should the appointment of the building contractor.

Whether changes in design are matters for the joint venturers, as opposed to the management team, must vary from project to project. However, if there are to be material changes to the design of the structure or the materials used then these need to be considered by the joint venturers. Lettable floor areas should not be reduced beyond stated tolerances without the participants' agreement.

Because of the current difficulties in obtaining meaningful design warranties from the professional team which are underwritten by insurers, careful consideration should be given to obtaining project insurance. Joint venturers are put in a particularly difficult position and it will be useful to summarise the position regarding responsibility for design, as it may affect the joint venturers and those financing them. For these purposes the project team consists of the architects, quantity surveyors, engineers and building contractors. They have two areas of responsibility, one in contract, the other in tort. The responsibility in contract, which is entered into with the project teams' employers and anyone to whom they have given a contractual, collateral warranty, extends to both direct loss (ie, replacement of damaged areas) and economic loss consequent upon their failing to comply with their agreements. The project teams' responsibility to third parties of whom they ought reasonably to have knowledge (eg, tenants, mortgagees, subsequent purchasers) is in negligence and does not extend to economic loss.

It would seem from the above that in law any person to whom a member of the professional team has given a collateral warranty would be adequately protected. This is not the case. The insurers who give building professionals indemnity insurance now often specifically exclude any cover for claims made by persons who have contractual obligations from the professional team, but who were not employers for the purposes of their building obligations.

If the joint venture vehicle is a limited liability company which then employs the project team, the shareholders in that company would have a right against the project team if they obtained a deed of collateral warranty from the team. However, if there had been a breach of that agreement, the relevant member of the project team would have a liability to the shareholder but would not be covered by their insurers. This would make the shareholders' rights far less valuable in practice then they should be, even though he could have suffered considerably from the breach of the agreement by a member of the project team. Whilst the shareholder has a sustainable action against the member of the team, whether he can recover damages will depend on the financial status of the defendant, who will not be covered by his professional indemnity insurance.

When the joint venture vehicle is a small company, lenders of development finance will generally require the shareholder to make contractual commitments to supervise the design and construction of the development. Project insurance can be obtained at a cost provided that it is taken up in the early stages of the development, in order to enable the insurers to instruct their own professional team. If the insurance is obtained, it will benefit the tenants and purchasers and ought to enable the joint venture to be wound up without concern over contingent liabilities.

The method of financing the development will be covered in the joint venture agreement and will require the partners to provide finance in tranches in the agreed proportions and in accordance with a timetable, so that it is provided simultaneously, consecutively or in any other agreed manner. In any event, the method of the provision of finance should be against architects' certificates or other approved vouchers. It is a matter for negotiation as to whether the finance bears interest and whether it is replaced by third party finance when available. In this event the parties should agree how loans owed to the participants should be repaid.

X PROFIT PAYMENTS

Once again, payment of profit is a matter for negotiation. There is no reason why profit payments have to be made strictly in accordance with the participants' respective holdings. The participants may agree that one receives a first tranche of profit before the others participate; alternatively one may receive his profit payment from a certain aspect of the development and not from others. In general terms, the parties should not be entitled to share in the profits until loans have been repaid in full and all interest paid. If any participant is entitled to a fee for work done (eg, a project management fee), this may be payable either as a charge on the scheme before profits are shared, or as part of the profit share of that partner. After 1 April 1989 the profit share will probably attract VAT as project management and other fees now do. The formula for profit participation can ensure that the fee element of the profit is paid out as works progress, should this be the parties' intention.

In general terms the profit will be that which is left after all the costs of the development have been paid. The joint venture agreement should make it clear how profit payments are to be made. If there is a potential for development costs to be expended after completion of the development, as will generally be the case, there should be a preliminary division of profits as soon as the bulk of the proceeds of sale are received. This assumes that the parties wish to receive their profit payment as quickly as possible and that the development is completed, let and sold shortly after practical completion. Additional development costs may be incurred for some time up to and after the issue of the final certificate under the building contract, after the making good of defects. If there are potential claims by contractors or others, substantial provision may be required and if this is the case, consideration should be given to paying out all sums subject to a suitable clawback. If there is concern that the partners may not be prepared to repay overpayments of profit, then the alternative is for the reserve to be made but with interest being paid out in accordance with profit shares. Where one of the participants is to retain the property, there will need to be a procedure for it to be valued on completion and letting and for the other participants' profit share to be paid on the basis of that valuation less the development costs.

Even though this may be an anathema to a developer, when considering how the profit participation works, thought should also be given to the way that losses will be paid when the joint venture agreement is entered into. It may be part of the terms of the transaction that even though there is an unlimited partnership, one of the partners will not have any liability for losses. If the document is silent and there is no other evidence of the parties' intention, the losses will be borne in the same proportion as profits would have been shared.

Even where the joint venture is a limited company, one shareholder might not wish to allow the company to fail for a number of reasons. At the time failure has occurred, it will be difficult for one shareholder to negotiate a contribution from his joint venture partner if there is no legal liability on the shareholders.

There have been successful joint ventures where property has been developed to be retained for investment by the joint venturers but these tend to be exceptional cases. The fundamental problem which makes joint ventures, other than quoted public companies, inappropriate is that of marketability of the parties' interests and the consequential adverse effect of the valuation of the participants' interests. The concerns are similar to those found in short-term joint ventures; the only practical solution is for one party to acquire the other's interest at an agreed valuation which disregards the discount which there would normally be for an undivided share in property. If an acquisition cannot take place on this basis, the only alternative is for one or other of the joint venturers to require the exercise of its right for the property to be sold under the trust for sale, if the venture is a partnership, and that is the approach that has been adopted.

The difficulty does not normally occur where there is a joint venture for development and sale, even where the property is held by trustees on a trust for sale. In the cases under consideration in this chapter, the parties have taken the view that their relationship will not continue into the indefinite future and that from its inception the joint venture is there to create a trading profit and to ensure that a sale will take place in a relatively short timescale.

XI   ENTERPRISE ZONE FINANCING

Although this chapter is not intended to deal with long-term joint venture developments which are intended as investment purchases an exception should be made for development for investment in enterprise zones. This is currently a significant area for joint ventures which is tax led and of interest to tax paying companies and individuals because of the capital allowances available on the construction costs involved.

The aim of the government in establishing enterprise zones is to provide taxation incentives and reduce statutory controls on the development of specified areas. These were chosen for their redevelopment potential, but felt to be in need of additional incentives in order to stimulate development.

Zone benefits are available for a period of ten years from designation, the first zones being designated in 1981. Benefits available include:

1. One hundred per cent initial allowances for capital expenditure on industrial or commercial buildings (this includes almost any building including offices or retail shops used for commercial purposes).

2. A simplified planning regime under which most forms of development have

deemed planning permission (within the parameters set out in the relevant Enterprise Zone Planning Scheme).

3. Exemption from general rates for industrial and commercial properties for the period of designation of the zone.

The government at present intends to create no new enterprise zones (EZs) in England. Some EZs have been more successful than others, but significant investment opportunities still exist.

The most successful to date is the Isle of Dogs (London Docklands). The cost to the public sector (in providing infrastructure and the taxation benefits) has been matched by private sector investment in the ratio of at least 1:7.

Since designation as an EZ, perceived development potential in Docklands has pushed land values from £70,000 per acre to in excess of £1.5m per acre. Rents currently being quoted for air conditioned office space are in the region of £18 per square foot, well below City rates and proving increasingly attractive to quality tenants.

The net yield which can be expected from a building in an enterprise zone is in the region of 6–8%, depending upon the quality and location of the building. This is before taking any account of the tax allowances.

XII   FUTURE TRENDS

Joint ventures are now an essential technique for property development financing. Their importance has grown and they will feature to a greater extent in the future, because of the changing requirements of the property owning institutions and tenants and the wider interest in property ownership.

Apart from property companies, the principal purchasers of commercial developments are the institutions, such as major pension funds and insurance companies and, to a greater extent today than for many years, owner occupiers.

Most institutional purchasers prefer buying let and completed developments or – if they carry out direct development or development funding – developments which are pre-let to approved tenants. This gives the institution the right to choose its tenants without having to debate the merits of the strength of covenant with a partner who is only looking to complete a letting to crystallise its profit.

A self-administered pension fund of a commercial company can buy or develop a building for the company which employs the eventual beneficiaries of the pension fund. On completion of the development, the pension fund will let it to the company on commercial terms. The beauty of the arrangement is that the rent paid by the tenant will be deductible from the profits of the company before assessing its tax liability, but the rent is not subject to tax in the hands of the trustees of the pension fund, as all non-trading income of the fund is free of tax.

It is likely that the pension fund trustees, if they decide to carry out the development themselves, will be advised to do so by means of a joint venture rather than carry the risk themselves so that they do not put the beneficiaries' funds completely at risk.

Whilst the economy remains strong and tax rates are relatively low, property development and therefore joint ventures will remain popular. In addition, the 1988 Budget changes in the tax structure, which means that there is no tax benefit in building property assets to ensure a capital gain rather than a trading profit, may encourage the turnover of schemes to make trading profits which will be available for further joint ventures.

There is an argument that we must be approaching the top of the present cycle of property development because of the number of developments which are being carried out by developers who do not have sufficient experience in their chosen field. It is when the inexperienced flood into a bull market that one knows that the market is likely to collapse. It is therefore essential now more than ever that any joint venture should include an experienced property expert.

The best joint ventures (and there are many of them) have succeeded because the potential problems underlying the relationship of the parties in the project have been underlined at the commencement of the venture and the documentation prepared accordingly. Because the parties have aired their respective positions on the material aspects of the project, they are understood and catered for. The mark of a good partnership in any field is that once the agreements have been exchanged it has not been necessary to consult them again.

Chapter 6

The Needs of the Property Company

Jim Beveridge

In this chapter I would like to consider, in some detail, the financing requirements of the property company, from a property company's perspective. The requirements are varied and I will expand on the differences which are apparent both by virtue of size and by virtue of function and intent within the sector. Throughout this chapter, I will be making reference principally to the needs of the public property companies although many of the observations will apply equally to the larger private property companies, of which there are many more.

I WHAT IS A PROPERTY COMPANY?

Property companies come in many different shapes and forms and, in particular, encompass the whole spectrum of size from the very small to the very large. Other contributors to this book have provided detailed analyses of types of property company. For the purposes of this chapter, I will confine my comments to a brief distinction between the two principal categories – the property investment company and the property trading company. I will then consider their respective financing requirements.

1 Property investment companies (PICs)

The largest element of the property sector comprises the property investment companies. These companies are primarily in business with a view to maximising growth in net asset value while, at the same time, maintaining a reasonable growth in revenue profits and also dividend payments to shareholders. The title 'property investment company' is a partial misnomer as often these companies can also be very active developers of property for long-term holding.

2 Property trading companies (PTCs)

The balance of the property sector, in general terms, comprises the property trading companies which take a variety of forms. The PTCs vary greatly in size but, in general, tend to have smaller market capitalisations than the PICs.

The PTCs develop or acquire properties with a view to their ultimate resale and realisation of income profits. They seek trading gains as opposed to net asset growth. While the PICs are essentially long-term investors taking a view over a period of many years, the PTCs must be viewed as akin to any conventional trading company with property as their 'stock in trade'. The shares of the PTCs tend to sell on a much lower multiple of earnings than the PICs.

The PTCs are normally at the smaller end of the sector but they have been growing in size of late and some have acquired investment portfolios with a view to taking a longer term perspective. However, primarily these companies remain in the market for short-term gain and should be regarded as trading companies in the conventional sense.

3 Comparable statistics

(a) *Property investment companies*

Company	Price 2.9.88	Market Capitalisation £m	Yield %
Land Securities	539	2713.8	3.1
MEPC	521	1647.1	3.4
Hammerson	612	1011.7	2.5
Slough Estates	292	811.1	3.6
British Land	303	680.2	1.8
Great Portland	335	546.7	3.2
Capital & Counties	368	484.6	3.4
Greycoat	384	333.0	1.3

(b) *Property trading companies*

Company	Price 2.9.88	Market Capitalisation £m	P/E	Yield %
Mountleigh	132	305.3	6.4	3.8
LET	125	203.9	10.4	2.1
Arlington	140	110.8	8.9	3.8

Company	Price 2.9.88	Market Capitalisation £m	P/E	Yield %
Local London	463	93.4	12.3	2.2
Clayform	235	78.8	8.0	4.8
Speyhawk	295	76.2	9.9	5.2

II CONSIDERATIONS – TYPES OF FINANCING

In considering the requirements of the property company the following types of finance, which are available, need to be examined. At the same time, it is also necessary to look at the differing requirements which arise by virtue of size which I have already defined as market capitalisation. While a generalisation can be made that all property companies have the same requirements, the differences in degree which result from the size of the companies are important and do exert a major influence on the property market.

The various types of financing available for consideration can be tabulated as follows:

1. The various types of equity or near equity financing which are available in the different market sectors. It is difficult to define exactly what is meant by equity finance but it encompasses the following specific areas:

   a. An offer for sale of part of the equity of a previously unlisted company. An offer for sale can include the shares currently held by an individual entrepreneur or can include the sale of the enlarged equity capital in the company where new cash is being raised for the business as opposed to an entrepreneur selling out his stake and realising the value of his investment.

   b. A vendor placing of shares where a company acquiring a business issues shares to the vendor of the business being acquired. The vendor, not wishing to retain the shares issued, normally arranges to place the shares for cash with institutions via the company's broker.

   c. A conventional rights issue of shares which is not unique to the property sector.

   d. A disguised equity issue by way of convertible debt or equity warrants attached to debt. This type of finance is normally restricted to the larger listed companies which have a quote for their shares and have a reputation and track record in the market which makes them attractive to institutional investors. Such institutional investors are frequently located in Continental Europe and the Far East.

2. Pure debt financing must address the following points. These points concern both the nature of the financing as well as the needs which have given rise to the various structures:

   a. Secured financing versus unsecured financing. Traditionally property companies have given security, but over the past few years the larger companies have been able to raise unsecured financing on terms equivalent to other commercial companies. Due to the ease of documentation and the lack of legal problems, unsecured finance has become an attractive option to the larger companies.

   b. Short-term financing versus long-term financing. This is also a consideration in the context of the cost at which a company is prepared to borrow. Property companies must be in a position to take a realistic view of all alternatives available and assess the likely short-term benefits, in terms of cost, which normally result from participation in the short end of the market, vis-à-vis the security obtained from the benefits of entering the longer end of the market, at fixed rates of interest.

      As a generalisation, the property trading companies tend to finance at the shorter end of the market while there is an obvious attraction to the longer end of the market for the investment companies. Where the property trading company can see a quick turnover of projects then susceptibility to fluctuations in interest rates does not create unmanageable problems. However, in the case of property investment companies, where investment properties are held as long-term assets, then there is sound logic in taking longer term financing and fixing the rate of interest. Traditionally, short-term rates of interest are lower than the rates of interest charged on a fixed rate on longer term borrowings. However, the greater certainty of controlling interest expense is the principal reason why investment companies tend to favour the longer term borrowings. By taking the long-term view on the value of the asset, it is advisable to match the liability with as long a maturity as possible. In essence the investment companies will trade margin for length of maturity.

   c. A separate topic to be considered is the issue of project financing versus general corporate financing. It is difficult, in many ways, to define this as a separate heading as it crosses the borders of secured versus unsecured and short-term versus long-term financing. However, there is something of a two-tier market in financing currently existing where the larger companies, principally the PICs looking towards long-term investment business, have taken corporate borrowings which involve giving the guarantee of the parent company to the lenders with a view to obtaining very cheap financing on a par with other commercial companies. This has to be looked at vis-à-vis the benefits of project financing which have been undertaken by the smaller companies, sometimes involving some degree of recourse only to the project in question. The various considerations are examined in further detail elsewhere in this book.

3. In considering the various types of financing avilable, it is always necessary to look at the implications of gearing, both in the context of risk/reward to the company and also in terms of risk/reward to the provider of finance.

   Under this heading, consideration will be given to levels of debt which are 'on balance sheet' with full recourse to the borrowing company, the various off-balance sheet structures which have been progressively evolving over the years while some reference will also be made to the growth of non-recourse/partial recourse types of facility which have been becoming more common in the market especially over the last two years.

While an attempt has been made to set out the different types of finance available, they are all to a certain degree inter-related and it is not possible to look at each one in isolation. Therefore, the following comments will of necessity overlap in certain respects. For instance, it is not normally possible to raise 100% debt financing for property acquisition or developments and a certain element of equity financing will always be required. The level of equity available does tend materially to influence the level of debt which can be realistically raised by the property company, whether the debt is on balance sheet with full resource or off-balance sheet or non-recourse/partially recourse.

1   Equity

Expanding property companies always have a requirement for additional equity, this is irrespective of whether they are PICs or PTCs. There are a variety of reasons why it is necessary to grow or expand the equity base in relation to the size of the property development or property acquisition being undertaken. I am not seeking to be exhaustive, but the following reasons are important:

1. The absolute level of gearing in the company, both 'on balance sheet' and 'off-balance sheet' is particularly important. As a generalisation, it is not normally feasible for a property development or a property acquisition to be financed entirely by borrowed funds. This comment is made in the knowledge that properties acquired or developed will normally have a yield on first letting which is a few percentage points below the prevailing cost of finance. This is of course a generalisation and certain types of property in certain parts of the world will give an immediate return over cost of funds but, as a rule of thumb, there is a 2–3% negative yield on first letting.

   Therefore, if the objective is to hold the properties longer term as investments, there needs to be a reasonable proportion of equity finance in each property situation to counter this initial negative yield which will be represented by a negative cash flow. The impact of high gearing is less important in the PTC where properties are developed for immediate sale and, by and large, they are able to sustain a higher level of debt across the portfolio.

2. I have already mentioned that it is difficult to isolate individual factors and,

once again, one has to look at the overall level of gearing in relation to the amount of development or acquisition risk being undertaken. Obviously if fully let buildings are being acquired, one part of the risk equation is removed, ie, the risk of having a vacant building. However, if properties are being acquired empty or are being developed on a speculative basis there is the ongoing risk that the property company will be unable to find a tenant. Therefore, it is unusual to see 100% gearing in development situations. Usually a reasonable amount of equity will be required to provide some cushion to both the property company and the lender in the event that a building remains vacant for some time after completion.

3. There is a need to maintain an acceptable ratio of debt to equity with equity being defined as the total of all shareholders' funds. This follows on from the previous point inasmuch that a level of gearing which is too high will render a company susceptible to market fluctuations and vacant buildings in the portfolio.

The property companies therefore need an active equity market which is capable of supplying funds in the quantities required from time to time. Equity comes in a variety of forms and I would like to summarise them as follows:

a. Rights issues are always available, but such issues, especially of PIC equity, traditionally, have not been generally well received by the existing shareholders.

Shares of PICs have in recent years with the exception of part of 1987 and 1988, traded at a discount to net asset value, normally in the range of 10–25%. There are a variety of reasons why the PIC shares have traded at such a discount and it is beyond the scope of this chapter to debate them. However, it must be stressed that the issue of equity by PICs, in the main, is not well received by the market unless the issue of equity is at a price above net asset value. Net asset value is difficult to ascertain because the market is constantly moving, but it is reasonable to refer to the last stated net asset value of the company as the yardstick. Straight equity issues, by way of rights issue, have therefore been difficult to achieve by the PICs because rights issues have always been at a discount to the market share price which, itself, has normally been at a discount to net asset value. This additional discount, coupled with the traditional discount at which PIC shares have stood in the market relative to net asset value, has meant an overall dilution in the asset backing of each share due to the new equity issue. With the greater emphasis of the PIC on asset growth, rights issues have been less common than other forms of capital raising.

However, the PTCs, whose share price has traditionally traded at a premium to net asset value, have been particularly active in using equity issues to finance asset acquisitions or to raise the equity portion of developments.

b. The smaller, unlisted companies have always been able to raise equity by means of a share placing via a full listing or, more recently, a listing on the Unlisted Securities Market. Amounts raised have, however, been relatively small in the overall context of total property company requirements.

c. Another form of equity raising is through a 'vendor placing'. This enables the company acquiring the asset (which itself might be another company) to issue shares to the vendor with such shares immediately placed in the market normally using the acquiring company's brokers to effect a successful distribution and placing of the shares. There are, of course, many bona fide reasons for doing a vendor placing, but many vendor placings have been no more than 'disguised' equity issues to augment the capital base of the companies in question.

d. Convertible or equity warrant issues, both domestic and via the Euromarkets, have enabled debt to be issued at beneficial rates of interest where there has been a right of conversion or warrant exercisable at a future date into ordinary equity. Such convertible or warrant issues have been at a 'strike price' of between 10–25% in excess of current market share price. This premium 'strike price' has normally enabled the issues to be successfully placed with no negative effect on the issuer's existing share price. The premium in the strike price has ensured that no net asset value dilution will occur and, hence, it overcomes the major problem of dilution caused by rights issues.

The previous paragraphs have set out the variety of types of equity which are available, from time to time, via the stock market. However, equity raising by property companies in general has not been as active as companies in other sectors for the reasons which have been highlighted. However, with the newer types of convertible and warrant issues, near equity can be successfully raised, in small quantities, without diluting net asset value per share and hence affecting the share price in the market.

2   Types of debt financing and nature of the company

In looking at the types of debt financing available to property companies, it is necessary to begin to draw more distinct differences between the PICs and the PTCs. It is also important to attempt to draw some distinctions between the acquisition of investment portfolios which are already fully tenanted and speculative developments, where no tenant has been contracted ahead of completion. In considering the two types of activity I will discuss the benefits of short-term financing versus long-term financing, fixed rate financing versus floating rate financing and the availability to the finance director of the various new flexible banking products currently available. These new products enable both currency risk and interest rate risk to be hedged at short notice with comparative ease of operation.

1 INVESTMENT PORTFOLIO ACQUISITION

Investment portfolio acquisition has largely been undertaken by the PICs although the PTCs have, of late, been more active in acquiring portfolios of fully leased investment properties.

Until recently, the acquisition of investment portfolios was restricted to the larger PICs with the larger market capitalisations. As has already been mentioned in earlier paragraphs, the difficulty facing property companies with an investment portfolio acquisition is that the initial yield on the acquisition cost of the portfolio is usually substantially lower than the interest costs of financing the acquisition. This is true even at the most competitive interest rates obtained by the largest property companies.

It is a feature of property valuation and market practice that the reversionary nature of leases is discounted and reflected in current valuations. This normally means that there is a low initial yield which can be expected to rise at the next rent review. This income deficit means that the investment portfolio acquisitions, (other than those which have been acquired via a share issue or a share placing), tend to be confined to the larger companies where there is a large element of equity value in their existing portfolio. The increases in rental income generated from that portfolio are sufficient to cover the short-term negative yield when gauged against the cost of finance on the new properties acquired. The ability effectively to finance this negative yield by way of income growth accruing from property portfolios already owned is one of the inherent strengths of the PICs and has enabled them to grow significantly in size over the last decades.

However, it is an over-simplification to state that investment portfolio acquisition has been the exclusive domain of the PICs, as existing investment portfolios have also been reasonably actively acquired over the past few years by the PTCs. It is a good example of how the PTCs have attempted to get a more secure long-term income base and hence a longer term secure cash flow to enable them to undertake their more speculative development activities with a greater degree of confidence. I have already mentioned earlier in this chapter the need to have a substantial amount of equity in each development and this is one of the ways in which the PTCs have sought to achieve this objective. More importantly this is a fair comment to make as such acquisitions have frequently involved the issue of shares to the vendor of the properties, but particularly, as it has involved a vendor placing, as described above. In conclusion, it has to be stated that the investment portfolio acquisitions by PTCs have substantially increased their equity bases and enabled the higher geared development activities to proceed.

In considering the acquisition of an investment portfolio, the pros and cons of fixed rate finance versus floating rate finance and the pros and cons of long-term finance versus short-term finance need to be examined.

In an investment portfolio purchase, it is possible to forecast the likely level of income flow with reasonable accuracy, given that, typically in the United Kingdom, rental income is reassessed on a five yearly pattern on an upwards only review basis. Whilst it is possible to forecast rental income flow, world market conditions tend to decide interest rates. Where portfolio acquisitions are being undertaken, the property company must have the ability to fix the cost of interest to take one variable out of the overall profitability equation of the portfolio acquisition. It is not the objective of this chapter to discuss the various sources but it will be clear from other chapters that numerous options are available.

For completeness, mention should be made here of mortgage and debenture finance, which are both forms of secured financing, as well as the more modern capital market products, which are unsecured, such as fixed rate Eurobonds or other floating rate capital market instruments. The latter instruments can be translated into fixed financing via such techniques as interest rate swaps which can include currency swaps, as required. Alternatively, the risks of interest rate fluctuations can be reduced by the use of so-called 'floors', 'caps' and 'collars'. These techniques can have beneficial profit and loss account consequences. More recently zero coupon or deep-discounted bonds have been available to assist in financing the initial negative yield on property acquisition. Other chapters describe these techniques and products in more detail.

2   PROPERTY DEVELOPMENT

The development of speculative buildings requires different considerations, some of which have already been mentioned earlier in this chapter. One cannot stress too much the importance of having a reasonable equity content in each development in order to cover the risks inherent in this type of activity, as discussed above.

Speculative property development is undertaken by both the PICs and the PTCs although developments normally form a much smaller proportion of the asset base of a PIC than of a PTC. No precise statistics are readily available but normally a PIC will have no more than one-quarter of its assets under development at any one time, often considerably less. In contrast, the PTC could have the bulk of its assets under development; this emphasises the relatively higher risk of the PTC's activities. On the other hand, the reward is also higher if the developments are successful.

For development activity, the need is to ensure that development finance can be obtained which is appropriate for the project, both in terms of cost and length of maturity. The development process, especially in the UK, can be long and tiresome, from the initial site assembly through planning to the completion of development and its successful letting to a tenant. This can take from two to five years or even longer in certain cases. Similarly, it is necessary to ensure that the available finance is of a sufficiently long maturity to enable the project to be successfully built out and let up to provide a good cash flow.

There are major differences of approach to development funding between property companies of varying sizes. In this context it is appropriate to consider project financing, secured on specific projects, as against general corporate financing. The availability of general corporate financing depends mainly on size. The larger property companies are able to borrow unsecured on terms equivalent to 'other corporates', with the various lenders looking only towards the corporate covenant without taking any security for their loan. In exchange, the large property corporate borrows most debt on its balance sheet and agrees certain corporate covenants. The availability of such corporate facilities enables the larger property corporates to use the 'state of the art' financial instruments to ensure maximum flexibility and cheapness. This chapter does not seek to discuss the various sources and methods, but, as an example from a user's viewpoint, the Multiple Option Facility (described in Richard Wolfe's chapter), with its ability to issue various types of commercial paper, is seen as particularly attractive in this context. The use of swaps, caps and collars are also relevant here.

Banks are prepared to provide unsecured finance in exchange for certain covenants which typically restrict the overall level of borrowing to a multiple of shareholders' funds. Shareholders' funds are defined as all sources of shareholders' funds including equity capital, share premium account, other reserves including profit and loss account and revaluation surplus. In addition, in certain cases, some interest cover covenant is often required, although this is usually waived for the larger companies. As already indicated in the context of investment portfolio acquisitions, large companies can absorb the initial interest deficit on letting up a development due to the strength of the income flowing from their existing portfolio via reviews and reversions on existing buildings.

For the smaller property company, it is unlikely that they will be able to secure beneficial corporate borrowing and they will seek specific project financing. Project financing usually has to be secured, which makes it more expensive and places more rigorous covenants on the borrowers.

However, in secured project lending, it is not unusual to arrange structured finance to include the deferment of interest via the 'roll-up' procedure, as the incremental value of the project during development will be considered by the lending sources as good security. For the smaller company, such structured finance is an essential requirement, as is the availability of 'off-balance sheet' finance. These are adequately covered in other chapters.

The previous paragraphs have considered the shorter term end of the market, but there is a need for longer term finance both for the PIC and PTC. The definition of longer term finance must necessarily be wide but it should include all types of mortgage and debenture finance and the longer end of the unsecured Eurobond market. Such finance tends to be used where the company is making a long-term investment in the property, whereas the long-term nature of such finance, usually with fixed interest rates, is inappropriate for the PTCs. Consideration should also be given to the various institutional sources of long-term funding, in particular the potential for an institutional 'take-out' following successful development and letting.

The PTCs have different needs as their objective is to develop buildings for resale at a profit at the first available opportunity. Their requirements are therefore of a shorter term duration, which traditional bank finance can usually fulfil. However, equity in a disguised form is often available by way of institutional funding for development projects where the institution typically takes a large proportion of the risk for some element of beneficial return.

3   GEARING CONSIDERATIONS

Property companies must be mindful of the overall level of gearing both 'on' and 'off-balance sheet'. It is very difficult to make comment on what is an appropriate level of gearing for a property company as it depends on a variety of factors, including:

a. The objective of the property company – whether it is a PIC, or a PTC, ie, whether the property assets are intended to be held for long-term investment or sold.

b. The level of floating rate debt as against fixed rate debt – which is a measure of the control the company has over its borrowing costs. This has to be viewed against the certainty of income, which itself depends on whether the company is developing for resale, with the attendant risk of sale, developing or acquiring for long-term investment, or indeed is a holder of investment properties having the risk of income voids in the portfolio. It is a question of balance in all situations.

c. Whether the company is borrowing secured or unsecured. If the company is borrowing unsecured the maximum permitted level of borrowings will normally be set relative to shareholders' funds, as noted above. In addition, there might also be some interest cover provision. If security is being given, banks will typically only lend a proportion of the security value up to approximately 66–75% of value, although certain banks have been prepared to lend a higher proportion on the basis of a more aggressive loan to value ratio. The bulk of lending on a secured basis, if mortgage finance and debenture finance is excluded, is from the banks who will traditionally require an equity contribution from the borrower, particularly in the case of developments. The input of this equity element and the proportion of value (or cost) which the banks are prepared to lend is therefore a constraint on development activity.

d. Constraints on gearing levels have meant that some companies have structured 'off-balance sheet' financing and development vehicles which enable the corporate gearing ratios to be contained. However critical the need, 'off-balance sheet' financing will invariably be taken into account in assessing overall risk, which to a large extent, determines the pricing of facilities. The Accounting Standards Committee of the UK Accounting Institutes has recently issued Exposure Draft 42 which specifically addresses 'off-balance sheet' financing. Michael Peat's chapter discusses this area in more detail.

III   SUMMARY

The PICs and PTCs require the following:

a. If needed, the ability to raise equity.

b. The flexibility of either fixed rate or floating rate financing, as required, and also to have access to a wide variety of secured and unsecured instruments.

c. The ability to achieve financing with a long maturity, even though longer maturity tends to imply higher interest rates. This is particularly important to PICs where length of maturity is more important than the absolute interest margin over an appropriate benchmark such as LIBOR. If the principal element of outgoings, namely interest, can be fixed then it is with some degree of accuracy that income can be forecast and both business confidence and the ability to grow can be predicated.

d. The importance of flexibility in financial structuring must be stressed, as each individual case is unique and the property company must be in a position to achieve the appropriate mix of financing required.

There is no crystal ball which can set out a formula for the appropriate level of fixed rate financing versus floating rate financing, mortgage financing versus debenture financing, long-term financing versus short-term financing. All that one can say is that there is a need to have all sources available to the property company so that the individual company board is able to make decisions as to the appropriate mix, given the prevailing market conditions.

Chapter 7

Property, Property Companies and Public Securities Markets*

Stewart Millman

The purpose of this chapter is, firstly, to review the property company sector and to consider, in particular, the ways in which the quoted property companies are now financed. In so doing, the different types of property company will be described and analysed, including the property investment company, the property development company and the various forms of 'hybrid', which tend to combine elements of both.

Secondly, the chapter examines the increasing use being made of the public securities markets to finance property, the various types of financial instrument most commonly used and whether the ends necessarily always justify the means.

The chapter concludes with a short comment on the trend towards the internationalisation of the capital markets and attitudes in the City post Big Bang.

I PROPERTY COMPANIES AS A SECTOR

Sections 1 to 4 aim to provide some background on the principles underlying the investment markets in property. Sections 5 to 7 sketch the three principal types of property company, before launching into the detailed discussion in the body of this chapter.

1 Overview of sector

Property has long had its own sector in the UK stock market (eg, in the FT All-Share Index). Furthermore, the sector is one whose boundaries are little beset by definitional disputes unlike, for example, the regular debates on whether a particular company fits better in the electrical or the electronics sector. Although

---

* I am most grateful to my colleagues David Tunstall, Richard Langford and Gary Baker for providing all the data which this paper includes, and to my secretary Linda Ball for typing the rather unappealing manuscripts.

we therefore seem intuitively to know what we mean by a property company, it is worth exploring what our intuition encompasses.

The property business obviously involves the economic exploitation of land and buildings. Yet most people would, I think, describe Brent Cross as a property development and hence Hammerson as a property company, but not Heathrow and BAA, although both Brent Cross and Heathrow derive the majority of their profits from shop rents, and a minority from service charges, and both incidentally have excellent location value. Why? Probably because Heathrow's income and value is inextricably tied to the health of the airline industry: in addition, neither the changes to, nor the number and identity of, Heathrow's airline users can be determined by BAA alone. Direct property investment and property companies therefore seem to involve control of physical land and buildings by a landlord whose return is relatively independent of the commercial success of the tenant's business.

Before a clutch of property company managing directors put pen to paper to tell me of the searching economic and commercial analyses which they demand, let me explain my point: property companies do not normally rent out hospitals, hotels or airports nor, less obviously, farms nor homes let to individuals, though all of these involve land, bricks and mortar and have location values. With a hotel or hospital, for instance, the choice is usually either to provide the full service (ie, operate the business) or not to get involved.

Thus, a better description of the property business is probably the extraction of value from land and buildings such that the landlord can take a creditor's view, rather than an equity holder's, of the occupiers. The clear identity of a 'property company' stems from this relative detachment from commercial profit cycles.

The quoted property sector owned property valued at nearly £17 billion at 31 March 1988. It owed its creditors (principally banks and other lenders) about £3 billion more than its cash, debtors and other assets. All the shares in all these companies at mid-market Stock Exchange prices on 31 March 1988 were worth nearly £13 billion. In the jargon of my trade, the property sector had property portfolios approximating £17 billion, net assets around £14 billion and a market capitalisation of nearly £13 billion. By contrast, BP had a market capitalisation of £15 billion, British Gas £7 billion and the commercial banking sector £16 billion (before Barclays' rights issue in May 1988). As with most of the UK stock market, about 70% of the shares in the property sector is owned by investment institutions.

Over 90% of the £17 billion is located in Great Britain with the remainder in the cities of North America and Australia and in Europe (principally France and the Low Countries), where high population densities limit site availability and generate high location values as in Britain. The quoted property sector is therefore much more domestic than both the average stock market company, which earns about one-third of its trading profits in a wide range of foreign countries, and the UK economy which has large import and export components.

Property company portfolios are often divided into three main categories – office, retail and industrial: residential investment is small, despite the construction sector's substantial production of housing. Our (ie, BZW's) estimate of the approximate composition of the £17 billion portfolio by value is:

Office	50% ie,	£8½ billion
Retail	20%	£3½ billion
Industrial	30%	£5 billion

'Industrial' here includes business parks although these are functionally in between the old office and industrial categories.

The office data suggests that, in physical terms, the quoted property sector owns about 30 million square feet of offices, in which perhaps a quarter of a million people work. Shops might total about 14 million square feet – equal to about 14,000 small High Street shops – plus about 100 million square feet of industrial space.

While UK property dominates the property sector of the UK stock market, the reverse is not the case. Financial statistics show the UK investment institutions as having approximately 10% of their approx £400 billion portfolios in property. I doubt if this figure is fully revalued to the current market and I would estimate that on a basis comparable to the quoted companies, the institutions have £40–50 billion in property, mainly but not entirely in Britain, plus maybe £1 billion more held in property unit trusts. Most long-term investment institutions are allowed to own direct property: perhaps 25% of long-term funds are in entities not allowed to do so, mainly Authorised Unit Trusts and Approved Investment Trusts. Foreign-resident pension funds and insurance companies also do not have significant property holdings. Thus, institutional property portfolios are about three times those of property companies: institutions own £40 billion or more of direct property versus about £10 billion worth of shares in property companies: for those institutions who can own direct property, the ratio exceeds 5:1.

In addition, there are three types of owners of investment-grade property whose portfolios are, so far as I know, unquantified but nevertheless massive – owner-occupiers; private investors, both personal and corporate; central and local government.

I have elaborated on the smaller proportion of property assets owned by quoted property companies not at all to demean them but to show one reason why the companies seem able to find a ready supply of counterparties for purchases and sales. In fact, the quoted property sector is more important to the property industry than the asset ratios suggest because their transaction frequency tends to be higher. For developments, the quoted sector is more important still, if not indeed pre-eminent with the rise of the 'new breed' of property development companies.

2 Property investment and inflation

Until the government started issuing index-linked Gilts in 1981, commercial property was the investment most directly linked to inflation. Rent is an overhead which businesses can usually afford to have rise roughly as fast as their wages bill. Thus, when I started in the City in 1971 my salary, as a graduate recruit, was £1,500 per annum and prime City rents had passed £10 per square foot per annum. In 1987 new City graduates were usually paid £7,500–£10,000 and comparable rents were £40–£50. This anecdotal evidence suggests City rent inflation of about $8\frac{1}{2}$% per annum compound and City wage inflation of about 11%: in the economy as a whole wage inflation has usually exceeded price inflation by around 2% per annum. Put another way, using an average of 100 City square feet per person, the rental of space for a graduate recruit cost about 65% of his base salary in 1971 and about 50% in 1987.

It is worth noting that corporate profits and dividends often do not track inflation as closely as wages or rents: shareholders receive what is left after everyone else has been paid. Profits can oscillate so sharply around the long-term inflationary trend as to appear to obscure it.

Inflation and the like are very long-term variables, but fortunately the mathematics of such trends have been relatively kind to us. The return, summed to infinity, on an investment with a growing income stream is the initial yield plus the growth rate at which it is compounding. (How nice to use simple arithmetic to foster the illusion of immortality!)

If the 1971 rent was £12.50 and represented an initial yield of $5\frac{1}{2}$% on the value of the property, and this compounded indefinitely at the anecdotal $8\frac{1}{2}$% rate, the return on the 1971 value would be 14% per annum. Furthermore, if the value continues to represent a $5\frac{1}{2}$% yield, an investor can sell at any time and have enjoyed a 14% per annum return. With 10% per annum growth and all else constant, the return would be $15\frac{1}{2}$% per annum, comprising $5\frac{1}{2}$% per annum income and 10% per annum capital growth. Thus, the higher the expected rate of rental inflation, the lower the acceptable initial yield and the higher the proportion of return which arises as capital, rather than income.

This simple model has powerful implications for investment in property, property companies and hence their shares. Further quantitative analysis is fairly easy.

In early 1988 long-term conventional Gilts yield about 9% per annum and unsecured loan stocks, whose credit risk is similar to leases, about $10\frac{1}{2}$% per annum, ie, $1\frac{1}{2}$% per annum over Gilts. Thus one should seek a net cash return of $11\frac{1}{2}$% per annum from property. In fact it costs more to manage property than bond portfolios and rent-review intervals cause rent receipts to lag inflation. Perhaps $1\frac{3}{4}$% per annum covers these two points, suggesting a 'required' apparent return from property of $3\frac{1}{4}$% over Gilts or around $12\frac{1}{4}$% per annum, comprising initial rental yield plus the rate of rental growth. An initial rental yield of 6% would therefore imply long-term rental growth of $6\frac{1}{4}$% per annum, about $2\frac{1}{4}$% per annum above recent price inflation of 4% and a similar relationship to wage inflation as my anecdotal example.

This approach therefore allows an investor to estimate the rental growth necessary to equate the long-term cash returns on property and long-term fixed interest. In this example, rental growth of $6\frac{1}{4}\%$ is necessary to 'break-even' on property: this is just over 2% above the recent rate of price inflation and therefore close to the rate of wage inflation one would expect if prices continue to increase at around 4% per annum.

An alternative approach is to compare property with index-linked Gilts and/or shares (equities) both of whose yields are related to inflation. This enables an investor to take inflation as a given number, and to estimate which type of asset is likely to yield larger real returns. Long-term index-linked Gilts presently offer 'real' yields (ie, yields in excess of the rate of price inflation) of about $3\frac{3}{4}\%$ per annum; using the same allowances on property of $1\frac{1}{2}\%$ per annum for credit risk and $1\frac{3}{4}\%$ for management and income lag suggests that investors should require an *actual* real return of $5\frac{1}{4}\%$ pa, or a 7% *apparent* real return from property.

The UK equity market at the end of March 1988 had a historic dividend yield of just under $4\frac{1}{2}\%$ per annum. As mentioned earlier, the risk in equity dividends is greater than property or bonds, hence the required returns should be higher, probably an *actual* margin of 3% over index-linked Gilts, or $3\frac{1}{2}\%$ *apparent* margin if we add $\frac{1}{2}\%$ per annum to cover management expenses.

The required apparent margin on equities of $3\frac{1}{2}\%$ over Gilts is slightly more than the $3\frac{1}{4}\%$ which we estimated for property. (It is composed of a higher risk margin, lower management expenses and no allowance for income lag.) However, shares yield rather less than direct property: dividends on equities need to grow about $1\frac{3}{4}\%$ per annum faster than rents to equate the long-term returns from 6% property yields and $4\frac{1}{2}\%$ share yields.

Many of the parameters in these calculations are rather subjective but this form of analysis is sufficiently robust to provide a basis on which to make investment judgments and, occasionally, to have predictive power. Two examples should suffice.

In the early 1980s, inflation and inflationary expectations fell sharply: yields on conventional Gilts fell but not so sharply, so that real interest rates rose significantly. Expectations of growth in equity dividends also rose. Property rental yields therefore had to rise if property was to maintain its relative attractiveness. Actually, property yields did not rise sufficiently and there was a consequent decline in the proportion of institutional investment directed to property. Property company shares also sharply underperformed the equity market from early 1981 to late 1983.

The second example is 1987/8. By 1987, equity yields had fallen, going as low as 3% in the third quarter, at which level they seemed out of line with property. In the event, since early 1987 institutional investment in property has been picking up; values have risen faster than inflation and property shares have outperformed the market for over a year.

The interaction of inflationary expectations and yields is probably the most revealing insight into long-term trends in commercial property and property companies. It is important, finally, to understand its limitations.

First, it is a form of very *long-term* analysis. However, one has to survive the short term in order to enjoy the long term: the casualties of the early 1970s property boom generally ran out of cash before long-term rental growth came through. Survival is a matter of cash flow, to which I have devoted most of a subsection of this chapter.

Second, looking at property market averages does not deny that there is room for selection skill to enhance returns in property. I would caution that the average return among all property portfolios must be the true market average: almost anyone with professional self-esteem believes he has above average selection skill, yet roughly half these beliefs are wrong! Within these bounds, there is room for people with proven selection skill. Indeed, I strongly suspect that the property market is less efficient than the equity market, in the technical sense that all information is less thoroughly disseminated, and variations from 'correct' pricing consequently more frequent.

Third, the above analysis cannot be applied in the same way to compare direct property with property companies' shares. This is because dividends from property companies, far from being independent of rental yields and growth, are derived directly from rents. Consequently, their relative values are much more a matter of micro-analysis.

3   Corporate and tax structure

Detachment from much of the commercial activity of the tenants is central to our conception of property investment. The relative predictability both of income flows and of many decision points (rent reviews, termination of leases, etc) facilitates fine structure financial planning. If the macro decision on property investment is driven mainly by the interaction of inflationary expectations and yield gaps, the tactical decisions on ownership structure and even portfolio turnover have often been driven more by tax, I believe, than is often realised. To appreciate why, it is necessary to go back to the immediate post-war period.

Inflationary expectations began to increase, and wartime building controls eased, in the early 1950s. Corporation tax was introduced in 1960 and, more importantly, full capital gains tax in 1965. Personal rates of tax on unearned income were very high. Consequently the 1950s was a period when large investors began to switch from bonds into property (and into shares – the famous Ross-Goobey switch[1]): not only were the prospects for better total returns but capital gains were tax-free. Thus there was little inhibition to using a company to hold investment property: taxation of income could hardly be worse than a personal receipt, even with shortfall directions, and there was no problem with capital gains taxation. It is not surprising, therefore, that many of the famous British investment property 'empires' accumulated their seed-corn in this period (Land Securities, MEPC, Hammerson, Stock Conversion) as well as High Street retailing groups such as GUS and Sears.

---

1   Mr Ross-Goobey is credited with being the driving force behind the Prudential's decision in the late 1940s to switch substantial quantities of Gilts into equities in order to increase yield, and incidentally generate very large capital gains.

However, capital gains tax paid by a company on its internal capital gains has never been available as a credit against tax incurred by a shareholder on his capital gains on the shares of that company. (Contrast this with the imputation system introduced in 1972 whereby UK shareholders receive tax credits with their dividends equal to advance corporation tax paid by their companies.) Finally, note that rollover relief is not available on properties in investment portfolios, only on properties whose owners trade in them (that detachment again!).

Owning investment properties through UK companies, or groups of companies, has therefore been systematically disadvantageous since 1972 relative to direct ownership of the same properties by UK tax-payers and gross funds and by non-residents. This point is worth reinforcing with an oversimplified example.

A notional Mammon House was purchased in 1965 for £4m, had £6m of capital spent on it and was sold in 1982 for £40m – these are realistic figures for a smallish, well-situated City office. Consider the position of direct ownership versus purchase by a UK company, Mammon Holdings, which is itself sold after Mammon House to put its shareholders in funds:

	£m
Sale proceeds	40
Cost	(10)
Gain	30

	Mammon Holdings	*Direct ownership*
Gross gain	30	30
Tax on capital gain	(9)	
Available to shareholders	21	

	Tax on CG	*Net proceeds*	*Tax on CG*	*Net proceeds*
UK gross funds	—	21	—	30
Non-resident	—	21	—	30
UK tax-payer	6.3	14.7	9	21

This is the reason why institutions' portfolios of direct property are so much larger than their holdings of property company shares.

The extra layer of tax on capital gains could have been deferred by not selling Mammon House but selling Mammon Holdings, but in this case the shareholders in Holdings would have taken a lower price to reflect the contingent tax liability. Alternatively, they could sell House but not Holdings, but have no cash. Either alternative only saves tax by diminishing the shareholders' position.

Indexation of base cost for capital gains tax since 1982 helped reduce the tax charge, but not its structure or the above consequences. The 1988 Budget went much further and moved the base date for taxation on capital gains forward from 1965 to 1982. I believe that this is the closest the property companies are ever likely to get to the pre-1962 position. Gains accruing from now on will be little better off – the tax rates are to be 35% on corporate capital gains and up to 40% on personal gains. Thus the main significance of the change is the endowment on longstanding property portfolios: contingent tax liabilities equivalent to 10% or more of the portfolios of quoted companies (ie, tax liabilities of around £2 billion) have been removed. This confers considerable freedom on property company managements before capital appreciation, and the attendant contingent tax liabilities, again accumulate.

Since property investors expect appreciation well in excess of inflation (if not why not buy index-linked Gilts?), the change in capital gains taxation alone seems unlikely to reverse the trend of the last 25 years against the formation of property investment companies.

4 Capital structure and cash flow

Yields on property portfolios are below rack-rent levels because not all the properties will have had their rent reviewed very recently: some elements may be highly reversionary, ie, have very old leases with no recent reviews. Consider, then, Mammon Holdings with a decent average rental yield on market value of 5.5%:

Gross rents	5.50%	
Expenses	(1.00)	
Pre-tax income	4.50	
Tax (35%)	(1.57)	
Net income	2.93	
Dividends	(1.63)	[=2.2% including
Retained income	1.30	ACT credit]

(Expenses have again been set at 1% and in practice may involve non-tax-deductible items; the dividend yield is aligned to that of the FTA Property Sector at end March 1988, allowing for a 10% discount to assets.)

Retained income of 1.3% of portfolio value is not going to finance much increase in the company's operations, so what can Mammon's board do to expand?

Rental income is stable and predictable, the type of income beloved of bankers and other lenders, so one possibility is to borrow. Let us assume that Mammon have found a modern building, Titan House, rack-rented to give a 7% yield on the all-in purchase cost of £50m. Mammon sets the borrowing so that the rent will pay all the interest, for which we will take the long-term rate of $10\frac{1}{2}$% used earlier.

Deducting 1% for expenses, etc, 6% is available for debt service, so that about 57% (ie, £$28\frac{1}{2}$m) of the cost of Titan House can be borrowed: put another way, Mammon has bought a £50m building with £$21\frac{1}{2}$m of its own money. After five years, the new rent, on review, is 35% higher, at 9.5% of original cost, showing $6\frac{1}{4}$% per annum compound growth. If rack-rent yields on Titan House are still 7%, the capital value will also have risen by 35%.

Has Mammon made money by gearing up to buy Titan House? Just about. Had Mammon bought Minnow House for the same £$21\frac{1}{2}$m at a yield of the same 7%, it would, after five years, have received rent less expenses of £6.45m and have an asset worth £29.5m. In Titan after five years, it has an asset worth £67.7m, less debt of £$28\frac{1}{2}$m, equals £39.2m; rent received and interest paid cancel each other out. Ignoring compounding effects, after five years Mammon is better off by about £$3\frac{1}{4}$m pre-tax or £2.1m after tax.

This is, I think, illustrative of two points. First, the difficulty of achieving very much with a static portfolio if rental yields are low and interest rates higher than the rate of inflation. Secondly, think how tight the cash position is in borrowing to buy Titan House – Mammon has a £50m risk but zero net cash for five years and has not repaid any of the loan. With reviews increasing the rent by 35% every five years, it takes about 15 years to repay the £$28\frac{1}{2}$m loan from internal cash flow.

Any rental void or increase in outgoings in the first five years will force Mammon to subsidise Titan House from the rest of its portfolio. If the whole portfolio is Titan-like, either Mammon must have understanding bankers or it must sell a property to realise cash – Mammon is, of course, insolvent if it cannot meet its liabilities as they arise, regardless of whether its total assets exceed its total liabilities.

The Titan House example is in some ways benign: interest rates are fixed and the building is rack-rented. Consider £50m for Sixties House which is highly reversionary, a 2% current yield for four years, needs £10m spent on it then and will be rented out for £$6\frac{1}{2}$m-plus after five years. Mammon borrows half the cost, rolling up the income deficit and, two years on, interest rates go to 15%. Now Mammon's bankers have to be *exceptionally* understanding or Mammon must sell up quickly. However, interest rates are high for everyone so many people are selling property and the market is depressed.

Sixties House is not such a far-fetched example. It is a parallel to the property crash in the early 1970s when highly-geared property investors often did not survive to test their long-term judgments.

Now, in the late 1980s, various factors should militate against a recurrence of these events. Down to medium sized private companies it is possible to fix interest rates for some years with interest rate swaps (see section 4.2, below), so there is no excuse for a rise in rates catching out a property company for some years. More importantly, many of the present managements of public property companies, and of their lenders, were around 10 or 15 years ago. They are, I hope, unlikely to make the same mistakes again, especially in an environment of low inflation.

What long-term strategy can Mammon adopt? I believe that there are four choices:

1. Continue to invest mainly its own money (if you like, the Minnow House approach), accepting relatively low activity.

2. Issue its own shares when their dividend cost is below rental yields. Here there are stock market constraints, discussed later.

3. Accept the need to sell properties regularly, and try to choose the timing to suit Mammon, the seller.

4. Conduct the property investment inside a group that has cash flow from other activities so that property investment decisions do not strain the whole edifice.

A fifth alternative, for Mammon to apply its expertise to foreign property markets with smaller yield gaps, is outside the scope of this book. The other four approaches are covered in this chapter.

5   Conventional property companies

'Conventional' labels companies which aim to create value for shareholders by means of a retained property portfolio and encompasses the first two choices offered for Mammon Holdings. The boundary between investment and trading companies is usually fairly clear because until the tax year 1987/8 companies paid lower tax rates on capital gains than income profits and were therefore careful to preserve the distinction. Large groups therefore often have separate trading and investment subsidiaries. Many borrow in order to finance either developments of existing properties or portfolio additions. Capitalising interest in the development phase, eg, until the first valuation, is quite common (ie, adding interest incurred to the book value of the asset, rather than charging to the profit and loss account). The principle of capitalisation seems supportable though the practice can be rather subjective. More important, I believe, is that regardless of the accounting policy, cash has been spent and needs somehow to be funded, just like all the other development expenditure.

The large public companies can raise long-term debt through the public market in order to raise funds. As discussed more fully in section 4.2, the very largest companies such as Land Securities, Slough Estates and MEPC have more choices available.

Smaller companies tend to be more dependent on bank loans, usually of shorter maturity than public market debt. At least the growth in interest rate swaps (also discussed in section 4.2) enables these companies to fix the rate of interest. Thus the nature of the interest cost can be separated from the draw-down and repayment of funds.

Issues of shares to raise cash for quoted conventional property companies are more problematic because the market price of their shares frequently stands at a discount to the apparent net asset value per share (NAV), calculated taking properties at current market value. Since asset appreciation is the primary objective, both the directors and the shareholders of such companies are reluctant to issue shares for a price below NAV.

The interaction of share prices and asset values is the main topic of section II of this chapter. Suffice it to say here that the effect of the discount is that, to my knowledge, there have been very few new flotations of property companies whose shares are priced in relation to their asset value for at least five years. On the rare occasions when the discount to NAV is narrow or non-existent, existing quoted companies may issue ordinary shares or convertibles, often by way of rights issues.

Quoted conventional property companies are merged from time to time or bought by companies outside the sector. Since this activity needs new flotations, the quoted conventional property companies have as a group been shrinking noticeably by number of names and rather more gradually by relative value. This is in marked contrast to the development companies described next.

Nevertheless, the tradition of property investment companies has been so long established in the UK that over 85% of the capitalisation of the quoted property sector is still represented by conventional property companies and under 15% by development companies, or service companies including chartered surveyors.

6 Development companies

Development companies have evolved logically as the extension of the third choice identified earlier for Mammon Holdings: if selling properties is inevitable, why not make a virtue out of necessity and exert as much effort in maximising the proceeds from these properties as on their acquisition and management?

The crucial switch in the managements' attitude is when they set out, first, to discover what the buyers want and then either to find it or make it, rather than seeking the best price for what they already have for sale. Successful housebuilders have long operated in this manner but only recently has any of the commercial property business adopted the jargon of design, production, marketing and closing of the deal, more common in manufacturing than the property sector.

The main consequence of the high transaction volume for the companies themselves is the need for medium-term finance. Public mortgage bonds are rarely appropriate for portfolios which turn over rapidly and are usually without a rent roll. Development financing is usually one of two forms: either (i) the completed development is pre-sold to an occupier, long-term investor and/or (ii) the site acquisition and construction phases are carried out in a joint venture partnership substantially funded by an external investor and normally 'off-balance sheet' to the development company. (Michael Peat's chapter discusses 'off-balance sheet' financing very fully. Note that the 'off-balance sheet' financing rules are currently under review by The Institute of Chartered Accountants.)

A number of the companies make a point of providing a range of financing packages on their developments to occupiers who do not wish to purchase outright. In arranging 'sales aid finance' for their customers the analogy with manufacturers of other industrial capital equipment becomes closer. Mortgage finance is equivalent to a long-term loan secured on plant. They also offer 'property finance leases', also discussed by Michael Peat, which are like mortgages in guaranteeing the lender full amortisation of his principal and do not necessarily cover the full value of the property: like a finance lease on plant, all the payments are tax deductible. Selling the property and taking back a conventional property lease is more closely equivalent to an equipment rental contract.

£1.7 billion, about 13%, of the nearly £13 billion capitalisation of the quoted property sector is accounted for by companies generally regarded as developers. The value primarily comprises Arlington Securities, London & Edinburgh Trust, London & Metropolitan, Regalian and Speyhawk, plus Mountleigh and Rosehaugh both of whose market statistics are, as will be seen, halfway between conventional and development companies.

The newness of the group is striking. Its market capitalisation has probably multiplied ten-fold in five years. Three of the seven names have come to the stock market in the last five years, compared to a dearth of flotations of investment companies. The greatest economic value contributed has probably been in helping accelerate the development cycle.

7 Hybrids

Hybrids represent the final option open to Mammon Holdings: funding property investment with cash flow from unconnected operations. While internally this can make an excellent fit, the stock market tends to value quoted companies either relative to their NAV (ie, property investment companies and investment trusts) or as a multiple of their earnings and dividends (almost everything else): the multiple for earnings-valued companies is only rarely increased to reflect a greater asset backing. Conversely, property yields are far too low for conventional property companies to sustain an earnings valuation: a 5% net rental yield is equivalent to a price/earnings ratio of over 30 compared to the current market averages of 10–12. However illogically, therefore, the valuation of combined trading/investment groups is often below the sum of their parts.

The hybrids which do exist most often combine civil engineering/contracting with a property portfolio: Trafalgar House and Taylor Woodrow are obvious examples. The logic of this combination is very close to that of property developers who like to retain a few properties to add some stability to their earnings: both groups are essentially choosing to keep for themselves the occasional choice morsel from their production line.

The most consistent, if quiet, proponent of aligning cashflow businesses with property portfolios is probably Sir Jeffrey Sterling. In the early 1970s Sterling Guarantee Trust, although regarded primarily as a property company, always had a clutch of service businesses. SGT was merged with Town & City a few years later, but the combined entity's recent amalgamation with Peninsular & Oriental has again created a group similar to Sterling Guarantee but on a much larger scale: P & O has a range of service businesses including, incidentally, both a large construction division in Bovis and two major 'Heathrow type' assets, Olympia and Earl's Court, acquired many years ago by SGT.

II   INVESTMENT IN DIRECT PROPERTY VERSUS PROPERTY INVESTMENT COMPANIES

1   Similarity of portfolios

It is, of course, the case that property portfolios are not as homogeneous as are share portfolios. Investors in UK shares select from a limited range of about 1,500 available assets, and all ordinary shares in ICI are identical to each other. In contrast, if one looks closely enough, almost every property is different from its neighbour and from all other properties in size, construction or location. More importantly, location values essentially recognise scarcity, ie, precisely the fact that it is impossible to expand the supply of high-value properties, in contrast to the way that a highly-rated company can issue more shares.

Standing back from the detail, however, institutional property portfolios *are* fairly similar to those of the quoted property investment companies (PICs). They share a similar view of credit risk (covenant), lease terms, size of investment and required yields. Both sets of portfolios are heavily weighted, by value, to Southern England, though perhaps institutions moved somewhat earlier, and hence more heavily, into retail property.

2   Asset-based valuations

It is not surprising that the value placed by stock market investors on shares in PICs is much more closely related to calculated asset values than to the 'normal' stock market parameters of Price Earnings Ratio (PER), where the PER is the ratio of the market value of a company's shares to its after-tax profits.

Table 1 shows the net asset value and market value figures for the larger PICs as at 25 March 1988. Two patterns are striking:

1. a. The market valuations are all close to the estimated NAVs.
   b. The scatter of the valuations relative to the average of a 10% NAV discount is small – the total range is 20% discount to 11% premium.

2. a. The average PER is very high.
   b. The scatter of PER is very wide – 6.3 to 47.9.

TABLE 1

Market Statistics of Major Asset-Valued Companies
as at the end of March 1988

	Price 25/3/88 p	Market cap £m	NAV p	Discount to NAV %	Yield %	Prospective Price/ earnings ratio
Bilton (P)	385	163	400	3	5.3	17.1
British Land	303	677	350	13	1.8	19.5
Brixton Estate	285	234	290	1	3.7	26.6
Capital & Counties	388	529	410	5	3.6	21.5
Chesterfield	650	155	820	20	3.1	21.6
Estates Property	267	78	240	−11	5.0	20.0
Frogmore Estates	340	134	350	2	4.2	6.3
Great Portland Est	301	506	310	2	3.8	28.6
Greycoat Group	360	318	360	0	1.3	21.3
Hammerson Prop A	583	941	670	12	2.9	27.1
Imry International	377	97	430	12	2.9	18.8
Laing Properties	413	275	465	11	3.4	15.1
Land Securities	532	2745	615	13	3.3	27.2
London Shop Props	229	206	240	4	4.3	20.2
Lynton	403	194	390	−3	2.1	47.9
MEPC	521	1682	580	10	3.8	24.2
Peachey Property	410	177	490	16	4.0	17.0
Peel Holdings	320	151	350	8	2.3	15.6
Property Security	171	142	175	2	2.5	34.4
Scottish Met	135	130	140	3	5.5	24.1
Slough Estates	280	790	280	0	3.8	18.3
Warnford Investments	920	88	1,150	20	2.1	27.2
Wates City	178	234	210	15	2.4	30.6
Capitalisation-weighted averages				10		24.3

Notes: (1) NAV, PER and yield figures are BZW estimates.
   (2) Negative figures for discount to NAV indicate premiums.
   (3) Prospective data is to the next full-year results due to be announced
       for each company.

By contrast, for the stock market as a whole (excluding property companies and investment trusts), market capitalisation is around $2\frac{1}{2}$ times NAV, mainly in a range 1 to 5, and the average prospective PER 11 in a range of 8 to 14.

The empirical evidence therefore points very strongly to PIC values in the stock market being driven by the Net Asset Value, ignoring the Price Earnings Ratio. Dividend yield is less determinant but PICs have lower average dividend yields than the market.

3   Long-term investment performance of direct property and shares in property investment companies

Two factors should substantially determine the investment performance of PIC shares relative to portfolios of direct property: the relative appreciation in the respective portfolios and the discount or premium at which PICs trade in relation to their Net Asset Values. In both cases, we shall use the NAVs estimated by property sector analysts for PICs, rather than those the companies publish, and ignoring contingent tax on capital gains. This is because companies differ in their valuation frequency, carrying value of developments, etc: a more standardised basis of comparison is needed. The evidence (not shown here) is that share prices correlate better with the market NAV estimates than published valuations.

Below is Richard Ellis' performance data for UK property (which is a composite of separate office, retail and industrial sectors) and BZW's estimates of the NAV growth of four major PICs with mainly UK portfolios (Land Securities, MEPC, British Land, Slough Estates).

It is apparent that the NAV of the PICs has outperformed the direct property index. Property portfolios are not publicly valued and traded (pending property securitisation, thus strictly 'not yet'), so one cannot be sure that the direct property index is a true reflection of portfolio experience. However, I know of no grounds to allege systematic error: the Jones Lang Wootton index has very similar figures. Until hard evidence to the contrary is adduced, we must accept the conclusion that the large PICs, and hence presumably the whole PIC sector, have increased NAV faster than the average direct property portfolio.

Four principal causes seem possible:

i. *Gearing*

The extra NAV generated for Mammon Holdings by investing in Titan House rather than Minnow House demonstrates this effect. Titan produced NAV appreciation of £$21\frac{1}{2}$m to £$39\frac{1}{2}$m, ie, 84% over five years, or 12.9% pa compound with Mammon geared through a debt: equity ratio of $28\frac{1}{2}$:$21\frac{1}{2}$ or 133%. With Minnow House Mammon's NAV growth was 37% or 6.5% pa compound, without gearing.

The debt:equity ratio of PICs is presently 25–30% and has probably averaged 35% since 1980/81, one quarter of Mammon's. Thus if the Mammon example is typical, gearing might account for about $1\frac{1}{2}$% pa of the higher NAV growth shown by the PICs.

TABLE 2

Increases in Property Values 1980–1988

	Richard Ellis Monthly Index of capital growth				*BZW estimates of NAV of major PICs*
	Office	Retail	Industrial	Total	
1980/81	20.7%	13.9%	2.1%	15.1%	+28.2%
1981/82	9.3%	12.1%	7.8%	9.8%	+8.4%
1982/83	3.6%	1.4%	−0.5%	2.1%	+6.7%
1983/84	−0.3%	9.1%	−4.3%	1.3%	+5.7%
1984/85	−0.1%	10.0%	−10.4%	0.7%	+3.6%
1985/86	−0.9%	9.2%	−4.0%	1.6%	+5.5%
1986/87	6.4%	6.8%	2.5%	6.0%	+28.4%
1987/88	15.8%	15.6%	19.3%	16.4%	+50.0%
Cumulative	66.2%	109.5%	10.2%	65.0%	230%
Compound rate pa	6.6%	9.7%	1.2%	6.5%	16%

Note: Years to 31 March   Years to 30 June

ii. *Sector Weighting*
   The PICs on average probably have lower weightings in industrial property (despite Slough being mainly industrial) than the Richard Ellis index or the institutional property market. However, PICs generally are also probably lighter in retail property than the index or the institutional market. Industrial property has under performed the average and retail over performed so these two sector differences produce opposite effects. My guess is that they roughly cancel each other out.

iii. *Size*
   Smaller portfolios can be more active than large ones but, as we see soon, direct property is not particularly liquid anyway, so among already very large portfolios, size differences do not seem adequate to explain the difference.

iv. *Individual Property Differences*
   The residual differences over the seven years seem to be attributable to differences in property selection, development, management and sale.

Many of these factors might very generally be grouped under the heading 'Management'. If so, we cannot escape the conclusion that the PICs' managements have been better than average at generating increasing property capital values.[2]

Before passing on, a word about gearing. Institutional property portfolios do not normally gear, ie, borrow. Unsurprisingly, you may think: pension funds and insurance companies are the dominant buyers of bonds issued in the public market and thus the dominant lenders of long-term money. PICs are among the more regular borrowers in the long-term fixed-interest markets, so the institutional investors are readily lending to PICs. If an institution's fixed-interest desk lends funds to a PIC, it should have terms on which it would lend on a mortgage secured on institutional property. One presumes therefore that institutional property managers have not sought to gear their property portfolios.

A second determinant of the investment performance of PIC shares is the discount to NAV at which they trade. Graph 1 below shows the discount, or premium, at which the shares of the same four large PICs have traded since 1980 to their estimated NAV. Over the long run, changes in valuation relative to NAV are of much less importance than the appreciation in NAV. In the shorter run, the valuation relative to NAV can be an indicator of overall confidence levels in the stock market as a whole, as well as a good measure of the *relative* value of shares in individual property companies.

The long-term element missing from the conventional analysis, from which the data on this graph is drawn, is tax on capital gains, which would be payable if the PIC sold the properties at the values on which the NAV calculations are based. This contingent tax liability is omitted from the NAV calculation. To this extent the NAV is overstated and the discount to NAV represented by the prices of PIC shares overstated.

4   Investment performance of property investment company shares

Graphs 2 and 3 on page 186 show the absolute performance (ie, in simple cash terms) of the property sector of the UK stock market since 1980 (Graph 2) and, again in more detail, since 1 January 1986 (Graph 3). The picture is one of good long-term appreciation: from the beginning of 1980 to end-March 1988, the property sector index (which is dominated by PICs) has appreciated, roughly, from 310 to 1,155 which is 273% appreciation or 17.2% pa compound. Furthermore, in Graph 3 the present level of 1,155 shows a good recovery from the 1987 crash low, being 15% off the high of 1,355 and 33% above the low around 870.

2   I have ignored income differentials in these comparisons, for simplicity's sake. Retained income makes a small positive contribution to PIC NAV performance because I have used the capital-only property index, but I have no data on relative rental income and management costs, and in the opposite direction any disposal by a PIC generates a tax charge to deduct from the NAV. Therefore, I doubt if omitting income invalidates the conclusion.

Graph 1. Valuation of PIC shares relative to estimated NAV

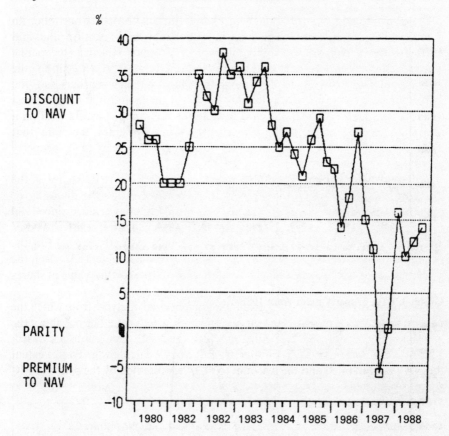

One comparison is with property capital values:

	8-year total	Annual rate
Appreciation in:		
Richard Ellis Property Index	92.1%	8.5%
NAV of major PICs	230%	16.1%
Property share prices	273%	17.2%

It is immediately evident that the general improvement in stock market ratings has been transmitted to property companies since their valuation has risen much faster than their NAVs, as we saw in the discounts.

Graph 2. FTA property index since 1980

HIGH:　1351.30 13/10/87,LOW:　309.57　8/ 1/80,LAST:　1155.30

Graph 3. FTA property index since 1986

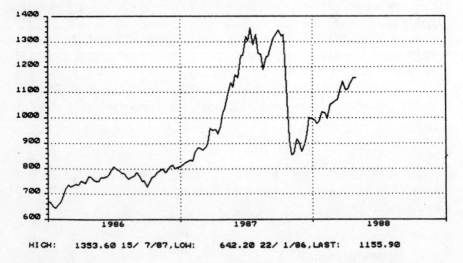

HIGH:　1353.60 15/ 7/87,LOW:　642.20 22/ 1/86,LAST:　1155.90

Have they been a good investment in stock market terms? The next pair of graphs (Graphs 4 and 5) shows the ratio of the property sector index to the overall UK stock market. The conclusion is that property shares under performed the overall market very severely – about 46% – from early 1981 to early 1987 as the ratio of the sector index to the market index fell from 1.63 to 0.88. Before and after this long, negative period the relative performance was positive.

The rationale for this performance pattern is simple and logical as shown in

Graph 4. Property sector relative performance since 1980

HIGH: 1.63   2/ 4/81, LOW: 0.88   5/ 3/87, LAST: 1.22

Graph 5. Property sector relative performance since 1986

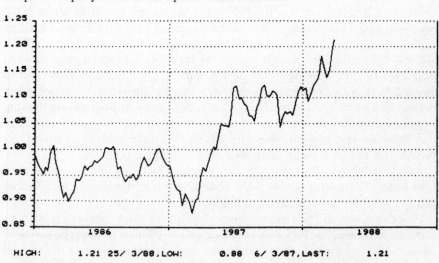

HIGH: 1.21   25/ 3/88, LOW: 0.88   6/ 3/87, LAST: 1.21

Table 2. The periods of outperformance of the overall stock market represent times when property values have been rising sharply. Relative underperformance arises when growth in property values lags other investment markets.

The performance of property shares as a group can be summarised as follows:

i. property shares should outperform both direct property and the stock market when values in both are rising strongly (1986 and the first half of 1987);

ii. property shares should outperform direct property but under perform the stock market when the stock market is rising but property is stagnant (1981–86); and

iii. good property markets and poor stock markets will cause property shares to under perform property and out perform equities in general (second half of 1987 – early 1988).

It seems logical to conjecture (supported by the experience of 1972–74) that property shares will under perform both direct property and the stock market if both are falling.

5   Property investment companies and their valuation relative to NAV

PIC shares appear to trade in the stock market on discounts to NAV similar to those at which Investment Trusts trade relative to the values of their portfolios of shares – in each case the range is apparently usually 10–15%.

In fact, this is not really the case – PIC shares really trade much closer to NAV. Quite apart from the fact that the PIC sector has traded close to or above NAV (eg, 1987) which Investment Trusts have not done as a group, allowance must be made for taxation. Investment Trusts are exempt from tax on capital gains, PICs are not. Before the 1988 Budget moved the base date for capital gains forward from 1965 to 1982, contingent tax on PIC capital gains probably amounted to about 20% of NAV. Subsequently this has probably fallen to 10%. Shareholders in PICs cannot receive the benefit of these capital gains without paying this tax, any more than they can enjoy income profits free of tax. Consequently, I believe that there is a very good argument for basing PIC share analysis on what I call NNAV (net net asset value, after deducting contingent tax).

Based on NNAV, PIC shares trade on small discounts, much smaller than Investment Trusts (for which NAV and NNAV are the same). Two factors account for this relatively higher valuation.

Property assets of PICs are relatively difficult for stock market investors to acquire for themselves. Not only may particular buildings or areas be scarce or unavailable, but even single properties are very large investments in financial terms and quite beyond the pockets of almost every stock market investor. Contrast this with Investment Trusts, most of whose portfolios comprise freely tradeable shares with the unit of investment the same as that for the Investment Trust shares themselves.

Secondly, liquidity in PIC shares is often better than in direct property, as regards time to transact, transaction costs and transaction size.

The difference in liquidity is even more striking, considering that the total direct property market is many times the size of the PIC market. This contrast provides the main impetus to property securitisation, as well as providing an

	PIC shares	Direct property
Time between initiation of purchase and completion of transaction	Minutes to days, occasionally weeks	Typically months
Total costs of purchase and sale as percentage of value	Usually 1–2%	Typically 5%
Size of transaction	Usually: Up to £100m or more quite feasible, if company large enough	Over £50m can be difficult. Over £100m can be very difficult

influence to lower discounts to NAV for PICs relative to their underlying assets, in contrast to Investment Trusts most of whose shares offer very similar liquidity to that of their underlying assets.

6 Impact of taxation on managements of property investment companies

Not deducting contingent tax on portfolio appreciation when estimating PIC NAVs may well have inhibited active management of the property portfolios of PICs. In the example in section 1.3, Mammon Holdings would have crystallised a contingent tax liability of $22\frac{1}{2}$% of the building's NAV contribution if it had sold Mammon House. Although an extreme example, it does illustrate how not deducting contingent tax in NAV calculations tends to inhibit portfolio optimisation: few PIC managers would be sufficiently confident judges of the relative merits of two properties to reduce the apparent NAV by $22\frac{1}{2}$% in order to switch.

This is another major difference between PICs and the developers. The latter take for granted that they will pay tax on the added value they generate, in their case through income profits. Here also is the origin of the jocular comment I once made to a friend that 'one or two PICs were dying of boredom turning £1 into 80p' (the discount to NAV was then 20% on PIC shares). The joke was an exaggeration to the extent that it ignored NAV appreciation and focused on the discount at which the shares stood. It did, however, identify one cause of the near-paralysis which has occurred in one or two cases in the property sector. Investment analysts would, in my opinion, do the company managements a very good turn, as well as giving themselves a fairer picture, by looking at net-of-tax NAVs—ie NNAVs.

7 Property unit trusts

Authorised Unit Trusts (AUTs) (ie, those which are regulated by The Department of Trade & Industry and available for sale to the public) have not until now been allowed to own property, probably because the intrinsic illiquidity of property greatly impairs redemption by unit holders. However, rules for property AUTs are about to be published for the first time. Until these come into effect, the only UK property unit trusts (PUTs) are those available to funds granted tax exemption by the Inland Revenue, normally charitable or pension fund investors.

The benefit offered by PUTs is to allow investment in properties which are too large for any individual holder to own outright. However, the PUTs' investment performance is generally described as disappointing. One reason is that they have usually been reverse geared, ie, uninvested cash has been accumulated until sufficient funds are available to acquire a new investment: all income is usually distributed. To go into net borrowing would greatly reduce a unit holder's hope of redeeming his investment. Thus the PUTs are placed between the rock of reducing already small liquidity for unit holders and the hard place of under performance.

Consequently, PUTs have not grown very fast and have been shrinking for most of the last few years. One or two PUTs have a backlog of redemption requests and one or two have been taken over entirely. Property unit trust assets probably approximate £2 billion.

In addition to these true PUTs, a number of insurance companies also manage unitised property pools for (tax-paying) policy holders and for the smaller pension funds, many of whom invest their assets mainly by selecting among many specialised unitised pools.

The improved capital performance of property-related investments in the past one or two years may well increase subscriptions to the property unit trusts and unitised pools. If not, this part of the industry would not appear to have a particularly bright future.

8 Prospects

To offer a view of the whole UK property market is beyond the scope of this chapter, and some more limited comments must suffice.

Yield comparisons seem presently quite favourable to property investment. However, to sustain much increase in property values may well need the occupiers of property to continue their strong trading performance and cashflow generation of the past few years, which is not beyond doubt. Graph 4 showed how the, basically earnings-driven, stock market has generally outperformed property-company values and by implication it illustrates how much corporate earnings have grown ahead of property values. This is particularly significant for industrial and business park property where owner-occupiers have been a significant force. Similarly, the Crash has taken the white heat out of City of London values and, elsewhere, a large volume of retail footage has been, or is being, built. Present forecasts are for a slowly declining trend in UK corporate profits until at least late 1989: I cannot yet guess if this would be adequate to maintain the rate of increase in property values.

As to the PICs, it would be very healthy if the tax windfall and consequent lower discounts to NAV were to stimulate greater activity in stock market and other corporate transactions. Inhibitions to portfolio optimisation are now much reduced and the stock market is usually fairly efficient at directing capital to managements who have demonstrated their good stewardship.

III EARNINGS-VALUED PROPERTY COMPANIES – THE 'DEVELOPERS'

1 Earnings valuations in general

Section 2 demonstrated three factors about stock market valuations of shares in PICs: how the values are driven mainly by NAV, how (like the other closed-end portfolio sector – investment trusts) the valuation tends to be either at or below NAV, and how, after allowing for contingent tax on portfolio appreciation, the discount on PICs is usually below that on investment trusts.

Most stock market shares, not only in London, are valued on an earnings, not an asset, basis. To ask why is probably the best way to understand the difference between the earnings-valued property companies (EVPs) and the PICs. The Industrial Group of the FT All-Share index comprises all sectors bar financials and oil companies: it is valued at 2 to $2\frac{1}{2}$ times NAV (my guess) and 11 times earnings for the 12 months to mid-1988. Expressed differently, the average industrial company has earnings of about 9% and NAV of about 40% of its market capitalisation.

The after-tax return on equity of the average industrial company is therefore 9%/40% or around 20% pa, whereas passive interest rates have been about 10% pre-tax or $6\frac{1}{2}$% after tax. Therein lies the reason for buying shares over NAV: the profits generated by the company are over three times those earned by putting its net assets on deposit.[3] Note that NAV mainly derives from the cost of buying the assets into an ongoing business, not the goodwill price for which a profitable business can be sold.

In general, the shares of companies which generate a high return on their invested capital, or NAV, stand at large multiples of that NAV: unsuccessful companies can trade at or below NAV. Interestingly, shares of banks whose return is composed of semi-passive interest receipts and outgoings are more

---

3 The NAV may be a little understated by over-depreciated plant and non-revalued property, but most of British company balance sheets comprise items far less likely to be mis-stated – cash, debtors, creditors, inventory – and the degree of error is insufficient to overturn the basic premise.

closely related to NAV than those of industrial companies. Return-on-equity considerations can be applied to shares in financial sectors such as insurance brokers, composite and life insurance companies, stockbrokers, etc. What view of the EVPs does this approach suggest?

2   Earnings-valued property companies

The EVP sector is one of the newest in the stock market. As recently as late 1983 BZW undertook the first widespread placing of shares in Arlington Securities, then a private company, and a few months later brought London & Edinburgh Trust to the public market. Both transactions met considerable initial scepticism, not so much whether the respective managements could deliver profits, but mainly whether the stock market would value a 'property company' well over NAV. The table opposite shows how rapidly events have moved since then:

The sector is valued, post crash, at nearly £2 billion, a fair slice of which has been provided by investors as cash or takeover consideration in only a few years. Even though EVP shares fell more sharply than the market in the late 1987 crash, many of them have been above average investments in the past few years. The capitalisation at a PER of ten implies net annual earnings of around £200m, equivalent to annual pre-tax profits of about £300m. This includes some rental income and some income from ancillary financial services, but the majority of the profits, say £200m pre-tax, comes from buying and selling land, developments and completed properties. If the average profit margin is between 10% and 20%, this implies that the EVPs are realising between £1 billion and £2 billion of property per annum. The early scepticism about the sector arose partly because of doubts that the companies could maintain a flow of deals so as to produce the predictable, long-term earnings streams necessary to accord reasonable PERs to their shares. That doubt has been largely overcome: the question now usually asked is how the EVPs can maintain their rate of profits growth, given the very large portfolios that they now need to turn over. Large growth rates in profits also tend to need increased working capital, which has hitherto come from the stock market.

Table 3 shows the EVPs to be generally valued much more on an earnings – rather than an asset – basis, quite differently from the PICs. The sector valuations also scatter more widely than the PICs: even leaving out Rosehaugh, the top-to-bottom range of PERs is 8 to 11.3, quite a wide range for a group of similar trading companies. This range is also a little below the current market average PER. So, incidentally, is the ratio of market capitalisation to NAV.

Finally, the table suggests a marked variation with size among the EVPs. For the large EVPs, the share price/NAV relationship is not very different from the PICs, though the smaller companies show large premiums to NAV. Before dismissing the EVPs, look at the Price Earnings Ratios: even the large EVP companies are on much lower PERs (average 10–11) than the PICs (average PER

TABLE 3

Market Statistics of Major Earnings-Valued Companies

	Price 25/3/88	Market cap	NAV	Premium to NAV	Yield	Prospective Price/ earnings ratio
	p	£m	p	%	%	
Arlington Secs	203	160	120	69	3.4	11.2
London & Edinburgh	141	319	115	22	2.5	10.0
London & Metropolitan	175	87	105	66	3.7	11.3
Mountleigh	165	460	250	−34	3.0	8.7
Regalian Properties	165	152	120	37	2.9	10.5
Rosehaugh	664	429	600	10	0.3	28.6
Speyhawk	359	90	250	43	4.7	9.4
Capitalisation-weighted averages				13		13.2
			ex Mountleigh	30	ex Rosehaugh	9.6

Notes: (1) NAV, PER and yield figures are BZW estimates.
(2) Negative figure for premium to NAV represents a discount.
(3) Prospective data is to the next full-year results due to be announced for each company.

24), which must mean that the NAV/Earnings relationship is different from the PICs.

3 Return on capital for earnings-valued property companies

Table 4 shows returns on equity for seven of the major EVPs calculated by dividing earnings per share into NAV. The second column shows the opening NAV calculated by deducting the year's earnings from the closing NAV. The adjustment in column 4 is to facilitate comparison with PICs, most of whose portfolio appreciation and hence return on equity is reported untaxed. The EVPs charge the full 35% on realised gains before computing their earnings. As a simple but crude approximation, column 4 shows EVP returns on equity grossed up by $17\frac{1}{2}\%$, ie, as if the tax were only charged on half of their earnings.[4]

This simple model assumes that no equity capital has been raised in the year in question. This is roughly true for 1988 but would not have been true for previous years.

The average UK listed company is expected to produce a return on shareholders' funds approaching 20% after tax in 1988, a figure rather above those in the table for the EVPs. Even more marked is the comparison with the PICs which are likely to show NAV appreciation (their measure of return on capital) of 35–50%, which, even allowing for the nil tax charge, is considerably above both the market average and the PIC average.

It is therefore fairly easy to see why the EVPs have underperformed both the property sector and the overall market since mid-1987: this year they seem to be earning a lower return on capital than either of the other comparison groups.

The table does not show equivalent figures for the previous year but it is a very fair guess that the returns on capital were substantially higher, mainly because the equity base of the industry was much lower before the large volume of fund-raising in 1986 and the first three quarters of 1987. The returns for the PICs were much lower in previous years – around 25–30% in 1986/87 and only 5% in 1985/86. In these years, the comparison made with EVPs would have been much more flattering to the EVPs, and therefore the strong performance of their shares was justifiable.

The analysis in terms of return on equity seems preferable to that based on earnings growth rates because there is some investor concern that the EVPs cannot sustain their earnings growth without regular recourse to the equity market for funds. If this is true of any particular company, the rating of its shares is likely to suffer. Return on capital helps avoid this problem because it provides a broad measure of a company's ability to finance its own growth.

At the foot of the table are shown the sector average returns on equity and the averages for the larger- and smaller-sized companies (excluding Rosehaugh which is anomalous in this group and probably closer to a PIC). It seems clear that the smaller companies earn higher returns on capital. This should not be seen as demeaning the large EVPs. Rather the message should be that raising capital to grow in size has no real advantage: it is the return which can be earned on the new capital which should be the principal criterion.

This in turn is an example of a point generally true for all listed companies whose shares, like EVPs, are valued on earnings criteria. It may seem strange in the property industry, but NAVs do not much matter; it is the return earned on those assets which counts.

4 The EVP's reported earnings generally exclude unrealised appreciation on the respective portfolios, which could be another source of potential inaccuracy. The impact of this inaccuracy may not be too great in estimating rates of return, because much of the profit realised in one year will have accrued earlier. The returns on equity are only distorted to the extent that the rate of unrealised appreciation carried out from one year is different from that brought forward into that year.

TABLE 4

Return on Equity of Major Earnings-Valued Property Companies
in 1988

	Earnings per share p	Opening NAV p	Return on equity %	Grossed up return on equity %
Note:	(1)	(2)	(3)	(4)
Arlington	18.1	102	17.8	21.5
London & Edinburgh	14.0	111	12.6	14.8
London & Metropolitan	19.4	90	16.7	19.6
Mountleigh	21.0	229	9.2	10.8
Regalian	28.2	114	14.0	16.5
Rosehaugh	25.0	579	3.6	4.3
Speyhawk	41.2	280	14.7	21.1

Overall capitalisation-weighted average ex Rosehaugh	12.1
Largest three companies ex Rosehaugh	13.2
Smallest three companies	20.8

Notes: (1) BZW estimate to next full-year results to be announced after June 1988.
(2) NAV from previous table minus column 1.
(3) Column 1 divided by column 2.
(4) Column 3 figures divided by 0.825.

IV CAPITAL MARKETS OTHER THAN EQUITIES

It may seem curious to define this section by exception: the other instruments are generally less familiar than shares ('equities'). Readers familiar with them can readily move on.

1 Securitised property

The rationale for trying to securitise single properties lies principally in the tables in, respectively, section 2.5, comparing the liquidity of PICs with direct property, and section 1.5, comparing their tax positions.

Liquidity might seem an abstract concept but many examples suggest that it is not so. There are a number of examples of borrowers with unlisted issues of very similar credit risk to negotiable issues, as well as wider examples of similar but not non-identical borrowers with comparable listed and unlisted issues. Unlisted sterling issues usually yield $\frac{3}{4}$ to 1% pa more, which is equivalent to listing providing an increase in capital value of about 4–8% depending on maturity. The difference in value between shares in a company before and after listing is much larger though difficult to measure. It is commonly estimated at 20–30%: I would expect a differential at the top of this range if the shares were as painstaking to transfer as are partial interests in property.

Thus the analytical rationale behind the various property securitisation schemes is to combine the liquidity of PICs and other listed companies with the 'tax neutrality' of direct property. ('Tax neutrality' implies that investors do not incur materially greater tax liabilities by investing through an indirect vehicle than by investing directly; other examples are unit trusts and investment trusts for investors in UK equities.)

The relative illiquidity of direct property creates one factor in favour of securitised property, namely the discount sometimes applied in valuing large properties, say over £100m. The small number of possible buyers of this size of property can depress its price just as a seller of a very large block of shares usually has to concede a little on price. Securitisation allows access to markets accustomed to such large transactions, but it is also possible to securitise part of a property, thereby maintaining the quality of the investment without swamping the market.

Securitised property is of particular interest to the earnings-driven property companies who are naturally keen to add to the range of outlets for their product. Both buyers and sellers are needed to make a healthy market and the success of securitised property may well depend on the success achieved by the various property securitisation instruments in attracting new investors not involved in the present UK direct property market. The initial market may well lie in those institutional investors, the majority by number of names if not necessarily by value of portfolios, who do not own property. This could be because of the difficulty in recruiting and retaining good quality management or because of considerations of required size of investment and relative illiquidity. It would be a pity, however, if private investors were excluded since the tradition of investment in property by wealthy individuals is well established in the UK.

The valuation parameters for securitised property will be related to asset values, not earnings: PICs shares should be the easiest comparison, since they have a value calculable every day. The natural question is why anyone will buy securitised property if PICs apparently trade at a discount to NAV, and are also highly liquid. One important reason is that the NAVs normally quoted for PICs do not deduct contingent tax on portfolio appreciation, now probably about 10% of stated NAV. Secondly, securitised property passes the rental yield through directly to investors: the prospects are probably for an income yield of 5% or more pa (comprising 6% rental yield less expenses) compared to 3% or less pa for property shares. On the principle that a new instrument has to be demonstrably attractive to find buyers, this suggests that securitised property should meet a reasonable acceptance if the apparent discount (ie, ignoring contingent tax) on PICs shares is not much over 10%. In these circumstances, PICs shares would be trading close to their true, net of tax, NAV and therefore to securitised property: the higher yield of the latter is a 'free' bonus. In addition, the valuation discount for very large properties is available to be split between buyer and seller.

To maintain its valuation relative to PIC shares it will be essential for securitised property to be of high quality and to demonstrate its motivated management: remember the evidence in Table 2, section 2.3, that NAV growth of the PICs has greatly exceeded the property averages. Ideally, perhaps the manager would have a proportionate investment in the securitised property as the best form of incentive. Here might conceivably lie an additional role for the PICs: they could securitise a portion of some of their investment properties and retain the management. Good management also requires access to capital to undertake refurbishments, etc to which investors in a securitised property will have to contribute, directly or indirectly.

Finally, a couple of warning notes. Liquidity allows an investor to buy or sell more readily. It is therefore certain that when markets move sharply, investors will trade preferentially in securitised property, rather than direct property, precisely because only liquid instruments can actually be traded. Therefore, values of securitised property will be more voltatile than direct property values have been to date, just as PIC values are also more volatile. One intriguing question is whether valuers will be able to maintain the present pattern of slow-moving property values in the face of swings in securitised property prices.

Secondly, it is possible to split out, and even securitise, different layers of interest in a property, eg, by inserting a ground rent or creating bonds entitled to income and capital payments ahead of the equity interest. Gearing is not itself either dangerous or undesirable, but it is in a high degree unlikely that a package of *different* types of paper will be worth more than the unified interest, especially if all the paper is negotiable. Investment trusts offer similar opportunities for slicing the cake into various layers and, so far as I am aware, no such layering has created (or destroyed) long-term value.

2 Debt and debt securities

GENERAL

Mammon Holdings introduced the concept of 'debt' borrowing in property companies as a means of increasing shareholders' return. Lenders have a quite different risk:reward profiles to equity investors. A lender seeks a very great degree of certainty that his money, and the interest on it, will be paid when due: in return he accepts a lower return than the entrepreneur or shareholder. Consider a typical bank balance sheet: total sums lent or invested are often *fifteen times* the bank's own long-term capital; of these sums maybe one-third is lent to other banks or invested in high-quality governmental obligations, leaving the remainder, say ten times the bank's capital, in commercial loans, leases, etc. A loan-loss provision above 1% on commercial loans, leases, etc. would be considered a poor performance: put more strictly, commercial banks need to get their risk-asset deployment about 99%, by value, correct.

Public debt markets are generally similar to this summation of the banks' position. Defaults on UK listed bonds are very rare indeed – the last clutch was probably on subordinated loans issued by small banks later caught up in the mid-1970s secondary banking/property crisis. Similarly, default (or rescheduling) on Eurobonds is extremely rare. Mezzanine debt and so-called 'Junk' bonds or loans created in the USA and now coming to the UK have moved the balance of a proportion of lenders' portfolios towards a higher-risk/higher-reward profile: nevertheless, even these lenders require strict covenants, specific payment dates for interest and principal and detailed cash flow forecasts. Although willing to accept a greater risk (for example in debt:equity ratios), their approach is nowhere near that of public shareholders who volunteer to receive a yield well below the cost of money in exchange for the expectation of much larger capital gains of indeterminate size and timescale.

For a property company incurring debt, the three major criteria are those for any commercial borrower, namely:

Maturity—When must the loan be repaid, and can either the lender or borrower accelerate repayment?

Terms—A breach of the terms of the loan will normally trigger immediate repayment, but even without such a default, the borrower may have to mortgage assets, seek the lender's permission for asset sales, maintain financial ratios, etc.

Interest Rate—There are two main types of interest (fixed and floating), a distinction often more important than the interest margin charged.

If these criteria are satisfactorily met, then the question of size, ie, availability, arises.

INTEREST RATE SWAPS

Swaps have grown into a very large business over the past five years or so and provide a major element of flexibility in corporate funding. It is one which I believe to be particularly important in an industry like property which is highly capital-intensive and has relatively low cashflow ratios.

In the simplest terms, interest rate swaps represent an exchange of interest payments of equal term and value but different type, one floating one fixed. An insurance company may have regular cash balances, eg, held against possible claims, on which it would prefer a fixed rate of return to fluctuating money-market rates: in the mirror-image position could be a property company with a medium-term bank loan priced at LIBOR plus a margin. A swap is normally arranged through a bank acting as principal so the two parties who exchange or 'swap' interest payments never know each other: the insurance company agrees to pay the bank interest at LIBOR on, say, £10m in exchange for receiving interest of, say, 10% on the same sum; the property company agrees to pay the bank interest of, say, $10\frac{1}{16}$% on £10m in exchange for receiving interest at LIBOR on this sum. As a result, the property company has now borrowed at a fixed rate ($10\frac{1}{16}$% plus the margin between LIBOR and the cost of its bank loan) and the insurance company receives a fixed rate (10% less the difference between LIBOR and its money market deposits).

One of the most important points to note is that in a swap, the principal itself (the £10m above) does not change hands, only the interest thereon. Consequently, a swap enables the actual incurring of debt to be completely separated from the determination of interest rate. Currency swaps can be used to switch the currency obligation as well.

Consequently, whereas a few years ago I would have written that bank loans are short- to medium-term and necessarily floating rate in contrast to the UK bond markets, being long-term and fixed rate, maturity is now nearly independent of whether rates are floating or fixed.

Another vital consequence is that fixed-rate debt is no longer limited to the very large companies able to sell long-term listed bonds, because the swap market is open to a very wide range of companies. Thus Mammon Holdings need no longer get into the mess with Sixties House described in section 1.4: if it is able to borrow £25m, it could use a swap in order to fix borrowing costs for some years, and become immune at least to the direct effects of a rise in interest rates.

MATURITY

The primary benefit enjoyed by issuers in the UK in the quoted bond market is the long maturities available. Pension funds and life insurance companies have liabilities stretching out literally for decades. Therefore, these investors have a strong preference for long-term fixed-interest bonds to match their long-term liabilities: shorter bonds involve a larger reinvestment risk, ie, the risk of not knowing the yields that will be available when a shorter term bond matures and the funds have to be reinvested for the remainder of the term.

Common maturities for public issues are therefore 20, 25 or even 30 years. However, to commit funds for such long periods, investors also need to be very sure of the borrower's creditworthiness. Hence the apparent paradox that the UK bond market tends to demand issues with very high capital risk in terms of price sensitivity to changes in interest rates, but very low credit risk. Very large public property companies (eg, Land Securities, MEPC, Slough Estates) have fairly free access to very long-term debt, as do many medium-sized companies. The small public property companies that have, after all, sold equity to investors may not be able to sell long-term debt at all easily. The Euromarkets, to the extent that they are different from UK domestic debt markets, aim at shorter maturities, typically five or ten years, but tend also to focus on very large companies.

Bank debt is generally available to creditworthy property companies of any size, and maturities are much shorter, rarely over five years. Such maturities are far too short for the cost of investment property to be repaid from rental income, as section 1.4 showed. Hence bank loans on property normally are either bridging loans – perhaps to developers – repaid by sale or long-term institutional funding, or medium-term loans in which the rent covers all the interest but not capital repayments[5].

Overdrafts are repayable on demand, the shortest maturity. This can work to borrowers' advantage since surplus funds can be used to repay expensive borrowing immediately. More generally, bank borrowings can be far more flexible in terms of drawdowns and repayments than bond issues.

TERMS

The very great majority of property loans are mortgages, ie, secured on specific properties. When issued in the UK domestic bond market, and often called debentures, the facility exists for the properties to be switched, subject to value criteria, during the life of the bond. Only the largest property companies can issue unsecured debt, whether in the domestic or Eurobond market.

INTEREST

At end-March 1988, yields on property company listed sterling bonds were as follows, with base-rate around 9%:

	10 years %	25 years %
Gilts	9	9
Unsecured loan stocks/Eurobonds	$10\frac{1}{4}$	$10\frac{1}{2}$
Debentures	10	10

Compare: base rate 9%, hence cost of bank funds 9–11%

5   Richard Wolfe examines the most common forms of bank lending to property companies in detail in his chapter.

Interest spreads over Gilts are therefore currently of similar order to the margin charged by banks over their cost of funds.

SIZE

Issues of debt securities are rarely under £10m. The common range is £25–100m with the largest sizes available only to the biggest companies. Bank loans are nearly all rather smaller, though very large syndicated loans can be arranged for specific projects.

3 Convertibles

A convertible bond is one which offers conventional interest and repayment and is also exchangeable at the option of the holder for another security, usually shares. The shares available on conversion are normally those of the same company as issued the convertible bond. The effective price at which the holder of the convertible can acquire the relevant ordinary shares is usually fixed in advance of the convertible being issued as a so-called 'conversion rate', eg, 50 shares per £100 nominal of convertible bond. This in turn determines the 'conversion price': if the £100 of bonds is issued at par, the conversion price is £2 per share. The conversion ratio is predetermined, except for adjustments to reflect rights issues, scrip dividends, etc. Convertibles can also be issued in the form of preference shares convertible into ordinary shares: the essential feature is an initial safe return exchangeable for the excitement of equity.

The holder of a convertible has greater capital security than a holder of ordinary shares (because the repayment of the nominal value ranks ahead of ordinary shares in a liquidation). In addition, the convertible holder enjoys greater income than an ordinary shareholder. In exchange for these benefits, the issuer naturally sets the terms of the convertible such that, at the issue price, the conversion price is above the then current price of the underlying ordinary shares.

The two valuation bases for convertibles reflect the choice that the holder enjoys between retaining the bond and exchanging for equity. For instance, using the 10.5% gross redemption yield for loan stocks mentioned earlier, a 25-year convertible loan stock with a $6\frac{1}{2}$% coupon is worth about 65% of par as a bond. As deferred equity, the value of the shares is added to the extra income receivable, a calculation which adds to the conversion price the estimated value, discounted to the present of the extra income likely to be received by the convertible holder (before conversion) compared to converting immediately at the conversion price. This calculation therefore depends on the conversion price, the present price of the shares, and the yields on the ordinary and convertible. For example, a coupon of $6\frac{1}{2}$%, conversion rights of 50 shares per £100 bond (ie, a conversion price of 200p), against a present price of 220p per share with an ordinary dividend of $3\frac{3}{4}$p net (ie 5p gross dividend and a yield of $2\frac{1}{4}$% on 220p) growing at 10% per annum, are worth about 105% of par (Euromarket convertibles are not always valued so analytically, but they too generally trade at a conversion premium).

Convertibles are not a different category of financing to equity and debt but a hybrid between the two. New issue terms of convertibles are usually set so that their issue price is justified by their value as deferred equity. The pure bond value is usually much lower – rather like the above example where the two values were 105% and 65% of par respectively. There is some special relevance to property companies since the range of conversion premiums – normally 5% to 15% – is similar to the discount to NAV on which PIC shares usually trade in the stock market. Consequently, the conversion price of a convertible may be sufficiently close to the NAV, for the fully diluted NAV per share not to be reduced as a consequence of the issue. Thus, with a little buoyancy in the stock market, PICs, can issue convertibles as rights issues or acquisition consideration without diluting their published NAV. Much of the advantage over straight equity is cosmetic however: the issuer has to buy the higher conversion price for his equity with higher service costs before conversion.

V   RAISING CAPITAL FOR PROPERTY COMPANIES

1   Capital needs

The decision on when and how to raise capital is, I believe, more important for PICs than for the great majority of public companies (including EVPs) whose *raison d'etre* is to increase earnings rather than build asset values. Retained cash flow for PICs was shown in section 1.4 to be very small, typically 1.3% of NAV, and hence PICs are not able to finance much growth internally.

PICs therefore tend to need to raise new capital for quite a high proportion of their portfolio expansion, if this expansion is to be at other than a rather pedestrian rate. Bank loans are usually bridging finance during the construction or development phase. This leaves the essential long-term choice between debt and equity, the various hybrid instruments (convertibles, bonds with warrants, etc) being combinations of these two. Since PICs are valued mainly on NAV per share, with earnings being rather secondary, their primary need is to retain the benefit of rising asset values. This inclines them to raise long-term finance as debentures or loans, ie, debt, rather than equity, especially as many PICs have a stock of large, let properties of the type which make excellent security for lenders. Finally, as we shall see, the price of PICs' shares relative to their NAV is a major constraint on capital raising.

EVPs should be much more self-financing. The tables in sections 3.2 and 3.3 imply retentions of about 12% of NAV; in addition, it is in the nature of their business that EVPs realise their asset portfolios quite quickly and therefore also release internal 'capital' cash for reinvestment. Indeed, in this sense the EVPs' greatest need for capital is not at all reflected in their balance sheets or in their recourse to the banking or securities markets: EVPs need customers to buy their 'product' – developed property. Occupiers confirm or enhance the value of the property on the basis of which the EVPs sell it to owner-occupiers or long-term investors. These sales release the EVPs' invested capital and profit. Since the completed value of a scheme is a multiple, often a large multiple, of the developers' initial commitment, EVPs are often reliant on much larger amounts of long-term funding to take out their projects than the amounts of capital they raise for their own balance sheet. The high level of fund-raising by EVPs in 1986 and 1987 must therefore, at least partly, reflect these companies' desire to expand very rapidly rather than the intrinsic character of their businesses.

EVPs need to raise capital in ways which enhance *earnings* per share, in contrast to the *NAV* per share for PICs. The service cost of debt is a direct charge on earnings, hence EVPs would be expected to look to equity financing, especially when their shares are on high price-earnings multiples. This has certainly been the pattern, again accentuated by another fact in which they are the mirror-image of PICs, namely that EVPs tend to hold relatively little let property capable of sustaining a long-term mortgage or debenture.

2 Rights issues

A rights issue is a method of issuing equity, rather than a different type of financing. It arises from the deeply enshrined belief in UK company law, and repeated in the attitudes of UK institutional investors, that the existing shareholders of a company are entitled to first refusal to participate pro rata to their existing holdings in any issues of ordinary shares made for cash. This so-called 'pre-emptive right' can only be overridden with the consent of 75% of the votes cast at a shareholders' meeting and applies to any equity-related security (eg, convertibles, warrants). It is implemented by the company writing to each shareholder offering the right (hence 'rights issue') to purchase new shares at a specified price in proportion to existing holdings – the right to buy, for example, two Mammon ordinary shares at 150p each for every five already held. Such an offer leaves Mammon on risk that, to the extent that any existing shareholder does not wish to subscribe, the capital raised by Mammon will fall short of the target amount.

This pre-emptive right, the necessary uncertainty and the mechanisms for handling this uncertainty are such an enduring characteristic of the UK securities markets that the tendency is to take the consequences as given. None of this section would be needed if shareholders were happy to allow their UK companies to sell new shares for cash to the highest bidder(s), as occurs in the USA for example. Pre-emptive rights are an important example of the greater control over company managements which UK investors seek to exercise than their US counterparts.

UK Stock Exchange rules require a rights offer to be open for three weeks. To ensure full subscription over three weeks of possible market vagaries is no mean feat – most US-style bought-deals are sold and signed in a very short period. The three principal means of so doing are pricing, transferability of rights and underwriting.

PRICING

Since the existing shareholders already own Mammon, the price at which they *all* subscribe for new shares does not matter to the value of their investment of their percentage ownership of Mammon. This seems so contrary to common-sense that proof through a worked example might be useful.

If Mammon shares are trading at 200p each immediately before a rights issue is launched, and the Board want to raise cash for 30% of the market capitalisation, pre-expenses, the 'conventional' choice might be a 10% 'discount', ie, a price of 180p per share. ('Discount' is in quotes advisedly since it is a peculiar form of discount to give someone their own money back.) A 1-for-3 issue at 180p will raise 60p per present share, 30% of the market capitalisation. After the issue all the shares are identical and therefore the (theoretical) post-rights price will be $[(3 \times 200) + 180] = 780 \div 4 = 195$p. Thus a Mammon shareholder originally with 750 shares worth £1,500 now has shares worth £1,950, and he has paid £450. However, the same result could have been achieved in a number of quite different ways, all based on an original holding of 750 shares priced at 200p each and an issue to raise 30% of the market capitalisation:

Rights ratio	Rights price	Resulting holding of shares		
		Number	Price	Value
2 for 1	30p	2,250	86.7p	£1,950
1 for 1	60p	1,500	130.0p	£1,950
1 for 2	120p	1,125	173.3p	£1,950
2 for 5	150p	1,250	185.6p	£1,950
1 for 3	180p	1,000	195.0p	£1,950
4 for 15	225p	950	205.3p	£1,950
1 for 5	300p	900	216.7p	£1,950
1 for 10	600p	825	236.4p	£1,950

The price at which a rights issue is conducted therefore does not matter provided each of the shareholders takes it up. In effect, the company has packaged together a scrip issue with the rights offer. Consequently, in computing per share data incorporating a period including a rights issue, an adjustment is made to all per share data, based on the initial market price of rights, just as if the company had split its shares. However, in the case of a rights offer this scrip issue is only received by shareholders who subscribe for their rights and the non-subscribers are only indifferent to the rights price if some means is available to them to recoup the value of the scrip issue which they have forgone. In the extreme case of the top line of the table above, the scrip issue is over half the value of the present shareholding, because a non-subscribing shareholder will be left with 750 shares worth £625, down from £1,500 pre-rights. On a per share basis, each right is worth $(86.7-30)=56.7p$ and the non-subscriber forgoes $1,500 \times 56.7p$.

TRANSFERABILITY OF RIGHTS

Rights to new shares may be renounced by a shareholder to whom they are first offered, but who does not want to increase his investment, and thereby transferred to someone else (not necessarily an existing shareholder) who may take them up. The advantage to the company is that this increases the chances of the issue being subscribed. An original shareholder is enabled to capture any surplus value in the right by demanding a premium from the purchaser. For this reason, all rights issues by UK listed companies have to be in the form of renounceable letters. Furthermore, after the issue closes the company must attempt to sell any rights not taken up ('lapsed') and distribute the proceeds pro rata to the shareholders who lapsed them. (They are sold paid-up to ensure receipt of the proceeds to the company.) Provided that the market in the shares and in the rights is efficient in the technical, economic sense, making the rights freely transferable enables each of the existing shareholders of Mammon to be indifferent to the pricing of any rights issue whether or not he takes up his rights. (This is provided that the issue is not above the market price. In this case, all shareholders still need to subscribe, or else the non-subscribers receive a free enhancement.)

Therefore, one obvious option in raising new equity through a renounceable rights issue is to offer the new shares at a price which includes a large scrip element and leave the market to sort out the transfer of value between subscribing and non-subscribing shareholders. This, a 'deep discount' rights issue, was the course followed by Barclays in early 1988 to raise over £900m.

UNDERWRITING

We have seen how the shareholder's position can be protected in a rights issue. Mammon has still to be sure of obtaining the capital it seeks. This can only be done by finding fallback investors to subscribe any of the issue not taken up by existing shareholders: if the rights are transferable, these fallback investors, or underwriters, only come into play after the market mechanism has also failed to find subscribers for lapsed rights.

A company launching an underwritten rights issue normally contracts with an intermediary (the 'underwriter') to subscribe or procure subscribers for any lapsed rights. The underwriter rarely retains all the risk but arranges for a wide range of institutional sub-underwriters to take on the risk in exchange for a further commission. The party procuring sub-underwriters, for historical reasons called broker to the issue, is also paid a commission.

The underwriters' risk is that the issue will be seen as unattractive, which mainly depends on the relative pricing of the existing and rights shares. Since rights issues for listed companies have to remain open for three weeks, a major component of risk is that the stock market falls, bringing the price of existing shares below the rights price – as happened almost universally in October 1987.

Rights issue pricing is therefore a far more sensitive issue for the sub-underwriters than for the shareholders of a listed company, who have a free option and will receive the cash value of any rights they do not subscribe. The risk that sub-underwriters are prepared to run is logically a function of the commission they are offered. In UK rights issues, it is normally the commission which is fixed ($1\frac{1}{4}$% for not more than 30 days' risk, $\frac{1}{8}$% for each successive seven days or part thereof) and the pricing which varies, typically a range of 10–20% below the previous price for the shares, ie, 160–180p in the Mammon example above. It is usual for the dividend paid on the post-rights share capital to be the same as that on the old capital.

The traditional commissions total 2% of the issue value: $\frac{1}{2}$% for underwriting, $\frac{1}{4}$% for finding sub-underwriters, $1\frac{1}{4}$% for the sub-underwriters themselves. Interestingly, very similar commission scales usually apply to underwriting and sub-underwriting cash alternatives to takeover offers and placings of shares, issued as acquisition consideration ('vendor placings'). In these latter cases, more complex commission structures involving different 'success' or 'failure' commissions are becoming more common.

Underwritten rights issues of convertible bonds or preference shares also contain a value buffer in order to contain underwriting costs to a reasonable level. This is done by setting the price at which the convertible can be exchanged for equity below the value calculation based on the discounted present value outlined in section 4.3, so that the convertible is initially worth more than the par value at which it is underwritten.

3   Equity pricing for property companies

Much of the discussion of PICs has emphasised how the main goal set by their shareholders and managements is growth in NAV per share. Consequently, PICs are very reluctant to issue equity at a price below NAV, since to do so would reduce overall NAV per share. If Mammon's share price is 200p when their NAV is, say, 240p, an issue of equity is unlikely to be well regarded. The same share price against an NAV of 180p would make an acceptable basis for an issue since NAV per share is enhanced, whether the issue proceeds are used to buy property, held as cash or used to repay debt. This approach is equally valid for a flotation (or other non-pre-emptive issue) and for a rights issue since the adjustment for the scrip element in the latter removes the sensitivity to the actual rights price.

Convertibles (bond or preference shares) usually offer a conversion price 5–$12\frac{1}{2}$% above that of the underlying ordinary shares at the time that the convertible is issued. This covers a fair part of the discount to NAV at which PIC shares normally trade, which makes it seem rather surprising that there have not been very many convertible issues by PICs. Nevertheless, convertibles are only a tactical gloss on a very deeply entrenched and far-reaching pattern in the property share market. PICs are very reluctant to issue equity below NAV, and very ready issuers over NAV.

This NAV-dependence is widely known to investors, indeed it is mainly a consequence of those investors' attitudes to the PICs, and is the principal reason that PIC shares rarely trade over NAV: a large volume of equity and equity-related securities is likely to be created at these higher prices. Thus the relative stagnation of the PIC sector in the stock market may be seen to result from property being a capital-intensive business in which the listed companies only rarely have access to the public risk-capital markets.

This dilemma is all the more poignant because the investment performance achieved by the PICs (see section 2.2) is quite creditable within their industry. The NAV/share price constraint is a relatively small one, say 0–20% over eight years, compared to the apparent relative superior investment performance (50–100% over the same period).

It is arguable that the industry, and the analysts who follow it, might be doing themselves a disservice by so clearly targeting NAV and ignoring the contingent tax and the consequent NNAV. This NNAV is the only figure that shareholders can enjoy since, unlike investment trusts, PICs pay tax on capital gains. However, if proof is needed that the stock market is already aware of these tax liabilities and unlikely to make shares lower if they are explicitly shown, witness the behaviour of PIC shares after the 1988 Budget. The sector rose 10%, roughly equal to the increase in NNAV: NAV, of course, was unaffected.

Pricing for equity issues by EVPs is not subject to as rigid a regime. The test for earnings-valued companies of all sorts is that equity issues do not reduce earnings per share. This is a long-term test and there has been some concern that EVPs can use share issues to buy assets on which there is a 'turn' but without fostering a long-term earnings stream. This is a very important, if highly judgmental, issue to be made for each EVP, as for most listed companies. While the fact that it is more judgmental than for PICs does not necessarily mean that EVPs' access to capital is more ready than PICs', it does mean that EVP new issues are more likely to be spread out since the pricing parameters for a non-dilutive issue by an EVP are particular to that EVP and the spread of market ratings for the sector is quite wide. This contrasts with PICs, which we have seen have closely bunched ratings.

If the EVPs are to retain this flexibility, they must remain jealous of their ratings and not issue equity when the price is low. Otherwise, the possibility is that their share price too will fall to their NAV and they too may be in the narrow equity pricing constraints suffered by the PICs.

4 Acquisitions and mergers

Issues of shares as consideration for purchase of property or another company are not restricted with pre-emption rights in the same way as cash issues. In addition, if the vendors are exchanging shares in their company for shares in the acquiror, the exchange should not be treated as a disposal for tax purposes. The pre-emption issue is now clouded by the requirement of UK institutional investors that they have the right to 'claw back' shares from large vendor placings (vendor placings are sales of shares on behalf of vendors to whom they have been issued as consideration for assets acquired from them). One attraction remains for acquisitions made for shares rather than rights issues for undisclosed or vaguely worded purposes: it is easier to convince both existing shareholders and prospective new investors of the merits of the capital raising if the intended use for the funds can be described and discussed at the same time as the funds are raised.

Some such acquisitions by or of property companies are essentially issues for cash by an indirect route, for example London & Edinburgh Trust's (an EVP) takeover of The 1928 Investment Trust and Singer & Friedlander's takeover of Centrovincial (a PIC). In addition, there are occasional purchases of properties for shares (again London & Edinburgh Trust is an example).

Other types of merger and acquisition activity in the PICs tend not to be hectic because both buyer and seller can see the same NAV. Occasionally a company wishes to be acquired (as when Chase Property was acquired by Trafalgar House in 1987); otherwise the seller will rarely agree to a price at which the buyer can see any added value for himself, unless he believes that property values are going to rise above the acquired company's NAV calculation, and the acquisition is a means of investing substantial funds quickly before the rise.

Finally, the use of NAV (ie, the non-deduction of contingent tax liabilities) tends to overstate the value of the portfolio to the buyer because the contingent tax will have to be paid if the portfolio is ever realised and its value enjoyed as cash. In the mid to late 1970s this liability could be mitigated by buying companies with capital losses for tax purposes. The supply of such casualties has been exhausted for some years, quite apart from changes in the tax legislation or its interpretation. These days the difference between NAV and NNAV is a real cost to the acquiror.

5 Debt issues

Straight debt (ie, non-convertible debt) involves no pre-emption rights and so can be sold to investors in an uncomplicated direct issue. One or more intermediaries usually underwrite the issue, again agreeing to subscribe or procure subscribers. As with equity or equity-related issues, the securities are usually sold on to a wide range of institutional investors on the basis of which a listing is usually obtained for the bonds, debentures loan stocks or Eurobonds as the case may be.

Beyond this, there are significant differences with equity issues. First, there are no sub-underwriters because there is no need to back-stop an offer open for some weeks. Issue costs are therefore lower. Second, the distribution of the securities may leave a proportion with the intermediaries, whereas with equities the intention is usually to sub-sell the whole issue. In the Euromarket, large blocks of the issue may stay in the market; in the domestic market only a small proportion, if any, may be held back. Bonds offer a much higher yield than equities, so the cost to an investment house of carrying an inventory of bonds is usually small and there may even be a benefit or positive carry. In addition, prices of different bonds move more closely together than do equities (where movements of 20–25% pa relative to the market index are not too uncommon) so that a large adverse price movement over time relative to the market is less likely to arise.

From a property company's standpoint, the first test is whether the market is available – section 4.2 indicated that generally larger companies are necessary for the bond markets. The second test is whether it has available properties to mortgage in order to issue a 'debenture'. For the minimum size of property companies with access to the long-term bond market, this may be the only form of issue acceptable to investors and even for the biggest company there is a cost of funds advantage in issuing secured debt.

If these tests are met, the next question is size. Every prudent man knows that too much debt is a Bad Thing. There is no single measure of how much is too much, but a good place to start is to remember that the worst aspect of debt is having to repay it. Consequently, borrowing 20 or 25 year money is very unlikely to get the borrower into trouble.

Income cover is the second criterion. Interest rate swaps should enable small- and medium-sized companies to avoid the worst effects of rising interest rates and falling property values, a protection previously confined to large companies. The logical prediction is that PICs should be less sensitive than EVPs to interest costs, because their shares are valued on an asset basis and because they have predictable streams of rental income which can be allocated to long-term debt service.

Consequently, it is unlikely that a PIC will come to serious harm by issuing long-term fixed-rate debt: the worst outcome is probably that property values are stagnant and a small reduction of NAV arises because of the 'funding gap' between rental yields and interest costs. At current long-term interest rates around 10% (section 4.2) and rental yields $5\frac{1}{2}$–$7\frac{1}{2}$% for most (non-industrial) property, the funding gap is fairly small except on highly reversional properties. The mid-1970s crisis was caused by interest costs in the mid-teens % pa and reversionary property yields as low as 1–2%.

EVPs are more sensitive to debt costs – borrowing long and immediately putting the funds on deposit may cost 2% or 3% pa – and they have much less mortgageable property. EVPs are much less common in the bond markets, but it is difficult to know whether this is due to the prospective borrowers not wanting to burden their profit and loss account or whether it is the relative scarcity of five to ten year fixed-rate money which is the more natural term for an EVP. One hopes it is the latter because it could be short-sighted to give up a tranche of long-term capital for a relatively small interest differential, especially post-crash when equity funds are more scarce.

VI   WIDER ASPECTS OF SECURITIES MARKETS FOR PROPERTY COMPANIES

1   Internationalisation of securities markets

One major trend, particularly apparent before the crash, was the increasing degree of international, cross-border investment. It is difficult now to remember that until 1979, exchange control had for 40 years strictly limited the amount of money which could be invested abroad by UK residents. Since then, not only have British investors moved substantial equity funds abroad, but American investors have diversified their equity portfolios into overseas companies and a number of continental European stock markets have at times been driven by the flow in or out of foreign money. Yet overseas comparisons and influence on UK property shares have been limited.

Sterling is not at all as international a currency as the US dollar or Deutschmark, so sterling bonds are a less important component of international bond markets than are UK shares in international equity markets.

Cross-border equity investors concentrate on very 'liquid', large capitalisation issues. By these standards, only a few property companies have large capitalisations. Furthermore, international equity investors often emphasise industries which are comparable in different countries, often because their products are traded internationally. These include pharmaceutical and chemical companies, oil industry, other mining or resources, international airlines and certain communications sectors. In contrast, industries very dependent on local conditions and knowledge are less familiar to foreigners and less likely investments for them.

Property is an industry whose importance and legal structure vary widely between countries, quite apart from the very strong dependence of property values on precise location. In Hong Kong, property values underpin a large proportion of the value of listed companies; in the USA real estate is relatively unimportant to the value of listed companies, although development and construction are major industries in themselves. The UK is in between, with a population density well above the US but below the rather unique data for Hong Kong.

It is understandable that UK property shares are less affected by overseas investors and that valuation parameters of property company shares are almost exclusively a domestic, UK affair. Despite the increasing, and generally welcome, involvement of the Europeans and Japanese in the UK property market and that of American securities houses as occupiers in the financial districts, property shares seem likely to remain towards the lower end of the scale in terms of overseas investor influence on share prices and of overseas involvement in equity financings.

2   The City post Big Bang

Ten or fifteen years ago, the City was composed of clusters of firms, each specialising in a particular form of financial intermediation and each relatively small. Thus there were about a dozen Accepting Houses, a dozen Discount Houses and ten or fifteen brokers capable of handling at least medium-sized companies. However jobbers were consolidated into a few key firms.

Big Bang was partly caused by overseas competition, represented by very large well-capitalised firms, dealing increasingly in UK securities and not being bound by the UK stock market's then rules which forbade the same Stock Exchange member firm to act as both principal and agent. The Big Bang changes were not discouraged, and were sometimes positively welcomed, by the major UK institutions who felt that it would lower dealing costs. Thirdly, the view expressed privately by a number of finance directors of listed companies that the 'one-stop shopping' available for issues, for example in the Eurobond market, seemed simpler and easier to use than the dual roles, and sometimes manoeuvring, of the UK bank/broker combination.

Therefore, in the first half of 1986, stock exchange member firms were allowed to engage in unlimited dual-capacity (agent and principal) trading; new electronic trading systems superseded the old, face-to-face, trading floor, and the firms were allowed to bring in outside capital, where previously the rule had been unlimited liability by the firms' principals.

It was predictable that the removal of competitive restraints and the admission of substantial outside capital would have caused a concentration of economic power in the UK financial markets – one of the government's objectives was to create such powerful combines to compete successfully with formidable foreigners in the securities industry. What could not be foreseen was that Big Bang would coincide with the final, tumultuous phase of a long-running bull market. In these conditions the new combines and the earnings of their star executives have attracted a high degree of attention. There may also be a tinge of apprehension at the apparent and actual influence wielded by the securities firms spawned by Big Bang and the reduction of choice necessarily arising from the concentration of the industry into larger units.

Despite these organisational upheavals, most of the basics of the securities markets are unchanged:

1. The major moves in securities prices are not created by the securities houses or any other intermediary but on a macro scale by economic and monetary trends, which even governments influence but do not necessarily control. On a micro scale, prices are heavily dependent on the success of the company managements concerned.

2. Investing institutions are the most influential participants in the UK markets. Their assets, mainly ungeared, are over $£\frac{1}{4}$ trillion. The institutional community is also relatively concentrated and well organised in the UK, compared for example to the USA.

3. Financial intermediation, between issuers and investors, always involves bringing together the interests of the two groups, which can be opposed in some terms such as price.

The meeting of minds which is required in financial intermediation has to be achieved whatever the mechanism used to intermediate. Experience suggests that companies (or at least their share prices) prosper better by regarding investors as a market whose demands are satisfied wherever reasonable, rather than opponents to be defeated. Post-Big Bang these fundamentals of the securities markets remain broadly true for property companies no less than others.

Chapter 8

Securitisation

Stephen Barter and Neil Sinclair

This chapter considers the relevance of securitisation to modern property financing techniques and to the property market. It reviews the legal and taxation hurdles which have had to be overcome in developing a securitisation vehicle suitable for the UK market and examines the SAPCO, SPOT and PINC approaches in detail. It considers the application of the PINCs approach to development finance in a worked example; finally, it discusses a number of the key issues about which the evolution of the securitisation market has provoked widespread debate.

I OVERVIEW

Securitisation simply means the conversion of an asset into tradeable paper securities. The concept has been common in other financial markets for many years as a way of transforming relatively illiquid assets into more readily tradeable investments.

Its application to property – such an obvious idea – is one which has eluded many in the past, largely because of the technical difficulties which UK land law and taxation practice presented.

Attention has concentrated on creating a method by which the equity interest in a single property investment can be securitised. In its simplest form, each equity security provides a direct share of the property's rental income flow and capital growth, but without the obligation of management. In contrast with a property company share, the investor selects specific assets rather than commits to a managed portfolio. As a result, the investor receives an income yield approximating to a direct property yield – currently, on average, double the dividend yield from property company shares.

A key objective has been to devise a vehicle which avoids the double taxation of companies, so that any income or capital received is taxed only once – in the hands of the investor, according to its own tax status. An additional objective has been to provide the potential for gearing the property, either by bank debt or by a bond issue, in order to provide additional funding flexibility. Investors can then be offered the choice of either equity and/or debt securities, backed by the same property investment, and tradeable on The Stock Exchange.

Its introduction confirms a significant change in traditional attitudes to property investment and is likely to have far-reaching effects on development finance and the property professions. In the context of this book, securitisation is the key innovation for funding property through the capital markets. In particular, it opens up the world of commercial property investment for the first time to the general public and potentially allows property to be traded internationally through the global securities markets.

It may help to overcome many of the intrinsic shortcomings of property as a price-efficient investment medium and it opens up an entirely new set of possibilities for property financing and property management. In particular, it raises a number of issues which those involved in property (and not just chartered surveyors) will need to resolve in the coming years.

II   THE BENEFITS OF SECURITISATION

Why is it so important? The ability to securitise a single property investment and to trade readily its shares on The Stock Exchange is intended to provide the following principal benefits:

i. *Liquidity*

Property has traditionally been regarded as a 'lumpy' investment, with a considerably higher unit cost than stocks or shares. This factor is exacerbated by the particularly long time which it takes to buy and sell property – anything from three months to three years. There is a particular difficulty in the UK in that single investments with capital values above £20m are considered 'big', and relatively few single investors (institutions or otherwise) have sufficient capital resources to purchase them. For properties worth more than £50m, potential single purchasers are in even shorter supply.

The sizeable unit cost of a single property has precluded the smaller institutions and the general public from participating directly in the commercial property market.

In a UK context, an increasing number of properties now fall into the large category, including not just City of London office buildings above about 20,000 sq ft (which is most of them), but also the new generation of out-of-town shopping centres, business parks and retail parks which are now being developed throughout the country. As a result, the market for these larger properties is notoriously illiquid and their pricing is inefficient.

The impact of this illiquidity on the characteristics of property performance in recent years is illustrated in the graphs contained in the Introduction to this book.

Securitisation overcomes these problems. By offering investors tradeable equity shares in large single properties at a small unit cost, new liquidity can be injected into a traditionally illiquid market.

ii. *Valuation Precision*

The illiquidity of the larger properties presents significant problems to valuers. The range of possible capital values for such a property is wide; the valuer has to use his best judgment in calculating a specific value, given the small number of potential buyers likely to be in the market at the time and the limited amount of credible, comparable evidence (if any) available. Inevitably, valuers reflect this uncertainty by applying a discount to their valuation figure, simply because of capital size. However, the quantum of discount is necessarily arbitrary and subjective. This creates consequential problems for investors, in accurately measuring investment performance, and for financiers, in pin-pointing a realistic completed value for appraisal purposes.

Securitisation potentially provides valuers with a much greater supply of evidence (albeit marginal prices) from which to make a more precise judgment of an individual property's value. Equally, for investors, the continuous pricing of the securities through The Stock Exchange provides an immediate indication of value and a more reliable indication of performance. The extent to which this may also reduce the apparent discount for bulk is discussed in further detail below.

iii. *Precise Investment Timing*

Property is traditionally seen as a long-term investment, partly because of its relative illiquidity. However, with securitisation, trading can be immediate; it allows investors to time their purchases and sales very precisely and to take short-term, as well as long-term, positions. Property investors will therefore be able to react more quickly to changes in market circumstances. So too will prices, thus reducing property's relative lack of volatility, a characteristic which was caused largely by property's illiquidity and the infrequency of formal valuations. It remains to be seen how far the introduction of securitisation weakens the counter-cyclical nature of property, relative to the equity and gilt markets.

iv. *Efficient Diversification*

It has always been difficult to assemble a reasonably diversified property portfolio. Theorists differ widely about what constitutes efficient diversification in a property context. At a practical level, the ability to acquire, say 20 single property investments, reasonably balanced in terms of type, location, capital size and performance characteristics, is unachievable other than over a period of many years. In practice, because of the fairly sporadic nature of property investment purchases, due to market circumstances, it would probably require substantially more than 20 properties to achieve anything like a reasonably diversified spread across the whole portfolio.

In contrast, securitisation offers two principal benefits here. First, the small unit size of perhaps £1 per share makes it much easier and quicker to build up a reasonably diversified portfolio which is tailored to the individual investor's overall capital allocation and risk aversion. In its simplest form, each security carries a direct share in the property's rental income flow and capital growth and, consequently, for £1 per share, the investor achieves similar performance to an investment worth several million pounds. As a result, the investor can be much more precise and potentially more adventurous in portfolio selection.

Second, the opportunity for immediate trading means that the investor can mix long-term with short-term holdings. This permits a further area of diversification – between time periods – and may, in the future, permit a basic form of hedging. It will certainly allow the more inspired fund manager to back his hunches on specific local markets, without necessarily risking his job!

v. *Choice of Return Through Gearing*

The opportunity to create both debt and equity securities from the same property provides the investor for the first time with a choice of investment return.

For example, assume a multi-let office building worth £50m, which produces a 6% initial yield, say £3m per annum. In simple terms, this income stream could support a debenture with a fixed coupon of 10% per annum, to raise capital of £30m. The remaining £20m of capital value could be raised by the issue of pure equity securities in the property, producing no income initially, but with the prospect of significant capital gains as the occupational rents are reviewed. If, two years later, following rent reviews, the property is producing a total rent of £5m per annum, the debenture holders continue to receive income fixed at £3m per annum and hence the remaining £2m of annual income will accrue to the equity shareholders, thus producing a leveraged potential capital gain for them.

This example, though simplistic, is viable in practice and illustrates one of the most important features which securitisation offers to investors. By creating different types of investment, backed by the same property, investors can choose between securities which yield largely income return and those which yield largely capital growth.

This type of 'layered securitisation' permits the precise targeting of investor groups. This could potentially make the distribution and trading of the securities more efficient, as well as making the overall approach to property financing more flexible, as will be shown below.

However, two points should be noted in relation to gearing. First, the equity and debt securities described above have quite different risk profiles. The debt securities will be relatively low risk as to income yield, because they are essentially secured on the covenants of the occupational leases. But, like other fixed interest stocks, their capital values will be susceptible to changes in prevailing interest rates.

The equity securities, on the other hand, because of the geared nature of their return, will carry a relatively higher risk as to both income and capital, in that the level of capital growth (and income yield) depends mainly on how far and how fast the property's rental income exceeds debt interest. Debt service to the debenture holders will always be a prior charge on total income.

Second, the 1988 Budget has had the effect of making investors more indifferent between income yield and capital gains, from a tax viewpoint. Capital gains tax is now charged at marginal income tax rates, rather than at a flat rate of 30%. However, for a variety of other reasons, the opportunity to distinguish between income-orientated and capital growth-orientated investments remains important. For example, mutual life assurance companies, by their very nature, will continue to prefer income yield to capital gains.

vi. *The Benefits to Developers*

For developers, securitisation provides a new source of long-term equity finance for the larger scheme. It enables developers to tap the capital markets direct for both longer-term equity and debt funding, and provides an alternative to outright sale of the entire development to a single purchaser, should one be available.

In recent years, the increasing use of the limited recourse construction loan has provided the developer with greater freedom in the timing and pricing of disposal of his completed scheme, by avoiding the need for a forward sale to an institution at a discounted price. But for the larger development, this approach can leave the bank which provides the construction loan with significant uncertainty over repayment, because of the illiquidity of the end product. Equally, it can leave the developer with uncertainty over the timing and amount of his profit. Securitisation offers greater certainty and flexibility to both borrower and lender. By floating the completed property on The Stock Exchange, the developer avoids dependence upon a single purchaser and has the opportunity to retain a stake for the future in a marketable form. Moreover, by issuing a blend of debt and equity securities, and thereby gearing the investment, the developer can raise a larger proportion of the property's capital value than the equity interest released, without necessarily losing management control.

The concept is readily applicable to joint venture developments, as an alternative to a more cumbersome side-by-side lease arrangement or the use of a taxable joint venture company. Each party simply holds a proportion of the shares, and the respective interests can be valued accordingly. The application of securitisation techniques to development funding is discussed in further detail below.

Critics may argue that, for the best of the larger developments, securitisation is unnecessary because 'there will always be an institution in the market for prime property'. They miss the point; the issue is one of price. Early in 1988, Beaufort House, a substantial office development in the City of London, was sold ahead of practical completion to a leading UK insurance company for a figure reported to be in the region of £200m. At the time, this deal was among the largest ever single investment purchases in the UK. What does this prove? Insufficient information has been published to permit a detailed analysis of the price, but the key questions are: how many other single purchasers made bids and what was the range of prices offered? At the time of writing, it is understood that the answer to the first was very few and to the second, very wide. This is all we really need to know, because these answers illustrate both the uncertainty which faces all developers of substantial schemes and the dilemma which faces those who finance them. It is indisputable that the price mechanism for property is inefficient for buildings worth more than £20m and particularly inadequate above £100m.

To the extent that securitisation injects greater liquidity and more efficient pricing into the market, it will be of significant benefit in the appraisal of large developments by providing greater precision in the assessment of completed value and greater opportunity for refinancing on completion.

III   LEGAL BACKGROUND TO SECURITISATION IN THE UK

1   Restrictions on the multiple ownership of land

As with any other asset, it is possible for land to be owned by a company and for the shares of the company to be freely transferable. If, however, a direct interest in the property is required, then the legal constraints which have developed over centuries in relation to land ownership become relevant.

A distinction is made in relation to land between the legal estate and the beneficial ownership. The former comprises the nominal entitlement to the land, the legal owners being those whose names appear in the title deeds or on the land register; the beneficial owners, on the other hand, are the true economic owners of the land. Legislation provides that the legal estate in land can be held by a maximum of four persons. Accordingly, where multiple ownership is required, there must be a separation between the legal and beneficial interests. If a number of investors wish to exploit land jointly, it is possible for them to form a partnership with the title to the land being held by a maximum of four of the investors whilst the rest have rights determined by a partnership agreement. This does not, however, provide a viable basis for establishing securitised interests in properties for two reasons:

a. The unlimited liability which results from being a member of a partnership, although this can to some extent be circumvented by taking advantage of the archaic provisions of the Limited Partnerships Act 1907.

b. The restriction imposed by what is now s 716 of the Companies Act 1985 upon the maximum number of people who can join together in a partnership, other than one that is carrying on a profession. The limit is 20 participants, which in practice imposes a wholly unacceptable constraint.

Apart from a company (discussed below), the only remaining form of multiple ownership which is suitable for securitisation is the unit trust. In principle, a unit trust arises where an asset – in this case land – is held by trustees on trust for members who are treated as holding transferable units in the asset. The unit trust will be constituted by a trust deed which will provide rules for the transfer of units, and the holding of meetings of unit holders and will specify the responsibilities of the trustees and the procedure for replacing them.

Historically, therefore, the two forms of ownership of land which are appropriate for securitisation have been ownership through the medium of a company and the use of a unit trust.

2 Historic constraints on securitisation

Consideration has been given on many occasions over the years to the possibility of securitising single properties, but the proposals have always foundered on one or more of the following:

a. *The Prevention of Fraud (Investments) Act 1958 (PFI)*

Until the introduction of the Financial Services Act 1986, this Act controlled many aspects of dealings in securities and, in particular, it made it a criminal offence to distribute circulars inviting participation in investments unless certain conditions were fulfilled. In practice, the restrictions did not apply to shares in companies, as compliance with the prospectus rules were felt to impose a sufficient degree of control. In the case of unit trusts, however, circulars inviting participation could be issued only if the unit trust was authorised or, in the case of an unauthorised unit trust, if approval was given by the Department of Trade and Industry (DTI). An authorised unit trust was one which was approved by the DTI for the purpose of the PFI. Although the legislation did not prohibit the authorisation of property unit trusts, the view of the DTI was that the way in which the Act was drafted was such that it felt unable to authorise property unit trusts, since the assets owned were not in the nature of shares or similar securities. The DTI had power to permit the issue of circulars for unauthorised unit trusts, but it declined to exercise the power in relation to single property unit trusts. It is understood that the DTI considered that such unit trusts should not be promoted as they offered a lack of spread of risk and insufficient liquidity.

As a result of the PFI, normal marketing of an unauthorised property unit trust was not possible and this in practice constituted an effective bar on the development of single property unit trusts.

b. *The Taxation Regime*
   i. *Companies*

Since capital gains tax was introduced in 1965, shareholders in companies have suffered from the disadvantage of what amounts to a double charge to capital gains tax. When the company disposes of an asset it is itself liable to corporation tax on the capital gain. When the investor disposes of his shares for a consideration which would normally reflect the net profit retained by the company, he in turn suffers personal capital gains tax on his profit. The effect of this can be demonstrated in rather crude terms with an example where a company makes a gain of £1,000. Its net gain, after paying corporation tax on capital gains at the rate of 35%, would be £650. If the investor is liable to capital gains tax at the top rate of 40%, he would, on disposing of his shares, pay 40% tax on the part of the purchase price reflecting the retained £650 profit, that is a further £260 of tax. The total tax liability would thus be £350 plus £260, that is £610. Had the investor held the property directly, the total tax liability on disposal would have been only £400.

In addition, with the increasing gap that is developing between the rate of income tax and the rate of corporation tax, there is an income tax disadvantage on dividends paid by a company. If a company makes a profit of £1,000, it pays corporation tax of £350, leaving £650 available for payment as a dividend. If it wishes to distribute the £650 as a dividend, it has to account for advance corporation tax (ACT) at a rate equivalent to the basic rate of income tax of 25%, on such an amount as, after deduction of the ACT, would leave the original £650. The amount of ACT payable on a dividend of £650 is accordingly £216 (ie, 25% of £866) which can be offset against the £350 corporation tax liability referred to above. The shareholder who receives the dividend of £650 is treated as having received a dividend of £866 from which income tax at the basic rate of £216 has been deducted. The net result is that the company is paying £350 of corporation tax against which there is available ACT of only £216 and the balance is a charge to taxation that would not have arisen if the investor had invested directly.

   ii. *Unit Trusts*

The position with unit trusts is more complicated, as a distinction has to be drawn between authorised and unauthorised unit trusts. For capital gains tax purposes, both types of trust are treated as if they were a company and as if the unit holders were shareholders in the company. In the case of authorised unit trusts, however, there is an exemption from capital gains tax upon gains made by the trust itself. Accordingly, there is tax transparency in relation to capital gains so far as authorised unit trusts are concerned – because the investors pay no more capital gains tax on a disposal than if they held the unit trust's assets in their own names – but the double charge which applies to a company applies also to unauthorised unit trusts.

In relation to income, authorised unit trusts are treated as companies and therefore have the same ACT problem as described above. Unauthorised unit trusts, however, are treated like ordinary trusts. The trustees pay income tax which is treated as a credit on distributions made to unit holders. There is thus effective tax transparency in the case of unauthorised unit trusts – but not authorised unit trusts – although a problem for unauthorised unit trusts is that there is no provision for deduction against the income tax liability for management charges incurred by the trustees.

c. *Market Place*

No available market existed for single property vehicles. The Stock Exchange would not permit the listing of single property vehicles, on the basis of lack of spread of risk and the difficulty of assessing the history of any relevant business.

3 Recent developments

There have been developments recently in the above areas, so that the present position is as follows:

a. *Collective Investment Schemes*

The PFI was replaced, with effect from 29 April 1988, by the provisions of the Financial Services Act 1986 (FSA). This introduced the concept of the 'collective investment scheme'. A collective investment scheme is defined as an arrangement with respect to property of any description, the purpose or effect of which is to enable persons taking part in the arrangement to participate in, or receive profit or income arising from, the acquisition, holding, management or disposal of property. One particular kind of investment scheme is the 'unit trust scheme', which is defined as a collective investment scheme under which the property in question is held on trust for the participants. The FSA prohibits the issue of advertisements in relation to collective investment schemes unless either the scheme is an authorised unit trust or, alternatively, the arrangements comply with regulations made by the DTI.

The concept of authorised unit trusts has been extended under the FSA so that, in particular, certain types of property trusts can, for the first time, be authorised. The provisions required to obtain authorisation are, however, very restrictive. In particular, a spread of investments is required so that no single property may account for more than 15% of the fund at the time it is acquired – although it does not have to be sold after acquisition until it accounts for at least 20% of the fund. Rental income must come from a range of tenants, with not more than 20% being derived from one company or group of companies. Not more than 20% of the fund can be in properties which are being developed or refurbished. It thus remains the position that a single property unit trust cannot be an authorised unit trust.

Unauthorised unit trusts and other collective investment schemes can be advertised only if the schemes meet the requirements laid down in the DTI regulations. These are examined in more detail below but they do specifically contemplate that a collective investment scheme may relate to a single property. The previous restrictive position on promotion has accordingly been significantly relaxed in that, provided that the DTI requirements as to the nature of the property and the scheme are satisfied, a single property scheme can now be promoted.

b. *The Taxation of Unit Trusts*

The taxation regime applicable to unit trusts was partially extended by the Finance Act 1987 (FA 1987). It remains the case that investors in unauthorised unit trusts effectively suffer from the double charge to capital gains tax but there is now substantial tax transparency on the income side. In particular, the FA 1987 provided that the income of an unauthorised unit trust is taxed in the hands of the trustees at basic rates (but not the additional rate normally applicable to discretionary trusts). Capital allowances are made available to the trustees and the unit holders are treated as receiving annual payments of distributed or accumulated income in proportion to their rights, equivalent to the grossed-up income with a basic rate credit. It remains the position that management expenses cannot be deducted.

c. *The Listing of Single Property Schemes*

In May 1987 The International Stock Exchange issued regulations permitting the listing of single property schemes. The Stock Exchange requirements are dealt with below.

Accordingly, it is now possible to promote and to obtain a listing for single property schemes but, as will be explained below, a single property scheme which is based on a trust structure continues to have certain taxation disadvantages in comparison with direct property ownership. As long as the authorities remain unwilling to authorise single property unit trusts, the taxation disadvantages of an unauthorised unit trust continue to apply.

IV APPROACHES TO SECURITISATION

In recent years, several attempts have been made to overcome the problems described above. The various securitisation vehicles developed are known respectively as the single asset property company (SAPCO), the single property ownership trust (SPOT) and the property income certificate scheme (PINCs).

V SAPCO

Definition

The SAPCO is not a new vehicle; it is simply a company which holds a single property as its only asset and has as its sole purpose the management of that property. The novel feature is that it can now be listed on The Stock Exchange in London. The interest to investors, therefore, is not in the SAPCO vehicle – which is merely a framework – but rather the layers of tradeable bonds and other securities which can be issued within it, all backed by the same single property.

The SAPCO is not tax transparent. It suffers tax to the same degree as any other company; but it can be geared and it offers a corporate style of management under the Companies Act, through the company's board of directors.

VI BILLINGSGATE

The first example in the UK of a quoted single asset property company was the flotation of the Samuel Montagu City headquarters at Billingsgate on the Luxembourg Stock Exchange in June 1986. At the time, this was a significant transaction, because it brilliantly demonstrated the philosophy behind layered securitisation. The flotation pre-dated the London Stock Exchange's decision to list single property vehicles by less than two months and hence the securities were initially listed in Luxembourg. In June 1988, securities in the property were listed on The London Stock Exchange. The transaction was not without its critics, but it achieved an attractive financing result for the owner, S & W Berisford, and established a useful precedent.

1 The property

The principal characteristics of the property are as follows:

Size: 185,000 sq ft, net lettable approximately.

Tenant: Samuel Montagu (now part of Midland Bank).

Terms: 35 years, full repairing and insuring, from 25 March 1985.

Rent:	£5m per annum exclusive, subject to five yearly upwards only rent reviews.
Capital value:	£79m to show 6.2% initial yield, as at June 1986. (Revalued in March 1988 at £110m.)

2 The objective

The property had been developed as a joint venture between S & W Berisford (Berisfords) and London & Edinburgh Trust (LET), and was completed in September 1985. Berisfords had subsequently bought out LET and were seeking to reduce their capital exposure to the property but to retain an equity interest for the longer term.

3 The solution

A single asset property company, known as Billingsgate City Securities Plc (the Company), was formed to hold the property and three different types of security were created:

—deep discount bonds;

—ordinary shares; and

—cumulative preferred ordinary shares.

Both the bonds and the preferred ordinary shares were listed and underwritten; the ordinary shares were not listed but were issued to and fully retained by Berisfords as an investment.

4 Key features of the deep discount bonds

Capital raised:	A nominal £52.5m issued at 32.5% discount to produce £35.5m.
Term:	20 years.
Security:	First fixed and floating charge on the property and the other assets of the company. Letter of credit protection equal to three interest payments.
Redemption yield:	Gross yield to maturity, 10.6% at issue price, representing 115 basis points above Treasury 13.5% 2004/2008 at the time of issue.
Coupon:	$6\frac{5}{8}$% nominal, equivalent to approximately 9.8% per annum on capital raised of £35.5m. Payable semi-annually in arrears.

[Photograph: Montagu House, Billingsgate, London]

Capital cover:	2.24 times at the issue price.
Interest cover:	1.44 times based on the then current rent of £5m per annum.

5 Key features of the preferred ordinary shares

Capital raised:	25.8 million 1p shares issued at £1.00 per share.
Security:	Entitlement to income and capital only after debt service.
Income:	Initial yield of 5.9% gross, payable as half yearly dividend, subject to increases as rental income increases up to a maximum of 30.44%.
Tax subsidy:	The preferred ordinary shares benefit from the deferral of the rights of the ordinary shares (see below) which are primarily liable for all corporation tax on income and any capital gains tax on disposal suffered by the Company.
Stock Exchange Listing:	The shares were listed initially in Luxembourg and subsequently on The International Stock Exchange in London.
Disposal of the property and winding up:	In December 2001 and at yearly intervals thereafter, the preferred shareholders will, upon the occurrence of certain specified events, have the right to instruct the directors to dispose of the property or to wind up the Company. This right is subject to the call option, described below.

6 Key features of the ordinary equity

 i. Full gearing benefit.

 ii. No dividend entitlement until the rent increases at the first rent review (March 1990).

iii. The shareholders are entitled to 69.56% of any rental and capital growth, after deducting 100% of the Company's tax liabilities.

 iv. The shareholders absorb all management costs not recoverable from the tenants, all corporate taxation and the risk of shortfall between the sale price (should the property be sold) and an independent valuation.

 v. The shareholders have an option to purchase the preferred shares, exercisable either:

    a. after the preferred shareholders have initiated the disposal procedure (described above); or

b. in January 2006 and at five yearly intervals thereafter.

The purchase price would be based on two contemporaneous independent professional valuations of the property, undertaken in accordance with RICS Guidance Notes.

7 Principal achievements

Billingsgate demonstrated how a geared securitisation vehicle could be used to raise some 75% (net of costs) of the property's capital value for the owners by releasing only some 30% of the equity value. To that extent, it set a helpful precedent for the securitisation market in the UK.

In a wider context, the transaction was a milestone in presenting the first limited recourse deep discount bond issued on a single property in the UK. This was made possible because the property's income flow was secured totally on Samuel Montagu's covenant for 35 years. Even if Montagu were to assign the lease, English property law acknowledges the privity of contract of the original lessee.

Since Billingsgate, deep discounted bonds have been applied to single developments. Two schemes by Greycoat Plc, for example Embankment Plaza at Charing Cross Station and Victoria Plaza Phase II at Victoria Station were partly financed by deep discount bonds in a zero coupon form. However, in both cases, the bonds were issued with full recourse to the borrower, because of the speculative development risk.

8 Principal weaknesses

Billingsgate suffered much criticism at the time because of the apparent difficulty in placing the preferred ordinary shares among a wider audience of investors, and because of the apparently limited trading market in the stock, at least initially. This may be partly explained by:

 i. *Lack of Gearing*

Many analysts considered the lack of gearing to the preferred ordinary shares to be a deterrent; the stock was regarded as 'unexciting'. All the gearing benefit was retained by the ordinary shareholders (Berisfords).

 ii. *Single Tenant*

The property was floated as a newly completed development, occupied by a single tenant on a lease subject to five yearly rent reviews. Consequently, there were to be no frequent changes in the income flow to encourage differing views on price. Increased trading activity could be anticipated as a rent review approached – as speculation increased as to its outcome – but little excitement in the intervening periods. Equally, as a brand new development, there was little immediate prospect of refurbishment. The regular, stepped income profile of the investment therefore left little to the imagination.

iii. *Lack of True Tax Transparency*

The total tax liability was the same as with any company. The structure merely shifted the burden to the ordinary shareholders, in return for which they enjoyed a more than proportionate part of the benefits. If, however, the tax liability happened to be so large that there was insufficient net income or net proceeds of sale to meet the rights of the preferred shareholders, then the preferred shareholders would suffer as a result.

iv. *Luxembourg Listing*

For many UK institutions, this was an initial disadvantage, for psychological as much as practical reasons. However, although the London listing made it easier for investors to track share price movements, it made little apparent difference to trading volume, probably for the reasons stated above.

v. *Refurbishment Uncertainty*

The prospectus was rather vague about how a future refurbishment of the property would be funded. This was not an immediate concern, but it may have distracted the longer term investor.

vi. *Call Option*

It was argued at the time that the ordinary shareholders' call option to redeem the preferred ordinary shares acted as a clog on the trading price. To an extent, this undermined the objective of securitisation, that of allowing the trading price to be set by free market forces.

Billingsgate will perhaps be remembered principally as a special vehicle designed for a special transaction. It was not intended to be part of a wider initiative to create an active securitisation market, although its timing was helpful to the cause and the transaction itself neatly demonstrated a number of important precedents. At the time of writing (August 1988), Berisfords have made a bid to buy back all the preferred shares to provide them with total control once more, thus removing this 'pilot' securitisation from the market.

VII   SPOTs

The objective of the SPOT is to provide for the multiple equity ownership of a single property investment through a trust based vehicle which can be floated on The Stock Exchange. The SPOT offers the unit holder a direct participation in the property's rental income and capital growth, combined with management rights via a trustee, which would retain the ownership of the property itself. However, it is not intended that the SPOT should be geared.

It is anticipated that the scheme would be constituted by a trust deed in a manner similar to an ordinary unit trust. This will set out the rights of the investors, the circumstances in which majority decisions have to be taken, the duties of the trustees, the duties of the managers and the circumstances in which the trustees and managers can be replaced.

Whereas PINCs (see below) achieved the key objectives of securitisation by working within the current law, the SPOT required the law to be changed, particularly in order to achieve full tax transparency. Although FSA permitted the concept of the SPOT, in June 1988 the Treasury confirmed that it would not grant the SPOT tax transparency as to capital gains. Consequently, the SPOT is currently in abeyance.

VIII PINCs

The third approach, PINCs, has been devised by Richard Ellis Financial Services and County NatWest Limited, in conjunction with Berwin Leighton, ANZ Merchant Bank, Peat Marwick McLintock and Lawrence Graham. Its development is now supported and encouraged by The PINCs Association.

A PINC is a tradeable share in a single property company. It entitles the holder to a direct participation in the property's rental income and capital value with the benefit of tax transparency, the potential for gearing and without the obligation of management. PINCs can be listed on the main market of The International Stock Exchange and can be held by both professional investors and the general public. A vendor can sell either a whole or part of its equity interest in a particular property through PINCs, but suffers a capital gains tax liability only on the part released and has the flexibility to release further tranches of its interest in the future. PINCs offer a corporate style of management, regulated by the Companies Act and the Takeover Code in the same way as for other listed companies. The PINC therefore achieves the key objectives of securitisation and is currently unique in being the only instrument capable of so doing in the UK.

1 Philosophy

The approach has been to devise a technique for securitising single properties to achieve the benefits required by investors and vendors, but within the current law. The starting point is the belief that investors wishing to participate in securitisation do not of necessity require an interest in the property as such. Their objectives will be satisfied if they can be put in a position achieving the same financial benefits and having the same management participation as if they were direct holders of a property interest. PINCs therefore separate the property interest on the one hand from the financial and management interest on the other in the manner described below.

2 The PINCs security

A PINC is a composite security encompassing two inseparable elements:

i. the right to receive a share of the property's quarterly income flow; and

ii. an ordinary share in a specially created company which exercises control and management over the property and in which the PINCs investors and the vendor (if it retains an equity interest) hold ordinary shares. Each ordinary share carries one vote.

These elements combine to provide the investors with a share of the property's capital value. A PINC is, in effect, a limited liability equity share in a tax transparent single asset property company.

3 Structure

1 PARTIAL DISPOSAL

The vendor can initially release whatever equity interest it chooses into the market, subject to a 25% minimum, as required by The Stock Exchange if the PINCs are to be listed. Diagram 1, opposite, illustrates the structure, assuming that the vendor owns the freehold and has released 70% of its equity interest in the property as PINCs and has retained 30%. It may subsequently release more; the potential disposal of its entire interest is described later and produces a simpler structure.

The basis of the structure is similar to the position of the vendor and the investors each holding shares in a single asset property company (NewCo), but with two principal differences:

i. The vendor and the investors receive their income and capital via a financial intermediary (FI). If the investors were to receive rent direct from NewCo, it would be taxed as a dividend.

ii. The vendor retains its interest as an interest in land, via a leasehold relationship with FI, rather than as PINCs. As will be explained below, this arrangement minimises the vendor's capital gains tax liability.

The roles of the parties in Diagram 1 are as follows:

NewCo

This is the management and controlling company for the property, in which

Diagram 1

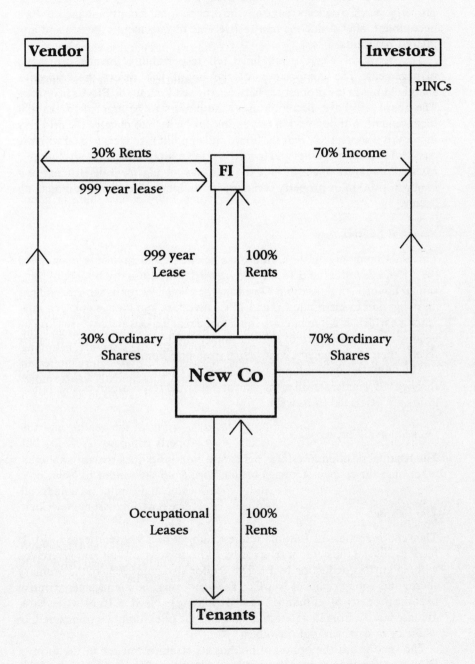

both the vendor and the PINCs investors hold ordinary shares pro rata to their share of rental income. NewCo is a public limited company which can be listed on The Stock Exchange. It would usually be known by the name of the property. NewCo collects rent from the occupational tenants and pays to FI a net amount, after deducting non-recoverable management expenses and any interest payments.

The board of NewCo will have full responsibility for the property's management. The composition of the board will reflect the respective shareholdings in the property as between the vendor and the PINCs investors. The board will have discretion as to the powers to be granted to external management. Although it will be possible for NewCo to manage the property directly, it is more likely that the board will appoint managers to deal with the day-to-day responsibilities and to advise upon management strategy. Suitable external managers might include the property management department of a major institution or property company, or an independent firm of managing agents.

Financial Intermediary

This is the company through which income and capital payments are made to the PINCs investors and to the vendors. FI would usually be a bank or a similar financial organisation. FI will charge a small fee for its services and has an obligation to distribute to the PINCs investors and the vendor, pro rata, amounts which, in aggregate, are equal to the rent it receives from NewCo. The vendor receives its share of the rent under the headlease and the investors receive their share under a contractual deed poll from FI.

Although the relationship between NewCo, FI and the vendor is expressed through 999 year leases, all management rights and responsibilities under these leases are delegated to NewCo.

Occupational Tenants

The tenants' position and their rights and responsibilities remain unaltered, other than the change of immediate landlord from the vendor to NewCo.

The Vendor

The vendor retains the freehold interest, subject to a 999 year lease to FI. It receives 30% of the net rent received by FI from NewCo. This rent is received without any tax deduction by FI. The vendor also holds 30% of the ordinary shares and voting rights of NewCo. The vendor has no management control over the property other than via its shareholding in NewCo. Its NewCo shares are inseparable from its interest in land and the one cannot be transferred, in whole or in part, without the other.

The vendor has the option of holding its retained interest in the form of PINCs, rather than as an interest in land. However, this would trigger a CGT liability on the value of the entire equity interest, rather than only that part released into the market.

When entering into its lease with the vendor, FI will undertake to pay to the vendor a premium for its 70% profit rental. The premium will be expressed to be equal to the amount which FI will raise from the issue of PINCs. Thus the vendor receives from the PINCs investors, via FI, a capital sum equal to 70% of the total value of the property.

Should the vendor wish to dispose of its retained interest, it can do so either as a conventional property transaction – selling the interest in land together with its ordinary shares in NewCo – or by making a further issue of PINCs. Disposals would be subject to the rules of the Takeover Code.

PINCs Investors

The investors hold 70% of the ordinary shares (and voting rights) of NewCo. They receive 70% of the net income of FI as a contractual payment under the deed poll, made quarterly in arrears and subject only to withholding tax (see below). Minority investors will benefit from similar protection as to those in other listed companies. Because of the composite nature of the PINC security, a transfer of a PINC automatically results in a transfer of an ordinary share in NewCo, together with the corresponding entitlement to income from FI.

2 TOTAL DISPOSAL

Diagram 2, overleaf, illustrates the structure, assuming that the vendor has released as PINCs, either initially or subsequently, 100% of its equity interest in the property.

This is a much simpler structure. In these circumstances, the freehold interest will be sold to NewCo for a nominal sum. It has no material value, since it carries no right to income or management. NewCo would grant a lease and leaseback of 999 years to FI at 100% of the net rents receivable, after deducting non-recoverable management expenses and interest payments. The lease granted by NewCo to FI would be at a peppercorn rent. The PINCs investors would own 100% of the ordinary shares and voting rights in NewCo and would receive income equal to 100% of the net rents from the property.

3 TAXATION

The taxation treatment of the PINCs arrangement is as follows:

The Vendor

The grant of the lease by the vendor to FI will be treated as a part disposal. Consequently, the vendor pays capital gains tax in respect of that part of its interest which is sold as PINCs. The release of a partial interest in the property through PINCs will not trigger the recapture of capital allowances; the full

Diagram 2

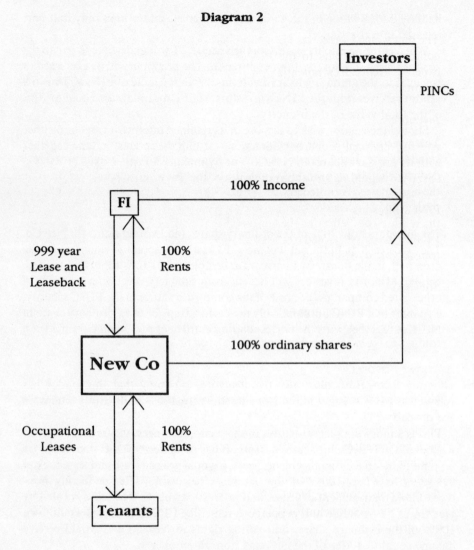

benefit of such allowances remains with the vendor. It receives rental income gross of tax.

NewCo

NewCo will be liable for corporation tax only to the extent that it makes profits on its management charges. However, should it choose to retain income to accumulate a sinking fund, perhaps for improvement works to the property, this would suffer corporation tax. In practice, such sinking funds are rarely used under modern leases.

Financial Intermediary

The rent which FI receives from NewCo is treated as a trading receipt, but the contractual payments to the PINCs investors are treated as an allowable expense. Hence FI's potential tax liability is effectively netted off. The tax treatment of FI in this way is the key to the tax transparency of PINCs.

Investors

The investors will suffer withholding tax on income received from FI at the standard rate. If the investor is a tax exempt pension fund or charity, the tax deducted will be recoverable. If not, the deduction will count as a tax credit in the normal way. As noted above, the investors will not be able to claim directly the benefit of the vendor's capital allowances. However, this would not prevent the vendor from reflecting the benefit of its allowances in the price at which the PINCs are first issued, although this benefit would not normally be transferable to a subsequent purchaser.

Stamp Duty

It is expected that a charge to stamp duty at 1% on the proceeds from the grant of the long lease to FI will arise. Investors will pay stamp duty at 0.5% on trading PINCs, as for other equity securities.

VAT

Under current legislation the grant of the long leases and the execution of the deed poll will be exempt supplies for VAT purposes. Once the currently proposed changes to VAT liability on construction and property supplies have been implemented in 1989, the grant of the headlease and the underlease will continue to be exempt from VAT. The subscription price payable by investors upon flotation will not be subject to VAT, nor will distributions by FI under the deed poll. However, NewCo will be given the option to charge VAT on rent and this will be a decision for the NewCo board, depending upon the prevailing circumstances.

The taxation treatment of PINCs, as described above, has been cleared by the Inland Revenue and Customs & Excise and creates a truly tax transparent medium for securitisation.

IX RAISING NEW CAPITAL

1 Equity

The PINCs structure allows rights issues to be made to provide new equity capital; the usual Stock Exchange procedure will be followed. The rights issue may be needed either to repay loans to NewCo (see below) or to raise additional capital to finance a major refurbishment of the property, should the available loan capital be insufficient. In either event, it would be for the board of NewCo to make a suitable case for the issue to its shareholders in the usual way and to arrange underwriting, as appropriate.

2   Debt

It is anticipated that from time to time it will be appropriate for gearing to be introduced into the PINCs structure. This could occur either at the time of the PINCs flotation or subsequently, perhaps for the purposes of refurbishment. The DTI regulations (see below) permit NewCo to borrow up to 75% of the property's capital value. Gearing in excess of this level is permitted for a specific purpose, subject to shareholders' approval. Interest payments on debt would be a prior charge on the rental stream received by NewCo from the occupational tenants. In order to provide additional security for borrowing, it has been suggested that NewCo would be granted an option to require FI's interest for £1 in order to provide a material interest in land. Such an option would only be exercised in the event of a default, as it would have the effect of collapsing the PINCs structure.

In all cases, the borrowing would be raised through NewCo, non-recourse to both the vendor and the PINCs investors, who retain limited liability. In the case of borrowing made at the time of flotation, funds raised would be passed to FI to form part of the consideration to be paid to the vendor; the balance would come from the issue of, in this case, geared PINCs. Funds borrowed for the purpose of refurbishing the property would remain with NewCo to be spent as appropriate.

It is the responsibility of NewCo to negotiate the terms of such loans and to obtain such shareholders' approval as may be necessary.

Repayment of loan capital can be undertaken in one of two ways. If it is repaid from retained income, interest payable by NewCo will be deductible in determining its taxation liability, but repayments of capital will not be. Repayments in this way can only be made out of taxed income, although this feature is one that is common to all borrowers on property assets. Consequently, it may prove more appropriate for loan capital to be repaid by making a rights issue of PINCs, as described above.

X   THE REGULATORY REGIME FOR SINGLE PROPERTY SCHEMES

All listed single property vehicles are subject to the rules laid down by the International Stock Exchange (ISE). In addition, unit trusts (including SPOTs) and PINCs are subject to the rules of the DTI and the Securities and Investments Board (SIB), which relate to collective investment schemes. The view has been expressed that PINCs are not strictly within the definition of collective investment schemes but it has been accepted that, as the position is not free from doubt, they should comply with the rules which are imposed upon collective investment schemes generally.

1 Definition of a single property

The ISE, DTI and SIB have each adopted the definition of a single property contained in s 76 of the FSA, as follows:

a. a single building (or a single building with ancillary buildings) managed by or on behalf of the operator of the scheme; or

b. a group of adjacent or contiguous buildings managed by him or on his behalf as a single entreprise, with or without ancillary land and with or without furniture, fittings or other contents of the building or buildings in question.

In the case of a PINCs scheme, the operator would be NewCo.

2 The ISE regulations

The ISE's special listing provisions for single property schemes were published in May 1987 and are set out in the Appendix to this chapter[1]. The key provisions are summarised below:

a. *Suitable Property*

The property must be freehold or a leasehold of at least 110 years unexpired. The single property scheme's activity has to be restricted to the management of the scheme for at least five years following listing and the property must be sufficiently let for its expected annual income to cover expected annual outgoings. The property which is the subject of the scheme must have a value of at least £10m. The scheme must provide for full distribution of net income.

The name of the scheme must include the name or address of the property. The scheme must be wound up if the property is sold. Both winding up and sale require approval by 75% of the shareholders. Normal pre-emption rights are to apply.

b. *Listing Particulars*

A prospectus for the property will be required. This is intended to provide a summary of all the information which a prudent purchaser of the property would normally require, in addition to information about the single property scheme itself and the securities to be held. Detailed information, including the occupational leases and various specialist reports, will be available for inspection. The property itself, at least externally, is there for all to see.

1 Reproduced with the kind permission of The International Stock Exchange of the United Kingdom and the Republic of Ireland Limited.

The prospectus will summarise the history of the property, together with details of its location, construction, layout, services and floor areas. Maps, plans and photographs can be used to illustrate these features. The tenancies have to be specified and, where any particular tenant accounts for more than 50% of the rental income, financial information so far as is publicly available has to be disclosed in relation to that tenant. The main terms of the leases have to be specified, including particularly the rent review clause and service charge provisions, and a pro forma summary has to be included.

An open market valuation of the property is to be undertaken by an external valuer in accordance with usual RICS guidelines. In addition there must be a full report on the physical condition of the property. Specialist engineers' reports may also be required, for example in connection with the property's air conditioning system. A solicitor's report on title is required together with details of current insurance arrangements.

The prospectus will describe the proposals for management. Under a PINCs scheme, for example, NewCo will have been formed specifically for the flotation and will not have a track record. Its board of directors and their management philosophy for the property should be described. If external managers are to be employed, it will be appropriate to include details of their relevant experience, as well as a summary of the terms of the management contract.

Clearly, as already noted, it is difficult to provide the five-year trading record normally required for a full listing but, insofar as the scheme has a trading record, an accountant's report on income and expenditure during the last five years, or such a lesser period as is available, has to be included.

c. *Continuing Management Obligations*

ISE has also imposed a number of special continuing obligations. The managers are obliged to produce annual reports which must provide projections of expenditure for the following financial year, together with details of major expenditure obligations reasonably foreseeable beyond that period. Independent building surveys are required at three-yearly intervals. Although annual valuations of the property are not required, independent valuations have to be provided when further issues of securities are made. A log book is to be maintained which has to be available for public inspection. This will contain details of title, physical structure, lettings and all other relevant information. There is a continuing obligation to provide information to the market of any significant matters which become known to the directors or managers including, for example, late payment of any material amount of rent, grant or major variation of significant leases and details of any material changes in the matters disclosed in the listing particulars.

The requirement for this degree of disclosure is discussed further below under 'Key Issues'.

3 The DTI regulations

At the time of writing (August 1988) the DTI regulations are in final draft form and should be published shortly. In general, the regulations follow those set down by ISE, but they are more detailed in some respects, particularly in relation to borrowing powers.

They cover two types of single property scheme – corporate-based schemes (such as PINCs) and trust-based schemes (such as SPOTs). The property interest involved must be worth at least £5m and must be freehold or leasehold having at least 110 years unexpired. At least 50% of the property's lettable floor area must be let for periods of not less than five years or, alternatively, at least 50% of the property must be pre-let with lettings of not less than 12 months to take place after completion of a refurbishment scheme.

In the case of corporate-based schemes such as PINCs, the investors must have the right to appoint a number of directors proportionate to their interest in the scheme as a whole. Both NewCo and FI under a PINCs scheme will have to be authorised investment businesses under FSA.

The income from the property must be sufficient to discharge its expected outgoings (subject to the gearing provisions, outlined below) and the whole income must be distributed, subject to certain necessary retentions for management purposes.

Borrowing by trust-based schemes will be restricted to borrowing for refurbishment purposes and may not exceed three times annual rental. Corporate-based schemes will have an additional right to borrow 75% of the current open market value of the property and the ability to maintain this gearing ratio in the future. The interest to be valued for this purpose is NewCo's, on the assumption that NewCo pays only a peppercorn rent under its lease from FI.

Certain transactions will require the approval of 75% of participants (including the refurbishment, refinancing and disposal of the property).

4 The SIB regulations

These cover a number of matters delegated by the DTI and, again, only draft regulations are currently available. Final publication is expected to coincide with the DTI rules, which may well have occurred before this book is published. However, the SIB have already made it clear that, for listed vehicles, compliance with the regulations of The Stock Exchange will suffice. For non-listed vehicles details will be laid down as to the contents of the initial scheme particulars, which will largely follow The Stock Exchange rules.

XI THE FLOTATION PROCESS

The flotation of a single property is a similar process to the flotation of any company. Aside from marketing and timing issues, key considerations will be:

i. the proportion of the equity interest in the property to be floated and whether or not the interest is to be geared;

ii. the responsibility for management;

iii. the method of flotation, ie, placing or an offer for sale;

iv. the pricing of the securities relative to the open market valuation.

The cost of the exercise will depend largely upon the complexity of the property, the capital sum to be raised and the method of flotation used. The process usually involves a number of different professional advisers and the vendor will inevitably compare the cost of flotation with the cost of disposal by private treaty through the conventional property market. A relevant consideration is that, if the initial offering is of a partial interest only, the release of further tranches in the future can usually be made at a much lower relative cost than the initial exercise, because much of the required information will already have been published. A further issue of 10% of the equity by a vendor will require listing particulars.

XII TRADING THE SECURITIES

Single property securities will be traded on The Stock Exchange in the same way as other main board listed securities. Current prices will be shown on SEAQ (Stock Exchange Automated Quotations). It is probable that the securities will initially be classified as gamma stocks, so prices on screen may be indicative rather than firm. Settlement will be via TALISMAN, The Stock Exchange's established settlement system. TOPIC will carry information on the properties as for other listed companies. Investors will be able to monitor price movements either on screen or in daily newspapers.

The Inland Revenue has ruled that PINCs (and probably also SPOTs if they appear) will be subject to the accrued income scheme. Prices quoted for PINCs will include the income accrued to date (ie, the prices will be 'dirty' prices). The Inland Revenue has agreed to the use of a national rate of accrual, which will be a proportion of the anticipated actual rate and will be agreed annually in advance between the Inland Revenue and each NewCo. The Stock Exchange will include details of notional accrued interest on PINCs in its regularly published list of accrued interest for account securities.

Broking houses will issue analysts' research and comments on individual properties and on the securitisation market generally, as they do for other stocks. There will be a number of market makers for each stock. Some firms of chartered surveyors are also likely to provide research material and may also act as agency brokers, provided they are authorised to do so under FSA.

The securities will be available to both professional and private investors, from the large financial institution to the private individual. Anyone who deals or arranges deals in the securities, or who advises or manages single property schemes must be authorised under FSA, usually as a member of a Recognised Professional Body or as a member of a Self-Regulating Organisation.

XIII THE APPLICATION OF SECURITISATION TO DEVELOPMENT FINANCE

1 Importance

The use of securitisation techniques in development finance is a potentially important application of the concept. Some of the key benefits were discussed at the beginning of this chapter.

Property development continues to have popular appeal. Many people would like to see themselves as a latter day Charles Clore or Harold Samuel. The vast fortunes of men such as Donald Trump and Alan Bond perpetuate the public image that property development is the key to wealth on a grand scale.

The willingness of the private individual to participate in major development schemes is therefore plausible; the issue in practice principally concerns risks and disclosure – a need to ensure that the private or professional investor is adequately protected. The application of securitisation techniques to property development will therefore be a gradual evolution, heavily labelled with health warnings.

2 The regulatory regime

Both the ISE's and the DTI's regulations potentially allow the flotation of a development in the course of construction, provided that it is pre-let. The DTI's rules specifically require pre-lettings of 50% of the property's net lettable floor area. These requirements are entirely prudent, but, in practice, because of the additional risks involved, the flotation of a development in progress seems unlikely until the market hs been operating successfully for several years.

However, the current regulations are sufficiently flexible to enable a developer to structure the financing of a development scheme in contemplation of its flotation on completion. This has particular advantages for joint venture developments and is illustrated in the following example:

3 Questions for the developer

The key questions for the developer in these circumstances are as follows:

i. What proportion of the equity interest does he wish to retain? The opportunity for gearing potentially allows the developer to release a smaller proportion of the equity interest than the proportion raised of the property's capital value.

ii. Does the developer wish to retain management control? This not only refers to the project management of the development, but, more particularly, to longer term management of the completed investment.

4   Achieving the funding aim

The following example, based on a PINCs structure, is simplified to emphasise the critical points. In practice, other, more sophisticated approaches could be used.

Assume a central City office building with a total development cost (including finance and voids) of £80m and a pro forma completed value of £100m. Assume the developer can raise a limited recourse construction loan (including interest) for 75% of the total cost; he will put in £5m of equity himself and needs to raise a further £15m elsewhere.

PINC HOUSE

	£m	£m
Completed value		100
Total development cost		
Financed by:		
Limited recourse loan (including rolled-up interest)	60	
Equity: Developer	5	
Investors	15	
		80
Profit		20

A not untypical scenario. How can it be funded?

One solution would be to structure a joint venture through the PINCs vehicle, taking advantage of its tax transparency, by a private placing of equity among a syndicate of investors to provide the required £15m in return for, say, 50% of the profit. Both the developer and the equity investors hold PINCs and the freehold title rests with NewCo, which becomes the joint venture company for the development. The limited recourse debt is raised by NewCo to cover the remainder of the construction costs. The scheme is then built out and let to produce a completed value of £100m. This structure is illustrated in Diagram 3 overleaf.

This is not an unusual arrangement, except that the joint venture is structured

Diagram 3

Joint Venture Structure

(Before profit distribution)

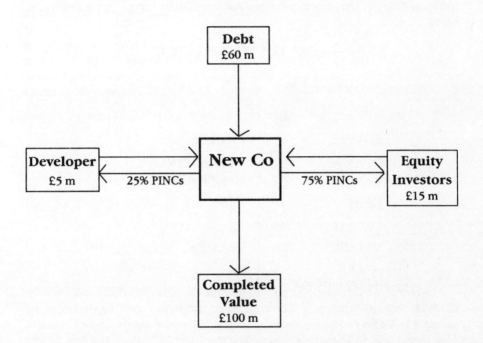

through PINCs, rather than by a leasehold arrangement or a conventional joint venture company. Each party simply holds a proportion of the PINCs. Although the equity contributions in this example mean that the developer has only a 25% shareholding in the joint venture company, arrangements would usually be made to ensure that for certain important decisions, (such as lettings and sales), the developer's position would be suitably protected. Alternatively, a small amount of equity could be held in equal shares and the rest of the required contributions could be subscribed in the form of loan stock. However, this would create a rather more complicated structure.

Once the development has been completed and let, in order to refinance the construction loan and to release profit, the joint venture can either remain as a private arrangement or it can be floated by a public issue of PINCs on The Stock Exchange. Within these parameters, a number of options are available.

A key decision will be whether the debt is to be fully repaid or refinanced to leave investors and the developer (if he wishes to retain an interest) with geared

PINCs. Equally it will be necessary to decide how much of each partner's shareholding is to be released into the market. This will have a direct bearing on management control.

One option would be a flotation to raise £75m of the £100m capital value by a new issue of conventional PINCs. This would be sufficient to pay off the debt of £60m and to buy out the developer for £15m (that is, his £5m of equity plus 50% of the profit of £20m), leaving the original equity investors holding 25% of the equity of NewCo, ignoring any further subscription by them. This is illustrated below:

PURE EQUITY TAKE-OUT

Pre-flotation		*Post-flotation*	
	£m		*£m*
EQUITY		EQUITY	
Developer	5	Partners' PINCs	25
Partners	15	New PINCs	75
DEBT	60		
PROFIT	20		
VALUE	100	VALUE	100

However, it would equally be possible to raise the £75m by refinancing the debt of £60m, perhaps through a debenture issue, and buying out the developer by issuing PINCs for £15m, representing 37.5% of the new equity base of NewCo. This would leave the original equity investors with 62.5% of the new equity interest between them in a highly geared form. This is illustrated below:

GEARED TAKE-OUT

Pre-flotation		*Post-flotation*	
	£m		*£m*
EQUITY		EQUITY	
Developer	5	New PINCs	15
Partners	15	Partners' PINCs	25
DEBT	60	DEBT	60
PROFIT	20		
VALUE	100	VALUE	100

The mechanics of this second example in practice are fairly complex. Of fundamental concern will be the price at which the new equity will be issued, because debt service will be a prior charge on rental income. Relevant considerations will include:

(1) The annual interest cost and whether this is fixed, floating or stepped. The Billingsgate example, as already described, used a deep discount bond at a fixed coupon;

(2) The levels of interest cover and capital cover on the debt which the market will require, assuming that the arrangements will be without recourse to the equity investors;

(3) The quality of tenants' covenants underpinning the rental income, the length of the leases and the timing of rent reviews;

(4) The level of return which an equity investor might reasonably expect, considering the risks involved.

Consideration of these factors will indicate the proportion of the total equity which will need to be offered to secure the amount required, in this example, £50m. Clearly, the answer will affect the position of the original PINCs investors and the value of their shares. Hence, although the geared take-out route offers potentially greater flexibility in refinancing a development, it also carries potentially higher risks for the equity investor than the pure equity take-out route.

5 Further variations

Conventional companies can already issue a variety of securities to achieve specific funding objectives. Similarly, it seems likely that single property companies in the future will be able to issue different types of security besides ordinary shares and debentures. Convertibles and warrants, for example, would seem to be well suited to developments, while the possibility of traded options in the more liquid property stocks would open up significant hedging opportunities. These variations permit not only more precise targeting of different investor groups, but also more precise pricing of the securities and therefore more efficient financing of the property itself.

However, because of the additional risks and technical complexity involved, it seems likely that the application of securitisation to developments, as well as the introduction of these further variations, will only gradually evolve in practice.

XIV   KEY ISSUES

Having now reviewed the need for securitisation, the vehicles available and the expected operation of the market, a number of key issues remain which only experience of the market in practice is likely to resolve.

1   Will there be a liquid market?

This is the billion dollar question. Liquidity is the principal objective of the whole exercise. Independent research commissioned by The PINCs Association in 1986, demonstrated an enthusiasm from institutional investors for the concept from an early stage in its development. Some 200 organisations of varying sizes were surveyed, drawn from insurance companies, pension funds, investment trusts, fund management groups, property companies and advisers. Although the majority considered themselves likely investors, there was little consensus about what would constitute a liquid market.

The Association's judgment is that the market will take some two or three years to prove itself, enough time for perhaps 20 properties to have been floated, say £500m of stock in issue. The depth of liquidity will depend on there being sufficient choice of opportunity for potential investors to review their positions in the market on a regular basis. As discussed above, in connection with Billingsgate, the characteristics of the initial properties will be crucial in achieving trading success. Investors are purchasing a share in an income stream and trading will be encouraged if there are features about the property which prompt speculation as to its future income flow or capital value. Multi-let or reversionary properties and the potential for gearing provide good examples, as well as the need to offer a spread of yield opportunities.

Perhaps the indisputable feature of this market, which is the most certain to encourage trading, is that there is no single value for any property investment. Investors in the conventional property market have differing views of a specific property's value; securitisation gives them the opportunity to express these views. The combination of short-term and long-term investors, arbitrageurs and opportunists, not least the appointed market makers, should enhance trading activity and potential liquidity.

2   Will the stock trade at a discount or premium?

The immediate answer must be, to what? If the question is intended to refer to the value of the property as a whole, the principal issue it begs is what is the value of the property?

The Stock Exchange's listing provisions for single property schemes require that the flotation prospectus must contain an open market valuation of the property as a whole on a conventional basis by an independent valuer. The valuation would include any discount for bulk which the valuer considered appropriate. The Stock Exchange does not require regular revaluations of the property, except where new capital is to be raised. It was strongly felt by those involved in drafting these rules that the trading price of the stock should be a free market price, unimpaired by an external valuation. In considering the first PINCs flotations, the objective was to price the stock initially as close as possible to par; on this basis, investors would receive approximately the same net initial yield and the vendor would receive approximately the same net proceeds as if the property had been sold on the conventional market at the prospectus valuation. Consequently, the issue price would not anticipate either a discount or a premium in the trading price but, at the same time, would give investors the benefit of any discount for bulk included in the prospectus valuation.

There is no technical justification for an automatic discount; PINCs, for example, are tax transparent and hence avoid an inherent potential capital gains tax (CGT) liability – the traditional reason for a discount to net asset value (NAV) of a property company share. The significance of this automatic discount has been emphasised by the effect of the 1988 Budget provisions on property company share prices. The 1988 Budget considerably reduced the impact of CGT on property companies by moving the base date for assessment from 1965 to 1982, with full indexation thereafter, and by an adjustment in the rate of tax from a flat 30% to the applicable marginal corporation tax rate. The effect of these changes significantly reduced the potential CGT liability on many property companies and the average discount to NAV fell sharply virtually overnight. Indeed, at the time of writing, (August 1988) property company shares are trading at an average discount to net asset value of below 10%. Should this be maintained, it may reduce any implied pressure on a securitised property stock to trade at an apparent discount in order to appear as attractive as an investment in a conventional property company.

Some commentators have pointed to the behaviour of investment trust shares in arguing that securitised property stock should trade at a discount. Scholars differ widely on the precise reasons why investment trusts tend to trade at substantial discounts to net asset value. It has been argued that it is partly due to uncertainty as to the underlying net asset value because of the effect of taxation and the costs of break-up. However, certainty of value is a key objective of property securitisation. Because comparable evidence and the number of potential single purchasers of any large property are limited, the range of possible values is wide. A valuer exercises his best judgment in settling on a specific figure, but even this could represent either a 'discount' or a 'premium' to another valuer's figure, based on identical information.

Herein lies the great Catch 22 – what is the base value for comparison and will securitisation make it more certain? It is at this point that the argument becomes circular. There is no objective value for any property investment, only the price that a buyer and seller can agree. Securitisation will provide a continuous pricing system offering an immediate indication of value from which investors will make their own judgments. The possible effects of securitisation on conventional valuations is discussed in the Introduction.

Does it really matter? At one level, the question of a discount or premium to an apparently objective value of the property as a whole to a single purchaser is irrelevant. The prevailing trading price of the stock is a matter of fact and the decision for the investor is whether it is cheap or expensive relative to the alternatives available, including shares in other properties. Certain types of investor (eg, small pension funds and private individuals) simply do not have the opportunity at present to buy direct property and so, for them, the comparison between the yield on a securitised stock and the apparent yield on the direct property is only of academic interest.

However, at another level, the comparison is important, not least to the managers, because of the threat of a takeover. That is, if the market believes that the trading price has fallen to an excessive discount relative to an apparent 'unified' value (perhaps due to inept management) a predator will no doubt emerge to put this to the test.

The two critical questions for investors in considering this issue are therefore, firstly, given the notional unified value, what premium if any, should be attached to the potential advantages of liquidity, limited liability, screen trading and independent management? Secondly, what effect will the emergence of the securitised market have on the notional unified value? To answer both questions, in general terms, we shall have to wait and see. All that can be said for now is that an important objective of the securitised market is to create greater certainty in the valuation of large properties. If it achieves that, it will have achieved a great deal.

3   What will be the implications for management?

1   THE MANAGER'S ROLE

The managers of a securitised property are responsible for the management of a listed investment scheme – in the case of a PINCs structure, a publicly quoted company. Consequently, the managers are the focal point of investor interest and are publicly accountable for their actions. Under PINCs or a SAPCO, the board of directors of the company must comply with the Companies Act.

The managers are responsible for two types of management:

—the day-to-day running of the property; and

—the financial and policy management of the business.

(Note: There is an additional role for the managers of a PINCs company in that, as a collective investment scheme, it will have to be an authorised investment business under FSA.)

Both types of management will demand new skills of the property manager, not least because of the responsibility of managing a business which is subject to public scrutiny. Rent reviews, decisions on refurbishment or on the raising of new capital will directly affect the trading price; these decisions will need sensitive handling to avoid giving the wrong signals to the market.

2 SUITABILITY OF MANAGERS

The composition of the management board will need careful consideration to ensure that it achieves an appropriate blend of specialist expertise and entrepreneurial flair. It is likely that the board members will have backgrounds in business and finance as much as in property. The management team will have to be credible for the particular property. For example, in the case of a shopping centre, it would be helpful to have a director who has an excellent track record in shopping centre management, or perhaps a retailer. Moreover, they will be the directors of a quoted company – an experience few institutional fund managers or chartered surveyors currently have. This will inevitably influence the selection process.

3 USE OF EXTERNAL AGENTS AND REMUNERATION

The managers can delegate some or all of their responsibilities to external agents. But this will have to be declared and a management contract published, to include disclosure of fees. It is likely that fees paid to external agents will be largely on a performance basis. Management costs will be closely scrutinised by investors; as a direct deduction from income, they must be competitive. In practice, under modern leases, a large proportion of the total management costs should be recoverable from the occupational tenants.

Similarly, it seems clear that in order to encourage the appropriate level of entrepreneurial flair, the remuneration of the managers themselves will need to be incentivised, perhaps related to the performance of earnings per share and possibly providing for equity shareholdings or stock options.

4 INTERNATIONAL COMPARISONS

The influence of the quality of management on the share price has been well demonstrated by examples of property securitisation in overseas markets. In his comparative survey for the College of Estate Management,[2] Bill Maxted observed that 'the experience of all the schemes in Australia and the USA is that asset management must achieve value enhancement', and that 'the trusts or partnerships whose units are sold at or above [net asset value] are those where the scheme and property management have a successful track record in terms of consistently increasing dividend payments'.

In Australia and the USA, this experience has tended to favour the securitisation of multi-let, 'landmark' buildings, which provide greater opportunities for management enterprise. Moreover, the higher value properties are

2 This report, commissioned by The College of Estate Management, describes the operation of listed pooled property investment schemes in Australia and the USA, and attempts to draw conclusions from this examination as to the possible implications for property securitisation in the UK. It was published in Autumn 1988.

preferred by the institutions because the larger volume of stock potentially available suits their higher minimum dealing levels.

Both observations are relevant to the UK. The latter point, in particular, emphasises the importance of encouraging participation by the private investor to ensure a liquid market. Private individuals with small amounts to invest are likely to deal more frequently than their institutional counterparts. In a climate of wider share ownership, many could become interested in commercial property investment in a securitised form. While some latent property tycoons may enjoy the excitement of creating their own portfolios, others may prefer to rely on selection by more experienced hands; for them, a managed portfolio – a unit trust of PINCs, for example – is likely to be a popular option.

This raises a further management opportunity, particularly if specialist funds are developed for specific types of property, such as shops or offices, or funds which offer either capital growth or income yield. Given the diversity of property types and potential vehicle structures, the permutations are numerous and several major insurance companies are already investigating them.

4 Will full disclosure inhibit trading?

The requirement for full disclosure presents the property world with a radical departure from its tradition of secrecy. Disclosure is clearly essential to continuous trading and The Stock Exchange, having taken advice from many interested parties, have provided a comprehensive set of disclosure requirements in their Yellow Book rules (see the Appendix). The contents were discussed above.

However, as is clear with conventional stocks, giving all investors the same information does not necessarily lead to identical pricing. Consequently, while full disclosure will remove something of property's mystique, it will not of itself provide all the answers. There is no one value for any property interest; each investor will have his own view – researched or intuitive – and the liquidity of the market will be enhanced as these differing views are put to the test.

5 What is the risk of insider dealing?

Some commentators have expressed concern that a tenant who is also a shareholder with access to full details of the other tenancies in the building, including the rents being paid, will inhibit management efficiency and pose an insider dealing threat. In practice, the impact of full disclosure is unlikely to weaken management efficiency as most substantial properties – particularly shopping centres – usually have well-informed tenants' associations, although care will be needed in the disclosure of turnover rents.

However, where a tenant has a significant shareholding and might expect a seat on the management board, and hence access to much more detailed information than smaller shareholders, different problems arise. The tenant's shares would need to be disenfranchised in certain respects, such as in connection with rent reviews, for so long as the shareholder remained a tenant. This is particularly relevant to the partial securitisation of owner-occupied property.

In all other respects and instances, the normal rules relating to insider dealing would apply. Hence, a tenant who seeks to use unpublished, price-sensitive information to his advantage does so at his peril.

Of particular concern to regulators, is the risk of apparent insider dealing at the interface between the non-regulated, secret conventional property market and the highly regulated, public securitised market, for example at the time of a rent review. The outcome of a rent review on non-securitised property A which is both comparable to and adjoining securitised property B, may be expected significantly to affect the latter's trading price, particularly if the securitised property is itself about to face a rent review. What is to stop those involved in the rent review on property A from anticipating the outcome and trading in shares in property B? Moreover, there is no legal requirement for the outcome of a rent review on a non-securitised property to be published, so the information need never be widely known.

The conundrum which this situation presents to regulators is obvious. Is it, in fact, insider dealing at all? Should it be prevented or does it reflect acceptable market speculation? There are a number of other potentially hazardous circumstances under this heading and it is beyond the scope of this book to analyse them further or to consider suitable forms of protection. These issues will need to be debated and suitable regulation may be required, in addition to chinese walls, in order to resolve these 'market inefficiencies'.

6 What will be the principal influences on the trading price of the securities?

There is much debate on this point and only the market's operation in practice will reveal the answers. To date, it is unclear from the attitudes of institutions how far pricing will reflect property as opposed to stock market criteria. The characteristics of the property will clearly provide the fundamental analysis; the timing of rent reviews, the perceived quality of the building, whether it befits the local market and the performance of the management team should all be important influences. To that extent, one might expect the performance of the stock to track the performance of the property.

However, there is little doubt that, as single property securities will be listed on the main board, the general health of the stock market is bound to have some influence on price volatility. It will be interesting to see which types of property are regarded as the more vulnerable in these circumstances. It was noticeable, for example, immediately following the October 1987 crash, that the share prices of the heavily asset-backed companies, such as Land Securities, Slough Estates and MEPC, held up more strongly than those of the merchant developers, such as London & Metropolitan and Arlington Securities. To the extent that single property securities are unquestionably asset-backed, this may imply a benchmark for performance.

It is unclear whether the institutions will allocate securitised properties to their equity department or their property department. The decision is bound to affect initial attitudes on pricing and investment policy. Of particular interest will be the benchmarks for pricing which are adopted. Having analysed the growth prospects of the income flow, what yield will the investor require?

In considering this issue, a distinction will need to be made between equity securities and debt securities. Evidence from the single property bond market on the Brussels Stock Exchange and from Maxted's survey in Australia, confirms that interest rates and other bond yields heavily influence the pricing of debt securities in single properties. The pricing of the deep discount bond on Billingsgate demonstrated this in a UK context. This influence is hardly surprising. However, the specific yield relationship between a bond issued from a single property and a bond issued by a trading company or by government is less clear. It will largely depend on the perceived strength of the covenants of the occupational tenants whose leases underpin debt service.

As for the equity securities, one of the novel benefits of the new market is that it allows investors to take short-term positions in specific properties. To that end, in making pricing judgments on equity securities in a particular property, investors will have explicitly to consider the expected time period of investment. Therefore, prevailing interest rates and bond yields for comparable time periods may well be influential. Of course, this result will largely depend on the confidence which investors have in the liquidity of the market, but because different investors may be seeking different holding periods for stock in the same property, this may, of itself, enhance the pricing variations, trading opportunities and liquidity.

The availability of gearing in a particular property will add a further dimension for analysis. Interest rate movements will clearly have an influence on pricing here, but because of the effect of gearing on capital value, an approaching reversion may have a far greater influence.

In summary, the basic objective for the analyst is not unfamiliar – what price today for the right to receive an expected future income flow? But the factors which might influence the answer are a completely new combination of ingredients.

XV CONCLUSIONS

The potential impact of securitisation on the property market cannot be underestimated. It represents the modernisation of property as an investment medium and may well trigger a minor revolution in the traditionally private and rather parochial UK real estate market. Property's inherent illiquidity has frustrated investors for decades, if not centuries, and has severely restricted their number and diversity. Illiquidity has therefore perpetuated illiquidity. It has required the determined efforts of a small number of highly motivated organisations, matched by a climate of innovation and liberalisation in financial markets, to break this vicious circle.

It has also required a fundamental change in attitudes to property both by the leading institutional investors and by the property profession. Management responsibility is the central issue here – will investors pay to have it or pay not to have it? What price the benefit of an investment in a specific property without the obligation of management but with immediate liquidity?

The answer is not so much concerned with discount or premium, but with certainty. Greater liquidity should produce greater certainty of both value and performance. If management control is the price of liquidity, certainty is the yield.

The dependence of investors upon the quality of the management team responsible for the securitised property will demand new standards in property management. Full disclosure and accountability are new disciplines for institutional owners and for most property companies at the individual property level. A new breed of entrepreneurial manager will be needed, financially astute yet shrewd and perceptive in property matters. Few individuals currently combine such qualities; the reality may be the creation of a new style of management agency, highly motivated and incentivised, available for appointment by a property's management board with varying degrees of discretion, paid by performance. Is this more than one expects from other public companies?

For the property market, securitisation represents a new form of ownership; one which immediately broadens participation to include many new players. The overseas investor, for example, seeking to test the market in a controlled way and, most important of all, the general public. The availability of bite sized chunks of property allows the private investor to enter the world of commercial real estate for the first time. The scope of this opportunity in the current climate for private investment is substantial and for political slogans even greater – not only can you buy your own house but you can now buy a piece of your own office!

The likely impact of the emergence of securitisation on valuation methodology and the property profession was discussed in more detail in the introduction to this book. There seems little doubt that in both cases, the effect will be radical and far reaching, demanding new techniques and fostering new competition.

The fear that full disclosure means perfect wisdom is unfounded. The need for professional judgment will remain just as strong. Investors will continue to seek advice on whether a share is cheap or expensive. However, the potential for insider dealing between the regulated securities market and the unregulated property market must be addressed.

Fundamentally, this new market recognises – and its liquidity relies upon – the firm belief that there is no single absolute value for any property; everyone has their own view. Let us hope that many will wish to test their judgment.

Appendix to Chapter 3

A TYPICAL FEASIBILITY STUDY

APPRAISAL OF SECURITY PACIFIC   Date: 23 Mar 1988

SALES

Let A1	160,000 sq ft @ 34.00 psf	5,440,000

Rental income	5,440,000
Yield in perpetuity	7.25%
Gross capital value	75,034,480
Less institutional funding fee at	2.75%
Institutional funding fee	2,008,224
Net capital value	73,026,256

TOTAL NET RENT 5,440,000   TOTAL CAPITALISATION   73,026,256

TOTAL SALES   73,026,256

COSTS

Site cost/premium		15,249,999	
Stamp duty @ 1.00%		152,500	15,402,499
Site legal fees @ 1.00%		152,500	
Site agency fees @ 1.00%		152,500	
Planning fees		100,000	
VAT on site acquisition fees @ 15.00%		60,750	
Initial payments		312,500	778,250
Construct	226,500 sf @ 127.00 psf	28,765,500	
Contingency @ 3.00%		862,965	
Professional fees @ 10.00%		2,962,847	
VAT on building @ 0.00%		0	
VAT on fees @ 15.00%		444,427	33,035,736
Interest			
Site + Stamp duty	18.0 months @ 12.00%	2,988,889	
Site fees + Init pmts etc	18.0 months @ 12.00%	151,021	
Build + Prof fees etc	16.0 months @ 12.00%	2,597,130	5,737,040

Void

Site + Stamp duty	6.0 months @ 12.00%	1,120,036	
Site fees + Init pmts etc	6.0 months @ 12.00%	56,593	
Build + Prof fees etc	6.0 months @ 12.00%	2,170,040	
Less: Void offset		0	3,346,669
Agent's letting fee @ 15.00% of gross rent		816,000	
Legal's on letting @ 0.50% of gross rent		27,200	
Agent's funding fee @ 1.00% of gross value		750,345	
Legal's on funding @ 0.50% of gross value		375,172	
VAT on selling fees @ 15.00%		295,308	
End payments		0	
Promotion		100,000	2,364,025

TOTAL COSTS   60,664,216

SUMMARY

TOTAL SALES	(pounds)	73,026,256
TOTAL COSTS	(pounds)	60,664,216
PROFIT	(pounds)	12,362,040
INTEREST COVER	(years)	1.63
RENTAL COVER	(years)	2.27
RENTAL YIELD	(%)	8.97
PROFIT YIELD	(%)	20.38
	(Annualised %	9.72)

Appendix

SINGLE PROPERTY SCHEMES

EXTRACT FROM CHAPTER 1, SECTION 10 OF ADMISSION OF
SECURITIES TO LISTING

**Basic criteria for
listing**

13. A single property scheme, with or without a
trading record, will be considered for listing
provided the following criteria are satisfied:

a. the scheme must own the freehold or a long
lease (of at least 110 years) of a single property,
which must be its only property and its only
material asset. A single property must satisfy the
characteristics set out in Section 76(6)(a) of the
Financial Services Act 1986;

b. the scheme's activity must be restricted solely to
the management of the scheme for at least the
next five years, although it is acceptable that the
property be managed by agents appointed by
the directors, trustees or managers;

c. the property must be sufficiently let for expected
annual income to cover expected annual
outgoings;

d. the property must have a value of at least £10m;

e. the name of the scheme should, except where it
would be misleading or unreasonable to obtain
or seek consent, include the name or address of
the property;

f. the scheme must provide that investors are
entitled to, or to payments equivalent to, rental
payments made by the tenants, and the same
should be fully distributed to them subject only
to deductions for:

   i. operating and service charges, debt service,
   insurance and taxation; and
   ii. reserves to finance prudent estate
   management requirements;

g. the scheme must provide that if the whole or

substantially the whole of the property is disposed of the scheme must be wound up, but, subject to the rights of secured credit holders, the property must not be disposed of nor the scheme wound up without equity shareholders' or unit-holders' approval, by special resolution in the case of a company, otherwise according to the terms of the trust; and

h. where listing is sought for equity capital, the scheme must provide that equity shareholders or unitholders have pre-emptive rights over further equity issues.

Where schemes are financed partly by equity securities and partly by debt securities, applications for the listing of equity securities may be refused if the ratio of debt to equity is considered by the Committee to be unacceptably high.

Information to be included in the listing particulars etc.

14. Paragraphs 15 to 20 deal with information required in listing particulars and offer documents issued by single property schemes. In addition, such documents issued in respect of any class of security of a company must comply with the relevant requirements of Chapter 2 of Section 3; and documents issued in respect of the units of trust based schemes must comply with the relevant requirements of Paragraph 5 of Chapter 4 of Section 10.

15. The following information must be provided:

a. history of the property;

b. summary details of location, construction, layout, services and floor areas;

c. details of tenancies, including schedules where necessary, to provide rent, lease expiry and rent review dates. Where any tenant accounts for more than 50% of the scheme's rental income there should be provided financial information relating to the tenant if and to the extent it is publicly available, together with details of the main activities and operations carried out by the tenant in the property;

d. main terms of lease(s) including rent review clauses and service charge provisions, and proforma lease extract with specific reference to any significant lease(s) that differ(s) materially from any standard which may be adopted for a multi-occupied property. Copies of the full lease(s) should be available for inspection; and

e. name, address and qualification of the scheme's property advisors.

16. The following must be included either in full, or in summarised form with detailed form available for inspection:

a. an 'open market' valuation of the property, prepared by an external valuer in accordance with the requirements of Chapter 1 Section 10;

b. a full report on the condition of the property to include its structure, finishes and services other than those covered in c. below, itemising in particular matters which:

  i. require repair or maintenance either immediately or within a period of three years; and

  ii. having regard to their nature and anticipated life cycle, will require substantial expenditure on repair or replacement in the foreseeable future;

c. a consultant's report on the air conditioning, mechanical and electrical equipment and services itemising in particular the matters required to be itemised under 16(b) above;

d. a solicitor's report to the scheme on title, including relevant searches. Details should be provided of relevant planning issues, in particular whether any planning conditions have not yet been satisfied;

e. details of current insurance arrangements, to include fire damage, third party liability, loss of rent, and other normal property risks.

17. If the scheme has a trading record, there should be provided an accountants' report on income and

expenditure during the past 5 years, or such lesser period as is available.

18. There must be disclosed, in so far as material, in relation to each of the promoters, managers trustees and directors of the scheme (or any subsidiary or holding company or subsidiary of any such holding company of such person):

   i. any direct or indirect interest of such person in relation to the property, the scheme or its management or the sale of the securities being undertaken;

   ii. the fact, if such is the case, that any such person is or has contracted to become a tenant of any part of the property; and

   iii. any relationship of such person with another person such as to place it in a position where its duty in relation to that other person conflicts with its duty to the scheme or to holders of its securities.

19. In the case of a property managed by agents, details must be given of their name, legal form, business address, terms of contract and remuneration, experience and qualifications.

20. Details must be given of the maximum amount of short term borrowings permitted without the approval of equity shareholders or unitholders.

Additional continuing obligations

21. Paragraphs 22 to 25 deal with Continuing Obligations which in the case of a corporate scheme are in addition to those in Section 5 and in the case of trust based schemes are in addition to those in Paragraph 8, Chapter 4, Section 10, so far as are relevant.

22. Annual reports should provide projections of expenditure for the next financial year and details of major expenditure obligations reasonably foreseeable beyond the next financial year. Independent building surveys should be carried out every three years, and independent valuations

should be carried out when further issues of securities are to be made. Appropriate details of the surveys and valuations should be disclosed in the annual accounts.

23. A 'log book' should be maintained for the building and be readily available for public inspection at a suitable location. The log book should contain comprehensive information including:

   a. title;

   b. physical structure;

   c. lettings; and

   d. all other relevant information including management reports.

24. The scheme should provide for minimum voting levels in respect of the following matters:

   a. making capital expenditure on redevelopment and refurbishment in excess of specified limits;

   b. approving any change of manager;

   c. raising further funds required in connection with the property;

   d. disposal of the whole of the property or any material part thereof;

   e. winding up the scheme.

25. The scheme should provide information to the market of any significant matters which are known to the directors, managers or trustees and which might reasonably be expected to affect investors' decisions including:

   a. late payment of any material amount of rent;

   b. grant, major variation, and surrender of significant leases;

   c. any significant variations between projected expenditure (as included in an annual report) and actual expenditure on repairs, maintenance or improvements;

d. specific notices (eg, Town & Country Planning Act 1971 or Landlord & Tenant Act 1954); and

e. details of any material change in any of the matters referred to in paragraph 18 which have arisen since publication of the latest listing particulars. In addition, details should be set out in the next annual report.

Glossary of Terms

This glossary attempts to define briefly a number of the terms to which the contributors refer in their chapters. It is therefore not an exhaustive list of financial terms. The definitions are not intended to be strict in a legal sense: many of the terms have a variety of interpretations depending upon the context in which they are used. In most cases, a more detailed explanation is contained in the relevant chapter.

All Risks Yield
The yield used to capitalise rent when valuing property by the *Years' Purchase Method*, being the initial yield on rack rented freeholds and the equivalent yield on reversionary property.

Articles of Association
The procedural regulations governing the activities of a limited company.

Authorised Unit Trust
A unit trust for which authorisation has been given by The Department of Trade and Industry and under s 78 of The Financial Services Act 1986. It can be marketed to the general public as well as to professional investors.

Cap
A technique whereby an interest payable on a loan.

Capital Cover
The capital value of the property (or portfolio) divided by the capital sum to be financed.

Capital Markets
A relatively vague term usually used to label financial markets in which

intermediaries raise money for companies by selling paper to third parties, rather than providing their own funds.

Chinese Wall

A device to ensure that the business of separate divisions, departments or teams within an organisation remain separate and that no improper or price sensitive, unpublished information passes from one to another.

Clawback

Refers specifically to equity (or equity-related) issues by UK companies. In a rights issue, the new shares are offered first to existing shareholders, and only go from them to outsiders if the rights are sold or have lapsed. Clawback is a similar idea but in reverse sequence: new shares in a vendor placing (qv) are first sold to outsiders subject to right of recall (or 'clawback') by existing shareholders. Under present rules, clawback is compulsory if the vendor placing represents 10% or more of the presently issued ordinary capital.

Collar

A technique which fixes the maximum and minimum interest rate payable on a loan.

Controlled Non-Subsidiary

A controlled non-subsidiary of a reporting enterprise is a company, trust or other vehicle which, though not fulfilling The Companies Act definition of a subsidiary, is directly or indirectly controlled by and a source of benefits or risks for the reporting enterprise or its subsidiaries that are in substance no different from those that would arise were the vehicle a subsidiary (ED 42 paragraph 54).

Convertible Warrant

A security (either bond or share) whose holder has the right to exchange it ('convert' it) for a different security. By far the most common form is a convertible which initially offers a steady income, fixed maturity value (and fixed value if the issuer is liquidated) – all independent of the profitability of the issuer. The holder also has the right (but not the obligation) to exchange the convertible for shares. The exchange ratio of shares issued for conversion is fixed in advance, as are the conversion intervals.

Occasionally, the convertible may be a bond exchangeable at the holder's option for another bond – there are one or two Gilts of this type.

Coupon

When securities were all issued in bearer form, the interest and redemption payments were made by the issuer only against surrender of the relevant one of a series of small, numbered coupons attached to the back of each bearer document. Eurobonds (qv), some US Treasury bonds and certain other securities are still issued in this form.

The term is now used more generally to mean the rate of interest payable on a security.

Debenture
Strictly speaking, it means a written acknowledgement of debt. Hence, for Eurobonds (qv) or US domestic issues, it can simply be a synonym for bond. However, in the UK domestic market, bonds tend only to be called 'debentures' if they are secured by a mortgage or charge over specified assets: hence property companies often issue 'first mortgage debentures', a bond with first charge over a property. Other companies may issue 'debentures' secured by a floating charge on their assets.

Debt/Equity Ratio
See Gearing Ratio.

Deep Discount Bond
A debenture (qv) on which the annual interest is payable at less than a market rate, but which is issued at a discount to its nominal value (ie to the amount to be repaid at the end of the borrowing term), such that the additional amount to be repaid (ie the discount on issue), together with the annual interest payments are equivalent to charging a market rate of interest over the life of the debenture.

Deferred Annuity
An income stream that begins at some time in the future.

Discounted Cash Flow
Analysis in which an appraiser specifies the quantity and timing of periodic income flows and discounts each to its present value at a specified discount rate.

Dominant & Servient Interests
Where one interest in land (dominant) enjoys certain rights over another (servient).

Duration
The (weighted) average time until an asset's cash flow begins.

ED 42
An ED, or exposure draft, is a draft SSAP (qv) issued for comment. ED42 'Accounting for Special Purpose Transactions', is a draft of the SSAP which it is intended, when issued, will substantially reduce the scope for off-balance sheet financing.

Enterprise Zone
A geographical area within the United Kingdom which central government has identified as being in need of commercial development and to which industry is to

be encouraged to relocate. Once an Enterprise Zone has been designated there are material tax advantages for businesses located there, namely:

i) 100% capital allowances giving relief against corporate tax;
ii) exemption from General Rates;
iii) exemption from Industrial Training Board Levies and statistical returns.

The benefits have in most cases applied for a 10-year period from designation.

Equivalent/Equated Yield
The total annual return to be received from a reversionary investment assuming no change in the property's rental value.

Eurobond/Euronote
A bond issued in the 'international format', ie paying interest without deduction of tax, available as bearer bonds and usually sold via a syndicate of international banks and securities houses. Unlike the position in Great Britain, Eurobonds are a common form of investment for private individuals on the Continent.

Fixed Charge
A charge over specified property (eg a company's office building or a property company's development). It is normally expressed by way of legal mortgage (ie a legal mortgage by deed) which gives the creditor a legal interest in the property which cannot be disposed of without the chargee's (the lender's) consent.

Floating Charge
A charge over a borrowing company's assets or on the whole of the company's undertakings. It basically floats over the assets which can be disposed of in the borrower's normal course of business and only becomes fixed or crystallises (ie is converted into a fixed charge on specified assets), whenever the borrower commits any breach of a loan agreement or otherwise gets into difficulties or when the chargee chooses to intervene and fix its charge.

Floor
A technique which fixes the minimum of interest rate payable on a loan.

Full Listing
Admission of securities to the Official List of The London Stock Exchange, ie quotation (qv) but not on the Unlisted Securities Market. (see also Quotation). A quotation on the main board of The Stock Exchange, rather than the Unlisted Securities or Third Market.

Gearing Ratio
A means of expressing the relative proportions of a company's or group's total financing met by debt (or borrowings) and equity.

General Partner
A partner within a limited partnership who has unlimited liability.

Ground Rent
Rent paid for the right to use and occupy land, or the portion of the total rent allocated to the underlying land. There are many different ways of calculating it, depending on the needs of the parties. For example, it can be a nominal amount (a peppercorn) or expressed as a percentage of the property's rack rental value or derived from a specific formula.

Historic Dividend Yield
The rate of dividend declared on a share for the most recent one year period, divided by the current market price of that share.

Index Linked Gilt
An obligation of the Government (strictly, a charge on the Consolidated Fund of the UK) whose interest and redemption payments are each increased pro-rata to increases in the Retail Price Index. For example, if the RPI was 300 when a particular $2\frac{1}{2}$% Index-Linked Gilt was issued, is 360 now and proves to be 600 when it is redeemed, interest payments will now be $(360 \div 300) \times 2\frac{1}{2}$% or 3% pa and the redemption value will be £$600 \div 30) \times 100 = 200$%. If this Gilt were issued at 100%, over its life it would offer a yield of $2\frac{1}{2}$% over the rate of inflation, ie a $2\frac{1}{2}$% real yield.

Initial Yield
The gross initial annual income from a property (or other investment) divided by the gross acquisition cost.

Interest Cover
A company's or group's net interest charge divided into profit before interest and tax. It indicates the extent to which profits can reduce before they become insufficient to meet the interest charge.

Internal Rate of Return
The compound annual rate of interest represented by the actual or expected receipts from an investment, expressed in relation to the cost(s) of making the investment.

Investment Trust
A listed company, not being a close company, which is approved by the Inland Revenue, under s 842 of The Income and Corporation Taxes Act 1988, as meeting certain investment and distribution requirements.

Junk Bonds
High risk bonds, usually promising a very high indicated return coupled with a substantial default risk and limited asset security.

Limited Partnership

A partnership where one or more partners are entitled to limit their liability to third parties so long as at least one partner has unlimited liability.

Limited Recourse Debt

Normally, limited recourse refers to loans made available by banks to developers where there is not a full right of action against the borrower in the event of a default. Typically, the loan will be secured on the project itself and, should the project be unsuccessful and the borrower unable to repay the finance, the only recourse the bank has is to possess the property being financed. Recourse is limited because certain undertakings will normally be given by the borrower.

Liquidity

For 'liquidity' read 'marketability', ie the ability to buy or sell. This covers the value which can be bought or sold, the speed with which it can be done and the variation from mid-market prices for large blocks.

Loan to Value Ratio

A ratio which states the maximum amount of a loan as a percentage of the capital value of the underlying asset charged to secure it.

Long Term Finance

Usually, loans having an initial maturity of more than five years. While such finance can be provided by banks, it is more typically provided by institutions, either directly or via some issue in the domestic or international capital markets.

Market Capitalisation

The market price of a company's shares multiplied by number of shares in issue. The market capitalisation of a company conventionally includes all equity and convertible securities, but excludes non-convertible ('straight') debt and preference shares.

Marriage Value

Latent value released by the merger of two or more interests in land.

Maturity

The date on which a bond is redeemed, or the time to go until the redemption date. Thus a bond issued in 1986 and redeemable in 2011 may in 1988 be described as either '2011 maturity' or 'a 23 year maturity'.

Mezzanine Finance

Literally, finance which, in terms of risk and reward, is at mezzanine level between pure debt and pure equity. It can take many different forms and can be secured or unsecured, but it usually earns a priority return after debt service and before equity. Mezzanine finance will usually seek a much higher rate of return than ordinary loan finance.

Mortgage
The document by which security is given to a person providing finance or owed a duty.

Memorandum
The objects for which a company has been constituted.

Merchant Developer
A developer who usually develops properties to trade rather than to retain as investments. (See also Property Trading Company.)

Multi Option Facility
Agreement between a borrower and one or more lenders to provide a specified range of loan and other credit facilities, often in a number of currencies.

Net Asset Value
Total assets less external (ie non-shareholder) liabilities. For property companies, net asset value is usually calculated using property assets at market value rather than cost and ignoring tax contingently payable if the assets were actually sold at these market values. For comparison with share prices, net asset value is quoted per share.

Off Balance Sheet Financing
Raising debt finance in a manner intended to ensure that the borrowings, and consequently the related assets, need not be included in the borrowing company's and/or group's balance sheet.

Off Profit and Loss Account Financing
Reducing interest payable on debt, and therefore the interest charge in the profit and loss account, to below a market rate by issuing debt which is convertible into equity or by issuing debt together with equity warrants.

PINC
Property Income Certificate, a tradeable equity security in a tax transparent single property company which entitles the holder to a direct share of the property's income flow and capital value. A PINC company can be geared.

Price Earnings Ratio
The market capitalisation (qv) of a company divided by its earnings (qv). This is arithmetically the same as the price per share divided by the earnings per share.

Prime Property
A property which commands the highest band of years' purchase for fully let property of that type, when calculating capital value at a given date.

Project Finance
Finance raised, typically from a bank, to finance the development of a building. Such finance will typically allow for the rolling up of interest during the construction phase. It is short-term in nature and is repaid on completion of the project. Project finance may or may not allow for a period of grace to find a tenant for the building.

Property Trading Company
A company which acquires or develops buildings with a view to selling them on to third parties at a profit. They are to be viewed as akin to trading companies in other sectors. The maximisation of revenue profit is more important than the maximisation of asset value. (See also Merchant Developer.)

Quotation
This has two meanings. The basic meaning is the price at which a security is quoted on The Stock Exchange (eg 200–210p). By extension 'quotation' is often used to mean the right or ability to have a security dealt on a Stock Exchange. It would be synonymous with 'listing' were not the second tier of The London Stock Exchange called the 'Unlisted Securities Market'. Thus 'Company A's shares are quoted on the USM'.

Redemption Yield
The internal rate of return (qv) enjoyed from a bond when buying it at a specified price and receiving all the income and capital payments due thereon.

Return on Equity
The value generated for shareholders in one year, divided by the net asset value (qv) at the beginning of that year. For trading companies, this is equal to the earnings (qv) divided by the initial net asset value. For property investment companies (qv), capital appreciation also has to be added to earnings to compute the value generated for shareholders when calculating return on equity.

Reversionary
The date at which the rent received from a property investment is reviewed (or when a new lease is granted), normally to rental value.

Rights Issue
Issue of new shares or convertibles by a company made by offering existing shareholders the right to subscribe for the new securities pro rata to the existing holding.

Risk Premium
The return in excess of that for a risk free investment.

Rollover Relief
General term used to apply to various circumstances in which a UK taxpayer is allowed to exchange one asset for another without triggering any taxable gain (or allowable loss) on the transaction. The tax base cost of the initial investment is 'rolled over' into the second investment.

SAPCo
Single asset property company.

Scrip Issue
Free issue of securities to shareholders pro rata to existing holdings (ie a rights issue at nil price). The nominal value of the new securities is paid up from the reserves of the company. Note that a share split is different, being merely a subdivision of existing shares with no effect on the accounts of the company.

Scenario Analysis
Assessing the future value of dependent variables given alternative future states of the world.

Securitisation
Conversion of a direct property asset into paper securities.

Sensitivity Analysis
Analysis of the impact of various factors in an investment decision on the rate of return to be earned from, or the investment value of, a property.

Short-Term Finance
There is no strict definition of short-term finance but it usually refers to finance which has a maturity of less than 5 years. Normally, it is provided from banking sources.

Side by Side Leases
A lease under which the net income received by the landlord is a predetermined proportion of the rents received (not receivable) by the tenant from sublettings.

Special Purpose Transaction
A special purpose transaction is one which combines or divides up the benefits and obligations flowing from it in such a way that they fall to be accounted for differently or in different periods, depending on whether the elements are taken step by step or whether the transaction is viewed as a whole (ED 42 paragraph 56).

SPOT
Single Property Ownership Trust. A securitisation arrangement which provides the investor with a specific share of a single property's income flow and capital value via a trust mechanism. Strictly, an investor would hold units in the trust rather than securities in a company.

Strike Price
A strike price is the price at which a convertible bond is converted into the shares of the issuing vehicle. Typically, strike prices for convertibles issued by property investment companies have ranged from 10% to 25% above the market price of the shares prevailing on the date of issue of the convertible.

SSAP
Statements of Standard Accounting Practice or SSAP's are issued by the Institute of Chartered Accountants in England and Wales in association with other UK accounting bodies. They describe methods of accounting for application to all financial accounts intended to show a true and fair view. Significant departures in financial accounts from SSAP's should be disclosed and explained.

Swap (Interest Rate)
An arrangement by which floating rate debt is converted into fixed rate debt and vice versa.

Swap (Currency)
An arrangement by which liabilities in one currency are converted into liabilities in a different currency.

Swaption
A swap option.

Swingline
A swingline facility is usually a part of a multiple option facility and enables the borrower to avail itself of funds on a same day basis when switching between domestic and euromarkets.

Take-Out
This usually refers to the repayment of a development loan either from sale of the completed investment or its refinancing on a longer term basis.

Tender Panel
A group of banks or financiers who undertake either on a committed or uncommitted basis to bid for loans or other financing paper on a competitive basis for a certain borrower usually as a part of a multi option facility.

Trust for Sale
A method by which the ownership of undivided shares in land is held in England and Wales. The legal interest is held by trustees on terms that the interest has to be sold and the proceeds of sale divided between the beneficiaries.

Unauthorised Unit Trust
A unit trust which is not an authorised unit trust and which therefore cannot be marketed to the general public.

Vendor Placing
Placing of shares (or convertibles) on behalf of the seller or sellers ('vendors') who have received the shares as partial or complete consideration for an asset (eg property or business) sold to the company issuing the shares.

Warrant
A certificate evidencing the holder's right to subscribe for a security, usually for shares. The subscription price is usually fixed in advance and is payable in cash or, occasionally, by a surrender of other securities.

Warranty/Collateral Warranty
An agreement or deed under which a person agreeing to provide goods or services covenants with the person to whom the provision is to be made as to the performance of work. A collateral warranty is where a warranty is given to a third party.

Zero Coupon Bond
A bond issued at a discount to mature at its face value and paying no interest.

Index